Inhabiting Contemporary Southern and Appalachian Literature

UNIVERSITY PRESS OF FLORIDA

Florida A&M University, Tallahassee
Florida Atlantic University, Boca Raton
Florida Gulf Coast University, Ft. Myers
Florida International University, Miami
Florida State University, Tallahassee
New College of Florida, Sarasota
University of Central Florida, Orlando
University of Florida, Gainesville
University of North Florida, Jacksonville
University of South Florida, Tampa
University of West Florida, Pensacola

Inhabiting Contemporary Southern and Appalachian Literature

Region and Place in the Twenty-First Century

CASEY CLABOUGH

University Press of Florida
Gainesville · Tallahassee · Tampa · Boca Raton
Pensacola · Orlando · Miami · Jacksonville · Ft. Myers · Sarasota

Printed in the United States of America. This book is printed on Glatfelter Natures Book, a paper certified under the standards of the Forestry Stewardship Council (FSC). It is a recycled stock that contains 30 percent post-consumer waste and is acid-free.
This book may be available in an electronic edition.

17 16 15 14 13 12 6 5 4 3 2 1

Library of Congress Cataloging-in-Publication Data
Clabough, Casey Howard, 1974-
Inhabiting contemporary Southern and Appalachian literature : region and place in the twenty-first century / Casey Clabough.
p. cm.
Includes bibliographical references and index.
ISBN 978-0-8130-4173-5 (alk. paper)
1. American literature—Southern States—History and criticism. 2. American literature—Appalachian Region—History and criticism. I. Title.
PS261.C49 2012
810.9'975—dc23
2012009810

University Press of Florida
15 Northwest 15th Street
Gainesville, FL 32611-2079
http://www.upf.com

For the places

There are places I remember all my life, though some have changed.

JOHN LENNON

No one lives in the world in general.

CLIFFORD GEERTZ

Most of the important things about the place of place in fiction have been said before and said by my betters. And so it is probably outrageous, bad form all around, to write about place again, to try to recapitulate the persuasive arguments so ably advanced that they are by now our unspoken assumptions, matters of faith and belief. Yet . . .

GEORGE GARRETT

Contents

Acknowledgments

As this book represents the culmination of my four previous scholarly books—the end of a decade-long intellectual odyssey which began with *Elements: The Novels of James Dickey*—I would like to thank *en masse* all the press and journal staffs I have worked with over those years who made it possible for me to realize my five-book cyclical vision. I know of staff members who have moved on from the positions they inhabited while working with me and still others who have moved on from this life. I am grateful to have my books counted among the work into which they poured their hearts as well as their minds. I hope the results do them some measure of justice.

For the book at hand, I offer my profound thanks to the staff of the University Press of Florida and especially Amy Gorelick, who has championed and shepherded both of my books listed in the Florida catalogue. Thanks also are in order to the editors of the following journals, who have allowed me to use revised material which initially appeared in their pages: *Appalachian Journal*, *Community Literacy*, *Elsewhere: A Journal of Place*, *Nantahala Review*, *North Carolina Literary Review*, *Sewanee Review*, *Shenandoah*, *South Carolina Review*, and *Southern Quarterly*. All translations are my own unless otherwise noted.

I offer special gratitude to the writers I discuss who materialized out of their work to answer my questions, especially George Garrett (1929–2008) and William Hoffman (1925–2009), both of whom I had the precious good fortune to count among my friends, and James Dickey (1923–1997), who served as my mentor for a short time before his death. "I want you to fight this thing through," he said in his final class. "Fight the thing through that we start with your own unconscious and your own dreams and see where it comes out." Well, sir, I have and will continue to do so.

I remain an ardent supporter of the Virginia Foundation for the Humanities and its fellowship program, which afforded me time and intellectual stimulation that helped result in material appearing in each of my five books since 2005, including the creative titles. I have experienced additional good fortune in the form of my most recent graduate assistants, Jen LaPlante and Katelyn Carey: the former proofing an early version of this book and the latter devising the index in addition to proofing. They are both promising young scholars and people I am proud to call friends.

I

Getting (Back) There

An Introduction and a Case Study

Why Read for Place?

An Introduction

> I have argued that place is unique. It is unique not as the first or highest member of a group, or part of a whole. It is unique as a single constitutive principle of the cosmos.
>
> Aristotle, *Physics*

Place: Spring Branch Farm, Appomattox County, Virginia, USA
Latitude: 37.41261
Longitude: -78.75932

Confusions of temporality aside, here we are, or as Henry James might say, "Here we wonderfully are": you, reader, for whom I am grateful, arriving only now, and myself seated at my writing desk, the rest of this book yet to take shape, facing south toward the hay fields of the farm I work and live on, the twenty-thousand-acre Appomattox-Buckingham State Forest spanning beyond them, the afternoon sun having begun its slow swinging round to the west. Between the fields and forest before me lies a series of springs conspiring to form a brook called Spring Branch, which is also the namesake of this farm. Spring Branch empties into Wolf Creek, which in turn winds through the state forest toward the Appomattox River. Less than a hundred miles to the east, at Hopewell (formerly City Point), Virginia, the Appomattox joins the James River, which bears its waters to the Chesapeake Bay only to have them plunged against and dispersed into the choppy currents of the Atlantic Ocean. It pleases me no end, sedentary scribbler that I am, to know that though the farm I live on lies over two hundred miles from the ocean as the crow flies, I could rise from my bed tomorrow morning, forsake my agricultural chores and writing ritual, and alternately walk and float my way to the Atlantic Ocean in a matter of days.

As this salutary description demonstrates, my abstract and visceral notions of place have become closely intertwined—perhaps hopelessly so—through my particular practice of thinking and living. In addition to having dwelt in the state of Virginia for thirty-four of my thirty-seven years, I also have served as literature section editor for the Virginia Foundation of the Humanities' *Encyclopedia Virginia* for the past five. For three of my decades I have lived on farms and thus interacted intimately with the grounded essence of the place at hand, my hands tearing and shaping great stretches the Piedmont's red-clay soil and stones even as they were torn and shaped by them. When I edit entries on writers from the places of the state I know, I not only catalog the particulars of their surroundings, but see and feel these places as my own: the slope of a ridge, the eddies of a tidal pool, the scent of a plowed field in the wake of soft spring rain.

How might one articulate the aspects of one's formative place, particularly when one is struck by the task of conveying it? How does one proceed beyond recognitions that are likely to appear fundamental and obvious to many? As if anticipating these central questions, Tim Cresswell offers the following basic statement in his book *Place: A Short Introduction*: "Place is clearly a complicated concept. It is all the more confusing because, at first glance, it appears to be obvious and common-sense" (50). Identifying some of those intricate elements which lie behind "the obvious and common-sense" is one of the chief aims of this book. While recognizing that place may sometimes function unfavorably as a variable in the workings of nostalgia, comfort, and tradition, place also remains an embarking point we never really leave over the course of our various physical journeys as well as during the mighty odyssey toward ourselves that is the great yearning endeavor of our lives.

As a matter of necessity, let us first take up the most basic word used in establishing place and location, the word *here*, and pose the question, what might it mean to be here? Here, that is, as opposed to someplace else? In an earlier book of mine entitled *The Warrior's Path,* the writing of which I had hoped would help me understand my personal relationship and that of my family to the long, tragic history of eastern Appalachia, I offered the following response at length:

> "Here," the word and idea, usually is something we take for granted, but its simplicity of connotation ever blurs in our minds its

> inherent insinuations of both position and time. The traveler asks herself, "How do I get there from here?" or, measuring the position of the sun against her own fatigue, suggests to her companions, "Let us stop here for the night and resume our journey at dawn." It may also refer to a minute topic or specific subject, as in "Here, I must disagree with you"; yet, more dynamically, it may too demand action: "Come here!" Beyond, in all these things, the word embodies an affirmation of life, of being, now. To the one who, uncertain of our presence, calls our name, we reply, "Here."
>
> "Here" is the bashful and more shadowy companion of "place." As with here, the idea of place, any place, remains one of our most basic yet slippery of concepts: it is a space with boundaries but its limits may be definite or indefinite; it might be construed as an abstract mental or spiritual location, "There is a place for you in my heart," or a literal blank domain, "This is the place where you write your name"; it may also refer to a small particular occupied spot, your finger touches the place where your head hurts, or a point someone has achieved or come to only to then lose it, as in a book: "I've lost my place." Place is irrevocably wedded to context, for the space your body occupies is a place, but so is the earth and what scientists call the solar system. And, at once more abstract and more central, it is also a proximity of yearning, of desire; as the writer Wendell Berry says, "The mind still hungers for its earth, its bounded and open space."(1)

As abstract as this rumination may appear, it was nonetheless the best I could manage at the time, and I find myself hard pressed to offer a better one now. Perhaps instead we might take a step backward and trace the journey of place toward us, toward our own time, with the aid of those who have helped establish our most fundamental understanding of it.

It is true the idea of place has always been of interest—though, admittedly, often of passing interest—to philosophers. In *De rerum natura* Lucretius posited, "All that is is place" (qtd. in Casey, *Fate* 79). Much later, Kant considered place as a prehension—a kind of unity of sensation—of the body rather than of the mind, and thus began a dialogue taken up later by a number of the phenomenologists, Husserl most notably. Place is afforded a powerful physical aspect since it is made up in part by live bodies, which are in turn placially shaped. Our bodies establish space and place by virtue of being in and sensing them. We move about and occupy, yet remain finite in terms of our movements, mass, and perceptions. Space may be infinite, but our apprehension of it is not. The boundary inside of which lies our awareness of space is a place. Beyond it are the places and spaces we do not know. Place, then, it turns out, can move; it can be active.

Consider the animals of this planet, ourselves included. We roam by nature, even when we do not have to, because we are built for it: from the evolutionary wiring of our central nervous systems to our means of locomotion. Contemporary humans have sped and deepened this process by means of technology, yet we have lost much in the process, including, some psychologists and philosophers have argued, ourselves. However, as one of these philosophers, indeed one of the best thinkers on place, Edward Casey, maintains, "Despite the costly character of an accelerated life, it remains the case that where we are—the place we occupy, however briefly—has everything to do with what and who we are (and finally, *that* we are)" (*Getting* xiii). Such an assertion, especially its italicized component, may jar some readers into reckoning it hyperbole. Yet, considered scientifically and anthropologically, the idea becomes somewhat more palatable. As David Jacobson notes in *Place and Belonging in America*, "The question of place, beyond territorial imperatives, is what distinguishes humans from other creatures. The temporal and spatial dimensions of place also indicate why the metaphysical dimension, large and small, from God to icons, from theology to the spatial tempo of funeral rites, is part of the definition of life" (192). Without place, Jacobson contends, we are cultureless rover-creatures bereft of metaphysics and religionlike systems of identity. As Wendell Berry laments in relating Jacobson's concern to language:

> Few now in our education system would suspect that loss of authentic local speech—based partly upon the familiar names of local places, people, plants, and animals, upon local weather, local topography, and local work—might be a loss, not only of cultural artifacts of interest and value, but also of a perhaps indispensable knowledge, propriety, and sensitivity. (42)

Stripped of such essential variables there is little chance of us knowing, not only who, but, as Casey puts it, "*that* we are."

Thus far we have referenced place without much reference to the void it operates in, against, and in concert with: space. And as each element is contingent upon the other, we cannot get out of addressing its crucial function any longer. "Place and space are notions that presuppose one another," writes Enrico Baraldi. "Space implies relationships and flow, proportions and relative distances, whereas place is located and bounded" (Baraldi, Fors, and Houltz xiii). Although useful for some scenarios, in literary practice the final portion of Baraldi's definition is restrictive and severe in application, for place does have the ability to break bonds and shift. As Casey notes, "Never having vanished into Space (or Time) altogether, place is abounding: this is so even when it is called by various names, and itself names different events and experiences" (*Getting* 339). While Baraldi restricts the movement of place, he does note the shifting of its boundaries, labeling them not "definite or unproblematic. Rather, they are permeable and constantly negotiated, disputed and maintained by the interests and actions of people. Places relate to the surrounding world and are perceived differently by different people" (Baraldi, Fors, and Houltz xiii). It is an anthropocentric notion, then, that shapes Baraldi's places, swelling and constricting them according to the various diasporas and namings performed by the nearly hairless bipeds who have inhabited them.

As with other fundamental concepts that intimately shape our everyday existences, place is a difficult, perhaps impossible, idea to stand outside of and consider. Indeed, interpreters of places, including regions, regardless of the abstract theories they employ and the topical content they choose to embrace, cannot help but be influenced by the *where* of their own existences, past and present. The Chinese scholar who conceptualizes the literature of the United States, for example, does so in the context of his own inescapable time-bound cultural influence and particular academic training. Yet being of the region one proposes to study and articulate poses additional and more immediate challenges. Where one consciously acknowledges firsthand knowledge and long acquaintance, there also exist the perhaps unavoidable cloaked, wayward-leading, and debilitating specters of personal identification and sentimentality.

On the other hand, however, is a pronounced and long-standing tendency in the academy to belittle or even dismiss altogether minute places and their inhabitants, scholarly or otherwise, simply because they are diminutive and remote. Scholars David Blackbourn and James Retallack, for instance, warn of the cosmopolitan temptation "to assume that what happens in localities and regions is necessarily more small-minded and cramped in spirit than what takes place on a larger and airier national stage" (Blackbourn and Retallack 15). Out of this assumption has arisen the idea of exceptionalism, which asserts that remote regional places consciously or unconsciously set themselves against national and/or global variables predominantly out of fear and ignorance. Assigned the labels of "less educated," "less traveled," and "less politically progressive," along with "more agricultural," "more religious," and "more materially impoverished," certain regions of the world, the American South and Appalachia among them, have been isolated and crammed into dichotomies that have served to perpetuate the myths established for them. Only recently, in fact, have scholars across disciplines begun to admit that constructions of regions are far too vast and complex to be limited to one discipline. There are simply too many bodies of data, too many gathering mechanisms for them, and too many theoretical approaches for managing them.

This book is in part a cautionary narrative set against the ongoing temptation to dismiss or assimilate regions. It is also a rehabilitative endeavor, for when we rediscover our places we enlarge our view and appreciation of the world, including new books, new writers, and new ways of thinking about ourselves. In doing so, we also deliver ourselves from personal, cultural, and psychological dispersal. In essence, we save ourselves.

* * *

The inquiring name of my introduction, "Why Read for Place?," constitutes in part a play upon the title of Dana Gioia's 1992 lightning-rod book *Can Poetry Matter?*, which spoke to a cultural crisis in literacy while also managing to touch upon the archetypal: although it sought to address enormous topics, the book was neither the first nor the last to ask these questions. And within and beneath the questions Gioia posed dwelt the smaller, humbler vestiges of particular places. Indeed, one of the best chapters in the book, entitled "The Anonymity of the Regional Poet," addresses the largely parochial subject matter of former United States Poet Laureate Ted Kooser and includes an epigraph from the poet William Stafford: "All events and experiences are local, somewhere" (98). Gioia, at least at the time of that book, believed the work of place often described as such because it was not up to national standards, though there sometimes develop coups and revolutions, episodes in which "regional writing attains prominence" (Gioia 99). Gioia's selection of Kooser as a definitively regional subject appears to have been an appropriate, even prophetic one, for years later, on Kooser's Internet homepage there would appear, next to his rustic Midwestern photo, an excerpt from a poem that describes a bat darting in and out of the glow of a streetlight, snagging and consuming moths. Of the doomed insects he writes, "They jerkily fly this way and that. But they can't escape this hungry little piece of darkness. Local wonders" (Kooser). *Local Wonders* is in fact the title of one of Kooser's books and may suggest, I believe, a felt tension between the parochial and the national, the bat functioning as a consumptively bland and hegemonizing national or global force, gobbling up its smaller, weaker prey. Incidentally, it is a relationship also described in regional historian Edward Ayers's playful science-fiction essay, "The Inevitable Future of the South," in which a fictional subpar student prepares a Fall 2076 presentation on an early-twenty-first-century phenomenon of the American southeast known as the Great Consolidation. As the student explains, "if you've seen one part of it you've seen a lot of it. That's the point, really, of consolidation" (Ayers 94). In light of Ayers's vision, we might imagine an enormous vampire bat blotting out Kooser's streetlight altogether.

Is a nationalizing or globalizing hegemonization, or, to use Ayers's term, "consolidation," appealing or terrifying within the context of place? A University of Virginia librarian tells me that when he picks up guests from the Charlottesville, Virginia, airport, he always brings them to town by way of a pastoral back route that highlights the Virginia countryside rather than via Highway 29, the corporate consolidation of that road being avoided in favor of ostensible residential variation and local color. In contrast, in one of his books, University of Virginia professor Mark Edmundson explicitly identifies the more sparsely populated expanse of Highway 29 South below Charlottesville—a largely bucolic stretch of road beyond the Ragged Mountains, a range of hills memorialized in a story by Poe—as the route a person might have followed to Lynchburg, Virginia, if she had wished to hold an audience with the Reverend Jerry Falwell Jr. while he was alive. Edmundson's 2004 book, *Why Read?*, is concerned with big universal questions of intellectual location: Does contemporary literary study suffer amid a theory-enforced, dehumanizing malaise? How do we make today's students care about reading, or anything else for that matter? Does a secular democratic humanism offer a kind of panacea for these issues or does it constitute yet another interpretive detour, or, worse, a regression? Rather than bury us in national, multi-institution assessment data, Edmundson addresses these questions locally: by depicting the academic community and larger region in which he teaches (Virginia); by recording student (most of them Virginians) comments and the tenor of the classes he teaches; and by relating these variables to his own formative working-class Massachusetts background. Edmundson is not a native of the Virginia spaces he inhabits, but in addressing his archetypal questions, he repeatedly draws on the place where he had been living for almost a quarter century when he embarked on writing the book. And in recording his place, he creates it, his immediate surroundings formulating the homegrown rudiments of answers to his large, homeless questions.

* * *

When not being outright ignored or belittled, regional study usually is sublimated into the often seemingly locale-less interdisciplinary concept known as globalization, which generally espouses the vision of a borderless world dominated by multinationals and markets, vanguards of a homogenized culture shaped by Western values and a grand narrative of reason. Yet beneath this imagined oneness reside a number of lingering, though perhaps doomed, places, systems and paradoxical elements. For example, the concept of nationalism continues to present itself as a complex sociopolitical phenomenon, constantly in formation, deformation, and reformation in response to various other place-based catalysts of change, such as soccer's World Cup. The dominant state form over the last five centuries or so, the nation-state emerged on a broad historical canvas out of dramatic processes of social change that incorporated empires, city-states, tribes, and feudal lords. Often taking the defensive in light of its tenuous mutability, the nation-state usually is portrayed by globalization proponents in terms of its narrowness, selfishness, and exclusiveness. And delving deeper, beyond nationalism, we spy the stubborn, familiar phenomenon of regionalism, nearer to each of us though sometimes more difficult to perceive. Often depicted by globalization thinkers as a smaller, meaner, more nostalgic form of nationalism, regionalism perpetuates a collective set of visions and values aimed at the establishment of a local system, formal or informal, within a specific geographical area. However, for all its perceived backward provincialism, the regional context finds itself attracting increasing recognition from observers of international relations, international political economies, and development, as well as governments and other stakeholders in civil society and the private sector. Increasingly, economic and cultural leaders find themselves searching for regional solutions to the problems and challenges presented by national and global forces. Much energy, therefore, now is being devoted to studying how regional processes relate to globalization: how regional trade arrangements may be stumbling blocks or stepping stones to ever-increasing free trade, and whether regional integration, economic as well as cultural, can be understood as a way of negotiating nationalism and globalization or of creating a social buffer against their potentially disturbing effects.

Things have begun to change, if for no other reason than many of the aspects of globalization, having been tracked and assessed for a few years now, are turning out to constitute bad business. As Baraldi summarizes at length:

> Explicit attempts by policy officials to copy and reproduce places, or even only a few chosen spatial features, seldom succeed. And even those actors who are expected to exert the strongest globalizing and homogenizing pressures, namely multinational corporations, simultaneously search for and foster variety and uniqueness in the places they aim to combine through their international networks. On the other side of the barricade, local authorities may well try to copy some successful recipes from abroad, but they do so only in order to make their place a truly unique, privileged spot on the world map capable of attracting investments and people. While all this goes on, neglecting the forces behind the heterogeneity of places in favor of a deterministic model that unilaterally predicts homogeneity is a severe limitation on our ability to understand the role of places and space in scientific, technical and business life. (Baraldi, Fors, and Houltz 387)

The cultural side of the globalization movement appears equally harried at present. Duke University Press, long a bastion and cheerleader for various manifestations of the movement, now finds itself publishing books such as Arturo Escobar's *Territories of Difference* that call into question the premises of a number of titles from its late-1990s and early-twenty-first-century publishing catalogue. As Escobar summarizes:

> Marginalization of place has had profound consequences for our understanding of culture, nature, and economy, all of which are now seen as determined almost exclusively by global forces. It is time to reverse this asymmetry by focusing anew on the continued vitality of place in the creation of culture, nature, and economy. Place continues to be important in the loves of most people, if by place we mean the engagement with and experience of a particular location with some measure of groundedness (however unstable), boundaries (however permeable), and connections to everyday life, even if its identity is constructed and never fixed. (Escobar 30)

Provocative books such as Ursula Heise's *Sense of Place and Sense of Planet* do a promising job of attempting to lay groundwork for a cosmopolitan ethic that weds the local and the global, but no convincing pragmatic plan has been offered to date. No, the pendulum (for the moment at least) seems to be swinging back to the local, globalization having become the unpleasant, homogenous, conservative edifice once occupied by *place* as a haven for nativism, parochialism, and sentimentality. Instead, it is the communal local—with its neighborly culture, agricultural and business exchanges, and deep sustainable care for its immediate surroundings—that has assumed practical and moral responsibility for human life as it proceeds deeper into the twenty-first century.

* * *

What I am proposing, in a literary context, is a New Regionalism: an idea of place which recognizes the individual and community as stewards of land and culture in attempting to realize a sustainable future for one's immediate environment and—if enough others choose a similar path—the planet. I do not mean to limit such an idea to a county, state, region, or country, though I believe lessons may be learned from investigations into the constructions and phenomena of each. I would merely second the following statement by Edward Casey: "Let us agree that a region is, minimally, *a coherent collection of places*—where the places are not necessarily the same in extent, composition, or overall character" (Casey xxx). In the interests of making this idea a little more open, my single caveat to Casey's definition is that the word *coherent* be preceded by *often* or *sometimes*.

I asserted earlier in this introduction that understanding our places helps us save ourselves, and I happen to mean that pragmatically as well as metaphorically. As ecology and environmental science make new and increasingly intricate links between natural and human systems, fundamental points (though certainly not all the points) made by agrarian thinkers as recent as Wendell Berry and as remote as Thomas Jefferson gradually are being proven by science. Indeed, the matrix of moral, political, and environmental ideals informing farming, which stretch back to the earliest human agricultural communities, are perhaps more relevant than ever as industrial agriculture and global economics experience anxiety over environmental collapse and world food shortages. This is not to say that agrarianism is useful as is, and certainly not in its most venerable forms. To argue that point would be to overlook racist, sexist, and colonial ideologies that have accompanied agrarianism on occasion and today would prove not only politically unacceptable, but also environmentally and economically counterproductive. Rather, an appreciation of food's function in local systems—for urbanites, suburbanites, country people, and all manner of folk in between—coupled with knowledge of the growing body of ecological and environmental science research seems destined to apply some of agrarianism's best and most fundamental ideals for sustainable existence as we find ourselves increasingly negotiating an era of dwindling world resources and dysfunctional global practices.

I noted earlier, too, that this book is a rehabilitative endeavor, for when we rediscover our places, we enlarge our view and appreciation of the world. It is also a work of literary scholarship. It leaves many of the cultural and economic variables of place to the experts most suited to their study. My avenue for conveying a new regionalism of place is through the investigation of academic literary matters and the books from which they arise. To attempt more would be presumptuous. I leave it to my sibling experts in their disciplines to hoe their own rows and tend their own gardens in the respective manners most befitting a robust harvest for us all.

* * *

Since we happen to be here, on this farm in Appomattox County, in North America, not far from where the Blue Ridge of eastern Appalachia meets the hard red clay of the Piedmont—a word which, by the way, means "foot of the mountains"—we might consider briefly, as an avenue for entering the literary fray, the specialty areas which identify themselves as southern literature and Appalachian literature, respectively. The following is a quote I sometimes use in class when introducing the idea of regionalism:

"The old sectional consciousnesses are rapidly fading. Except for certain slight and diminishing habits of speech, it is impossible to distinguish a Southerner from a Northerner or a Californian from a Yankee" (Hubbell 473). This observation might have been written or uttered yesterday or last week depending on the area of the United States, yet it appears in an essay entitled "The Decay of the Provinces: A Study of Nationalism and Sectionalism" from a 1927 volume of the *Sewanee Review*. That the author, a Virginian named Jay B. Hubbell, should have proclaimed a marked diminishing of regional sensibility almost a century ago may strike many readers of contemporary American literature as odd, especially in light of the numerous regionally focused journals and small presses quietly publishing across the United States today. However, the age of the observation also may direct some of us to question the authenticity of contemporary regional identities in the face of seemingly unavoidable and influential national and global commercial forces. How much contemporary literary regionalism reveals the true essence of a distinctive place and its people? How much is merely a kind of act: a formulated drama unfolding on a set, draped partially in nostalgia, that no longer exists save within the confines of the writer's mind?

Of special note in his senescent essay, Hubbell—also the author of the still-useful, nearly one-thousand-page literary history *The South in American Literature, 1607–1900* (1954)—identified the American South as a region "which represents the sectional extreme in our literature" ("Decay" 477). The act of pointing to the South as the country's most powerfully distinctive literary region hardly would have surprised anyone, even during the 1920s. Yet, if we accept Hubbell's observation that regional consciousness had become tenuous in his own time, we cannot help but wonder at the real nature of the South he was discussing or the one that exists—if, indeed, it really does exist—now. Hubbell provides part of the answer himself, for he specifies an image, a "representation," of the region rather than the region itself. Three quarters of a century later, in his foreword to a twenty-first-century essay collection called *South to a New Place*, scholar Richard Gray agrees that the South is portrayed and considered most fruitfully as a series of representational mimetic abstractions: "The South is an imagined community made up of a multiplicity of communities, similarly imagined" ("Foreward" xxiii).

This makes for confusing identification, but then conscious symbolic identity is not something with which southerners, except for a small handful of writers and academics, really concern themselves. As Gray points out, everyday southerners still are driven "to position themselves *with* others in their locality, communality of interest or area, and *against* or *apart from* others elsewhere," a sectional sensibility we might identify as generally familiar and traditional ("Foreward" xxiii). The editors of *South to a New Place,* Suzanne Jones and Sharon Monteith, espouse new articulations of the South based on places recently established within it or on meanings that arise from looking away from it, purposefully considering its various aspects peripherally while gazing at various international phenomena and other disciplines. The overarching critical approach of the book constitutes an early example of an interdisciplinary scholarly trend that proposes to evaluate the South, its literature, and its history in a global context, abjuring traditional considerations of specific places for a much larger interlocking perspective. Many current literary scholars who study the South have chosen to work out the various theories and paradigms they champion in comparative world contexts: the Gulf Coast, for instance, set against the south of France, or the commonalities of slavery's legacy in the United States with its history in the Caribbean and/or South America. Accordingly, such work considers subjects such as culture, race, and homosexuality across novels, decades, and hemispheres. Collectively, there emerges what might kindly be labeled a "montage" or negatively termed a "big interpretive mess": a magnificently agitated field of vision.

What we have then at this particular moment in southern literary studies is a series of shifty, occasionally overlapping, scholarly metanarratives creating various abstract formulations of the South: his South, her South, their South, our South. Diane Roberts's afterword to *South to a New Place* begins, "It was supposed to be gone, the South, all difference swept away in America's mass-culture tsunami" (Roberts 363). It seems Roberts has read and endorses Hubbell, for a little later on she remarks, "The South has always been disappearing, or about to disappear" (363). I would go further than Roberts and claim that whatever authentic collective identity the South may have possessed departed much earlier. As far back as 1939, Benjamin T. Spencer, in another bygone essay from the *Sewanee Review,* offered that if it fails in establishing any fundamental meaning, "then the term 'Southern' as applied to literature, like 'American,' might almost as well be abandoned" (Spencer 500). Nevertheless, almost a century later, academics and the scholarly publishing scene appear reluctant to allow that to happen just yet. As Roberts prophesies at the end of her afterword, "The 'newcomers' will invent and invest in their own Souths and so change the region. . . . Keeping up mythic property is hard work" (373).

* * *

Of special interest to this book, over the course of *South to a New Place*'s nearly four hundred pages, the South's Appalachian region, the communities that exist along and within thousands of square miles of hills, hollows, and mountains, is mentioned but once and only in passing, while places such as Italy and East Germany each receive full chapters. Indeed, the Souths that are imagined in the book seem more or less flat, tropical, cosmopolitan places: akin to each other in essence despite the disparate abstractions that are created within them. It is probably unfair, though, to criticize the book's wholesale neglect of the entire southern Appalachian region since works of southern literary criticism have been doing so for decades, accounting for it only rarely. In fact, such omissions generally have come to be expected and understood among readers and writers of Appalachian literature. Over the last two decades, however, scholars familiar with the dynamics of Appalachia have taken it upon themselves to establish an Appalachian studies almost entirely independent of those scholars who purport to explicate the South as a whole. Theirs is the excitement of a dynamic and promising field still in the process of establishing itself. As is noted by professors Danny Miller, Sharon Hatfield, and Gurney Norman, the editors of *An American Vein*, the most comprehensive collection of Appalachian literary criticism to date:

> Despite growing enthusiasm for Appalachian literature among readers who know it, there is no denying that this unique part of American literature remains largely unrecognized by the rest of the country. Many individual writers from the mountains have found success and acclaim beyond the region, but awareness of the *region itself* as a thriving center of literary creativity is not widespread. It is hoped that this collection of critical essays will help new readers, nationally and internationally, discover Appalachian literature and its relevance to our times. (Miller, Hatfield, and Norman xiii)

As scholarly books about the South continue to demonstrate, the editors' identification of a widespread lack of attention is an accurate observation. For instance, the scant reference Appalachia received in the seminal book

The History of Southern Literature is limited to Merrill Skaggs's chapter on local color, in which she identifies a few Appalachian writers either as "mountaineers" or by the states from which they hail. Likewise, theme-based scholarly studies of the South generally have been remiss in noting the numerous differences between the southern Appalachian region and the South's lower elevations. Anthologies of southern literature also have avoided and ignored the (sub)region, for the most part. In fact, the editors of *An American Vein* specifically note having greeted the one-hundred-page section, "Appalachia Recognized," in the contemporary anthology *The South in Perspective* with "surprise and delight."

Southern writers, ever a step or two ahead of the people who write about them, have been quicker to embrace the Appalachian literary scene than have the region's scholars, the active roll of the Fellowship of Southern Writers including such mountain folk as Fred Chappell, R.H.W. Dillard, Charles Frazier, Robert Morgan, Ron Rash, Lee Smith, and Charles Wright. Of special note, Chappell has recounted that Smith was the first writer he ever encountered who described herself as Appalachian rather than southern, a position for which Chappell greatly admired her and which he began adopting himself. Both writers grew up in counties—Smith's a Virginia coal community, Chappell's a North Carolina agricultural district—that lacked extensive old-family land holdings, Lost Cause nostalgia, or even minimal African American populations. For them, most of the scholarly renderings of and assumptions about southern literature, old and new, simply do not fit their experiences or work. Thus, *An American Vein* succeeds where many southern scholarly studies fail, considering the work of Smith, Chappell, and a host of other writers, living and dead, as articulations of the mountain cultures that produced them, in many ways divorced from the history and ways of the larger, lower-elevation South. In this way the book relieves and rehabilitates the aims and achievements of writers previously forced into ill-fitting paradigms that struggled awkwardly to articulate their cultures and concerns.

The final goal of the editors of *An American Vein* is "to present Appalachian literary criticism as a vital part of the American literary tradition" (Miller, Hatfield, and Norman xvii). Gathering for the first time more than a half-century's worth of literary scholarship on the region, the essays, as a whole, are not as fashionable, innovative, or theoretically sophisticated as those appearing in a collection such as *South to a New Place*. However, because they constitute the discipline's first comprehensive scholarly collection, interpretive abstraction probably should not be their aim. Many of the essays rightly take the time to offer plot summaries and biographical information on works and authors that will appear unfamiliar to many readers. The theory-laden formulations, the metanarratives, will come in time, but a scholarly foundation must be laid initially in order for those phenomena to function, to work either in concert with or against. *An American Vein* then has been a long time coming and most certainly is a book that is overdue. Its arrival, however, is timely nonetheless: it is a much-needed, indispensable resource for scholars, teachers, and serious readers of Appalachian literature.

Several times at readings or on panels, I have heard Lee Smith refer to southern Appalachia as "the South's South," not unlike that related mountain cousin many family members choose to disown. Yet, out of Appalachia's legacy of difference and disadvantage is arising a distinctive and dynamic period of unmistakable change: a rich milieu for those contemporary regional writers and scholars who are taking the mountains for their own and exploring the region's complexities. It seems inevitable, too, that readers and scholars of southern literature in general will increasingly take note of Appalachia's evolution. As much as the South and southern Appalachia constitute different places viscerally and culturally, they also occupy different points both in terms of their respective imaginative developments and the scholarly discourses that seek to explicate them. In looking away—scanning and scavenging the global horizon for the things we hope to install into our respective Souths—those of us who share an interest in the region as a whole must continue to take care not to trip over the neglected visceral things before us: a lump of coal, perhaps, or a petrified chestnut stump. For there *are* mountains in the South, and more and more people are beginning to imagine them.

The way in which I have described the respective and overlapping states of the place-based southern and Appalachian discursive communities—and I am aware there are those who would take issue with my summary—gives me hope there is good work to be accomplished in each of these regional academic arenas that would help enrich our understandings of other distinctive neighborhoods as well. Or is that the best way to go about it? Should theory-based, abstract scholarship, or metascholarship, continue as the current dominant mode for regional, place-specific inquiry? I ask these questions in light of two calls for papers that came across my computer screen. One, a proposed book entitled *The Limits of History* describes itself as follows:

> This volume is guided by the assumption that the current dominance of historicist approaches to literary study has often distorted the discipline, that historical methodology as it has been applied in contemporary literary scholarship is often heedless of its own methodological inconsistency, blind to its dependence on other disciplines, and incapable of clearly articulating many of its own most deeply held values. The essays in this volume will address the flaws of literary historicism as it is currently practiced and suggest more productive roles for historical scholarship with the ultimate purpose of clarifying the goals and values of literary study.

Blind? Incapable? Flawed? Indeed, that is pretty strong medicine for a millennial PhD such as myself, for whom historically based cultural-studies approaches constituted the framework for nearly every graduate-school paper I wrote. Now here is the other CFP which struck me as oddly connected:

> Essays are invited for a proposed collection on the theme of critical friction, a term which denotes the potential possibilities, opportunities, conflicts, and problems in the work of critics who write fiction, as well as creative writers who are also literary critics. In today's marketplace, many authors of literary fiction come from a background in academic criticism. Even those who do not are likely to have been through a higher education system which has exposed them to modern critical techniques, theories, and approaches to the interpretation of literature. This collection seeks to probe this relationship between the literary and the critical, and the slippages between the two.

Perhaps I can best elaborate on these two calls for papers with a brief anecdote. A few years back at the small liberal arts college where I teach, lack of space dictated that I share an office with a part-time writing instructor named Christian Wiman. A poet and essayist by trade, Wiman passionately wrote for literary magazines yet reluctantly relied on his teaching job for income, a familiar situation for many writers, young and not so young. Although this state of affairs irritated him, Wiman tolerated for a time the college structure, its dogmas, and its clear preferences for academically inclined research. As a kind of hybrid literary being myself—someone who periodically alternates between jargon-riddled articles in refereed journals and essays or creative pieces in literary magazines—I could sympathize with Wiman's frustration. Whereas I might always retreat safely into the purely scholarly academic side of things, my officemate was decidedly out on a limb with the other writers and artists for whom the higher education system often becomes odious, burdensome, and ultimately intolerable in conjunction with their artistic aims. Eventually for Wiman it came to constitute just those very things, and he forsook Lynchburg College for Chicago, where he now edits a magazine called *Poetry*. Much to the detriment of the college, the last laugh was his, and it pleases me even now to have had a small role in that mirth. Yet the happy ending I just have related constitutes a decided anomaly in a profession which sends its apprentices out into a world with sparse jobs and possesses a reputation for commonly terminating those few who hang on in annually renewable positions, especially those lacking terminal degrees who publish creative work.

Dissatisfied with the state of affairs and mindful of the uneasy and not always successful relationship between scholarly academic scribbling and largely nonacademic creative writing, I began increasingly to question the underpinnings of the former. And, as those two calls for papers attest, so, it seems, have others. In my particular case, however, the practice of investigating and accepting my academic work has taken on a decidedly personal and autobiographical hue: the attractive prospect—attractive anyway to me—of abstract scholarly data merged with personal experience: with the space and place of existence itself—each enriching the other. Fortunately, there exist already many fine exemplars in this mode, Barry Lopez's *Arctic Dreams*, for example, which celebrate and deepen the stories of their respective places by powerfully relating the experiences of their tellers within them.

My particular appreciation for and resolve to apply a similar approach came, appropriately enough, not from a book, not from vicarious experience, but from experience itself. As a participant in an NEH Regional Studies seminar, I, along with another literary scholar, were charged with devising a writing workshop manual for battered women, to be housed in the Caretta Community Center in McDowell County, West Virginia.

Ours was one of many service projects aimed at applying the latest studies in place, globalization, and public policy to the community needs of McDowell County, at the time the poorest and most illiterate district in West Virginia, and the sixth-poorest county in the United States. Having absorbed various theoretical and artistic constructions of southern Appalachia, in general, and coal country, in particular, we had winded our way into southern West Virginia with the challenge of attempting to translate our intellectual abstractions and techniques into some variety of community benefit. We had studied the history, culture, and economics of the region very closely. We arrived with a sound grasp of globalization theory and a new understanding of public policy. We hoped we could employ these abstractions as a means of doing some good for the folks of McDowell County. We were, of course, very ignorant and naïve.

Even now in McDowell County—three hundred miles from Washington, D.C., yet consistently rated one of the top ten poorest counties in the United States, eight-tenths of its land owned by people who don't live there, home to staggering rates of illness, illiteracy, and drug and domestic abuse—there exists, to a notable degree, a troubling marketing of victimization, an advertised human deprivation that openly attracts and recruits philanthropic groups and tolerates their various ideologies for the purpose of attaining whatever material benefits may be involved. Sometimes, a measure of genuine good is accomplished. Overall though, one cannot help but feel troubled that those who arrive with aid are, in some sense, not all that different in their paternalistic material capacities from the coal companies of old: a new benevolent crutch to replace the old malignant one, though a crutch remains a crutch, as the saying goes.

My colleague and I worried about slipping into this trap and considered the best ways by which to apply our knowledge in a manner that would prove helpful without appearing unduly prescriptive or, worse, condescending (our eventual solution was to spend as much money as we could in local bars and restaurants). Over the course of a previous summer I had attended a month-long seminar on the globalization of culture at Research Triangle's National Humanities Center, where one of the recurring questions had been how exactly to apply the theoretical salves and prescriptions of globalization theory through the visceral arm of regional public policy. One of the visiting lecturers, Rey Chow, confessed that this was something that had troubled and haunted her with regard to her own work, especially her writings on China. Another scholar, Timothy Brennan, appeared less concerned, offering that theorists should probably just do their jobs and policymakers, theirs.

I believe my own intellectual sensibility and visceral West Virginia experience align me, at least on this particular issue, more closely with Chow's position. Hoping to reconcile my abstract regional assumptions with the autobiographical aspects of experiential learning, I set out to perform nearly six hundred miles of hiking, following secondary roads along a route hugging the western slope of the Blue Ridge Mountains and descending into the Holston River Valley (from western Maryland to eastern Tennessee) that once was called Athowominee, which is Iroquoian for the "Warrior's Path." At one time the route had connected the nations of the Iroquois in the northeast and the Cherokee in the south, and was used by the first European settlers to enter and settle what was then considered the frontier. It is estimated now that as many as three out of every four Americans have an ancestor who used this trail at one time or another. My own German ancestors had followed the path from the Catoctin Mountain area of western Maryland to the Smoky Mountains at the end of the 1790s, and I resolved to make the same trip, comparing, along the way, that portion of contemporary eastern Appalachia against the accounts of early explorers. My hope was to generate a narrative of the natural and cultural development of that region, and connect those historical variables to the cultural and environmental realities that exist in the area now—the ongoing relevance of a place fundamental to the history of the United States and most individual Americans. Though the book is now available in print (*The Warrior's Path: Reflections Along an Ancient Route*), only time will tell if the narrative even will have begun to have done its job.

I relate these autobiographical elements since they necessarily inform both the concerns of this book, including my first-person narrative departures in two of the later chapters, as well as my recent forays into Virginia literature from European colonization to the present, performed in order to identify material for inclusion in the Virginia Foundation for the Humanities' *Encyclopedia Virginia*, for which I continue to edit the literature section. Academics often are fond of saying how their work is their life. However, for me—of Virginia, though in some sense culturally displaced *into* it—it can never be anything else.

But what of others? Why should the disinterested writer or scholar, with an already burdensome research agenda and beset with other alluring theories, even bother to read for place? For at its worst, regional study admittedly remains as small and limiting as the sectional or provincial boundaries that confine it. At its worst it dogmatically subordinates intellectual and/or artistic achievement and merit to geography. It lionizes exclusion, segregating identities and meanings, ethnic or otherwise, chaining them to invisible boundaries. Yet, conversely, the best sort of place-based study does just the opposite: it embraces variation, delineates diaspora; it demonstrates that the places we inhabit are forever changing, although, like time-lapse photography, the process may remain altogether invisible to the naked eye. It shows us, too, if only for an instant, our constantly evolving selves amid our ever-changing surroundings.

* * *

This book is organized to underscore the time-lapse process I refer to via words. Part I, the section we currently are inhabiting, entitled "Getting (Back) There: An Introduction and a Case Study," introduces a number of avenues for investigating region and place while critiquing some of their predecessors, new and old. It is followed, tested placially and spatially, by chapter 1, in which a character finds himself in a situation where he must adapt to a place with his life hanging in the balance. Landscape, diverse environments, and interactions between the human and natural worlds inform this chapter.

One way to think of this book is as a microscope, beginning with our academic selves, before magnifying the apparatus and upping the specificity. Hence, Part II, "A Matter of Context: Region and Place," zeroes in on two troubling and ambiguous overlapping places: the American South and Appalachia. When place and region are used interchangeably, a war of identity ensues, yet one that reveals the nuances of place in a way that a larger context—a nation-state, for instance—cannot. One writer's view of a changing South; another's experience of urban Appalachia; a piece both essay and interview addressing both the South and Appalachia; and a collection of reviews which function as a kind of microcosm, inform this section's meditation on the complexities and blendings of regional identification. Part III, "Looking Closer: A State of Place," intensifies the magnification even more, focusing on a single state, Virginia, which falls beneath the regional labels of both the American South and Appalachia. As inferred in the introduction, it is these county-based—even village-based—investigations of place that are most apt to yield the wisdom of the world and bring us closest to ourselves, wherever we may be. The book's epilogue closes with a pragmatic application of some of its abstract assertions, recounting the full experience of myself and another academic in our attempt to effect the humblest of positive local impacts in southern West Virginia.

* * *

Partially throwing his hands up in the air, J. E. Malpas notes in his book *Place and Experience: A Philosophical Topography* that "place cannot be reduced to any one of the elements situated within its compass, but must instead be understood as a structure comprising spatiality *and* temporality, subjectivity *and* objectivity, self *and* other" (163). At the risk of attempting to afford an overview of what I take to be the current state—or, at least, *one* current state—of place-based study with regard to contemporary literature, I have not always explored in great depth some of the specific modes of interpretive inquiry that currently are yielding rich results: ethnic, gendered, and comparative formulations, to name but a few. The key point here, however, within the temporal confines of this soon-to-be-concluded introduction, is that reading for place, making use of the theoretical and experiential tools which lie within easy reach of each of us, remains both a provocative and accessible mode of inquiry *for* each of us. This book, then, is a beginning and an invitation: a beginning and an invitation for us all. In delineating various understandings of our places, we necessarily enrich our comprehension of the variable equations that conspire to create others. In this sense, reading for place possesses the capacity to perceive the world passionately and deeply. And to writers, scholars, and artists, what could matter more?

1

"To Blend in the Place You're In, but with a Mind to Do Something"

The Practice of Merging in James Dickey's *To the White Sea*

> Genius resides in instinct; goodness likewise. One acts perfectly only when one acts instinctively.
>
> Nietzsche, *Werke: Kritische Gesamtausgabe*

> If I were to tell you that the rise of any free bird
> Is better
>
> the larger the bird is,
>
> And that I found myself one of these
> Without surprise, you would understand
>
> That this makes of air a thing that would be liberty
> Enough for any world but this one,
> And could see how I should have gone
>
> Up and out of all
>
> all of it. . . .
>
> James Dickey, "Eagles"

> I am not dead, I have only become inhuman.
>
> Robinson Jeffers, "Inscription for a Gravestone"

Despite its Second World War Japanese milieu and singular narrator/protagonist, the third and final novel of James Dickey, *To the White Sea* (1993), is possessed of close symbolic and thematic associations with each of the author's preceding two published fictional works. As in Dickey's best-known book *Deliverance*, water—in this case, the ocean—constitutes an identifying imaginative trope. In fact, Dickey originally called the work *Thalatta*, a variation of a Greek word meaning "sea." The book's conceptual similarities to Dickey's massive second novel *Alnilam* are equally notable. At its conclusion the protagonist's essence, like Joel Cahill's ghost in *Alnilam*, constitutes "a voice in the wind" (*To the White Sea [TS]* 274). However, although over the course of *To the White Sea* the protagonist, known only by the one-word name Muldrow, journeys across and through the elements of earth, air, water, and fire, his general sensibility remains acutely earth based. A child of the frozen Arctic wastes, Muldrow thinks of the cold of high-altitude aircraft as "the wrong cold": "The cold of high air is not real, it's not honest. Cold should be connected to the ground, even if it's at the top of a mountain" (*TS* 20). Muldrow's strong association with the landscape, as well as his use of and extended meditations on camouflage, make *To the White Sea* one of the most unique explorations of place in contemporary fiction. And it is the protagonist's powerful and peculiar desire to merge seamlessly with his place—"to blend in the place you're in, but with a mind to do something" (*TS* 273)—which makes the book haunting and resonant beyond its final pages.

Among the unpublished notes for his third novel, Dickey lists Muldrow's resources as "his cool," "his purpose: to get to . . . the sea 'with ice in it,'" "concealment," and "his ruthlessness." Following a discussion of Muldrow's background and its sources—his imaginative places of origin—I will be examining *To the White Sea* largely in terms of the qualities Dickey identifies. The first and last of Muldrow's listed assets, his "cool" and "ruthlessness," are expressions Dickey uses in depicting Muldrow's conscienceless personality, and I will seek to illustrate how Muldrow's circumstances and Dickey's background materials mold the character into an unrepentant killer. Even so, despite Muldrow's pitiless love of bloodshed, many readers sympathize with him through much of the novel. This is due largely to his semantic appeal, which—possessing an unusual combination of stunning poetic imagery and glib common sense—seduces the reader into his world view. Establishing the importance of Muldrow's discourse, I go on to demonstrate how it leads to his *Umwelt*, or self-world, which is based largely on a philosophy of later-day Epicureanism. This is apparent both in his dialogue with an American monk and his obsessive cataloguing of equipment. Muldrow's interest in matter and space also intersects with his need to arrive at the "sea with ice in it," the spatial and material environment in which he feels most comfortable. Correspondingly, I reveal how his magnetic drive northward in Japan takes on the quality of migration as he begins associating himself with various animals through his practice of dreaming. Amid his identifications with creatures and the compulsion to move northward, Muldrow develops and perfects his method of camouflage or "concealment," which feeds upon a dynamic of inhumanism that, in turn, makes his final transformation into place possible. Having waited throughout the novel, like the speaker in Dickey's poem "Fog Envelops the Animals," to feel "Long-sought invisibility / Come forth from my solid body" (*The Whole Motion* 80), he arrives at a cumulative juncture in space, time, and place where he presumes such a metamorphosis is possible.

* * *

Scion of the frozen north and product of its icy wastes, the character Muldrow is shaped, both inside and out, by the environment that surrounds him. At the beginning of the novel, he explains that he grew up on the north side of "the Brooks Range, which is away from everything, facing away from the States . . ." (*TS* 10). Even at this early stage, before we know much about him, Muldrow stresses the lonely autonomy of the habitat that forged him. It exists not "away from" specific places and objects, but rather "away from everything," a condition that reflects back upon the place itself, "the Brooks Range," and on the person who inhabits it: Muldrow. Significantly, Muldrow identifies his home by a geographical feature, a range of mountains, instead of evoking a principality or his national allegiance. Although Alaska is part of the United States, Muldrow characterizes his section of the Brooks Range as "facing away from the States," symbolically turning its back upon and rejecting the country that claims dominion over it. In fact, he says of his military service philosophy, "I had a way of doing things that was about half the Air Force's and half mine" (*TS* 20). Muldrow conceives of himself and his home as looking outward, northward—to an even colder and wilder environment—as opposed to gazing inward, toward the culture and civilization of the United States.

Dickey used Barry Lopez's book, *Arctic Dreams: Imagination and Desire in a Northern Landscape*, as a major background source for both portraying Muldrow's Arctic landscape and establishing his connection with Eskimos. Lopez attributes the genesis of this book to "two moments," one of which takes place near Muldrow's Alaskan habitat, in "the western Brooks Range of Alaska" (xvii). He recalls watching with lonely fascination, as Muldrow does in his youth, the herds of caribou, the wolverine, the elusive fox, and various migratory birds—all flourishing in a seemingly barren landscape, nearly devoid of people. Throughout Lopez's book—a fluid arrangement of history, science, and memoir—the dynamics of desolation, beauty, alienation, and death constantly reappear, culminating in an act of homage. Asserting at the book's conclusion that "the landscape and the animals were like something found at the end of a dream" (371), Lopez faces northward and bows to the inscrutable Arctic, a worshipful act that suggests Muldrow's repeated idealizations of his Alaskan environment.

In addition to drawing on the rich frozen wildness of Lopez's book, Dickey employed Vardis Fisher's novels *Mountain Man* and *Dark Bidwell* as source texts for Muldrow's upbringing and personality. *Mountain Man* takes place in the American West, north of the Oregon Trail, during the 1840s and follows Sam Minard, a scout and trapper, whose pregnant Crow wife is murdered by a band of renegade Crow. Vowing revenge, Minard declares war on the entire Crow nation, and much of the novel is spent describing his battles with various Black Feet and Crow, to whom he becomes known simply as "The Terror." Minard's interest in woodcraft and fighting strategies (which he compares to the tactics of various wild animals) and his single-handed attack on an enemy nation are highly suggestive of Muldrow, although their characters and circumstances are otherwise quite different.

More of Muldrow's character, especially his childhood development, is drawn from *Dark Bidwell*'s Jed Bidwell, a boy raised in a rattler-infested Idaho gorge on the Snake River in the early 1900s. The narrator's summary of Jed's childhood development is notable for its remarkable similarity to Muldrow's:

> Everything around him [Jed], for that matter, invited him to solitude or to reckless deeds. The great mountains, the untamed headstrong river, the wild animal life and the lonely blockade of winter months—he felt the power of all these, and their ruthlessness, and their savage ways. He took the spirit of them into his soul. The people whom he met, besides his own kin, were coarse in speech and thought. Sly sheepherders became his tutor, feeding his hungry imagination, suggesting deeds that he had never done. The early events of his life, often the tasks which his father gave him to do, shaped his emotions into a pattern of pride and revenge.
>
> And so he grew, schooled by savagery. Cruelty in his life was a meaningless word. Suffering and pain he was accustomed to from

> his first years. The agony of a tortured thing meant no more to him than the flow of the river or the cutting down of a tree; and he looked upon death as calmly as he looked upon life. (151–52)

Like Muldrow Jed is shaped by the environment in which he is raised, taking its qualities into himself—"into his soul." The morals of civilization mean nothing because they are such alien, nearly nonexistent, concepts; their only representatives are wandering sheepherders and occasional traveling settlers, themselves not very civilized.

In this vacuum of morality and collective human existence, Jed Bidwell gives himself over almost entirely to the qualities of the inhuman natural world. The sheepherders who rarely visit, like Muldrow's Eskimo acquaintances, offer a weak sampling of human interaction, but, being "coarse" and uneducated, there is nothing overly civilized about them, and their existence too depends on nature and animals. Also significant in Jed's development is the importance of the father—described by people who knew him as "a little bit out of his wits" (16)—whose reasons for coming west "remained a dark riddle" (18), a play on his name, Dark Bidwell. Muldrow's father's basis for moving from Virginia to Alaska is equally ambiguous, even to his only son. Muldrow speculates:

> He had his own reasons for being there, which he never did get around to telling me, or that I ever really understood. It may have been he got into some kind of trouble, back in Virginia or somewhere in the States, though I don't think it had anything to do with the law. But something had happened to him that made him want to be by himself, or maybe he was just that way all the time. Like I say, he never did give me the straight of it. (*TS* 19)

Echoing the eccentricity and possible madness of Jed's father, Muldrow says of his own, "The red wall was my father's only strangeness, though other people might have told you different" (*TS* 213). While other civilized humans regard Jed's and Muldrow's fathers as peculiar or perhaps even mad, the sons—raised without the benefit of any substantial comparative references—accept their sires' behaviors as customary, allowing them to shape their own.

It is Jed Bidwell's father who, for practical reasons—the protection of crops and livestock—encourages Jed to kill woodchucks and wipe out the snake population on their property. Yet the result of assuming this responsibility is a nurtured love of killing in Jed, a desire to outwit and destroy the entire species of whatever animal happens to threaten him. In order to eradicate them, Jed, like Muldrow, dedicates untold hours to the study of creatures: following them, watching them, and imitating them. He shares with Muldrow the obsessive poetic love of an animal's appearance and manner. Having built a snake pit, into which he casts dozens of captive rattlesnakes, Jed sits "on the stone wall, staring with pride into his venomous den. His breath would come slow and deep, and his eyes would darken, as he sensed fully their tamelessness and their power. He loved their jungle ferocity, and the lidless cunning hatred of their eyes" (177). Identifying himself with the powerful aspects of nature and its predatory creatures, Jed, like Muldrow, develops a strong inhuman and conscienceless personality from which he draws his opinions on existence: "'Some things is good,' Jed declared, 'and some things is bad. The bad things should ought-a-be killed. Human or beast, it's all the same to me'" (210).

A dominant byproduct of Jed's and Muldrow's upbringings is their predatory inhuman ruthlessness, which resembles the indifferent environments that produced them. Possessing an animalistic poetic sensibility, Muldrow conceives of the Alaskan landscape as Robinson Jeffers portrays the coastal hills at Sovranes Creek: "This is the noblest thing I have ever seen. / No imaginable / Human presence here could do anything / But dilute the lonely self-watchful passion" (358). Because Muldrow is so irrevocably alienated from human society, some readers have labeled him the victim of a de-evolution. Yet, it is Muldrow's very *Götterdämmerung*, his downfall from the communal order of societal norms and mores, which enables him to survive as long as he does. Mindful of this dynamic, Dickey constructs a provocative scenario in which a human being's subsistence hinges on the strength and effectiveness of his apparent inhumanity.

According to Dickey, Muldrow's lack of a conscience is based on Xenophon's *Anabasis*, the ancient historical account of ten thousand Greek soldiers who fought their way home fifteen hundred miles through rugged terrain and numerous barbarian hordes. Like Muldrow, the Hellenes in Xenophon's tale find themselves far behind enemy lines in an alien culture. After several Greeks are beheaded—as is the downed airman in Dickey's novel—while negotiating a truce, the survivors vow to use any means necessary that they might glimpse the Hellespont again. Like Muldrow, who also wishes to reach a specific geographic destination, the

Greeks repeatedly commit what most twenty-first-century readers would consider atrocities or war crimes. Throughout the campaign they liberally kidnap young boys and women of all ages from various villages to keep them as unwilling sexual companions and hostages. More suggestive of *To the White Sea*, in one incident, after repulsing a contingent of Persians, the Hellenes resolve to maim and behead the bodies of the fallen in an effort to discourage the enemy's morale. This episode calls to mind both the firebombing of Tokyo, which is partly an "anti-morale" raid, and Muldrow's decapitation of the old woman. Although Muldrow clearly is amused by his handiwork, his action, like that of the Greeks, accomplishes the practical military objective of spreading fear and confusion in the enemy's homeland. Furthermore, Xenophon, the advisor of the Hellenes and narrator of the account, never hesitates to make human sacrifices of prisoners when consulting the gods on matters of military strategy. Like Muldrow's path, the swath cut by the Greeks is littered with enemy corpses.

Dickey also claimed that Muldrow's conscienceless demeanor was drawn in part from the personality of Ted Bundy, the famous twentieth-century serial killer. Like Muldrow, Bundy enjoyed manipulating his personal appearance for the purpose of luring his victims to him. Using crutches or placing an arm in a sling, he often asked attractive female undergraduates to help him carry books to his Volkswagen Bug, at which point he would force them into the vehicle and spirit them away to a secluded place where, having eliminated the possibility of detection, he could rape and kill them at his leisure. However, although Bundy was an ingenious predator who displayed little guilt and, like Muldrow, targeted women, his similarities with Dickey's protagonist end there. With his good looks, magnetic charisma, and keen intellect, Bundy relied on conventions of humanity—qualities such as physical attractiveness and civic virtue—as props for his premeditated crimes.

Coinciding with Muldrow's developmental background and "ruthless" personality are the linguistic explanations he gives for his actions. Dickey maintained, "The hardest part of writing *To the White Sea* was to establish a tone or voice for Muldrow which would be convincing and yet distinctive to him. He's practically illiterate, but he has a highly developed personal mystique, which he states as a matter of course as though anybody would understand it. Actually, nobody but he understands it" (Kirschten 68). Dickey strengthens the appeal of Muldrow's unique discourse early in the novel by setting it in relief against less attractive language. In the book's first few pages, Muldrow's discriminating commentary appears reasonable versus the hyperbolic *Krieglust* of the Colonel's firebombing speech: "Fire. . . . We're going to put it in his eyes and up his asshole, in his wife's twat, and in his baby's diaper'" (*TS* 1). Beyond his negative use of military semantics, Dickey further attracts the reader to Muldrow's language by contrasting it with that of Arlen and the "Florida boy," the green airmen who approach him in the barracks. The larger of the two, Arlen, comes across as an insecure bully, flaunting his juvenile snake tattoo and badgering Muldrow with idle threats. In the face of Arlen's aggressive language ("I could bust his back with one chop" [*TS* 6]), Muldrow appears patient and forgiving, returning the money he wins from Arlen in their pinch-grip competition. He is equally tolerant of the Florida boy, who reveals his naïveté and fear of combat in the numerous questions he asks, which threaten to annoy both Muldrow and the reader. In his interaction with the young airmen, Muldrow's language seems neither boastful, like Arlen's, nor unsure, like the Floridian's. Against the inadequacies of the inexperienced fliers, Dickey portrays him as a patient and mature soldier who happens to excel at his job.

Muldrow continues to attract our understanding along dialogic lines once his plane is shot down, justifying his violent actions through repeated references to the emasculating and "decapitation-happy" Japanese, who have pledged to maim and execute any American airman found in Japan. Having stressed this dynamic to the reader, Dickey uses two events in order to finally undermine Muldrow's credibility: his seemingly gratuitous decapitation of an old woman and his confessed responsibility for the prewar death of a female identified only as the "Kansas girl." After inviting the reader's allegiance through the first half of the book, Muldrow performs alienating acts, both apparently committed on nothing more than a whim. *To the White Sea*, like *Deliverance*, is a first-person narrative; however, in the later novel Dickey upsets the reader's relationship with his narrator/protagonist in order to make her/him examine more fully both the nature of the narrator/protagonist and the practices of the reader. Dickey plays with the idea of reader/text merging by forcing the reader either to condemn Muldrow on the basis of his actions or to accept him, subordinating his destructive deeds to the aesthetic value of his philosophical vision. Through Muldrow, Dickey flirts with an aspect of the eternal debate involving art and morality: should, for example, a brilliant work of art be celebrated for its raw aesthetic genius or condemned for its unconscionable ethics if written by or about a serial killer, a racist, a sexist, or someone equally "immoral"? Faced with such a dilemma, the reader must determine whether to reject Muldrow and the novel on ethical grounds or to defer passing judgment on his indiscriminate killing in favor of his compelling artistic imagination.

Through Muldrow's poetic sensibility, rendered in sparse, penetrating language, the reader is made privy to the world he sees around him: his *Umwelt*, or self-world. Muldrow's interpretive outlook is essentially epicurean in that its foundation rests on material objects and the space in which they exist. Dickey accentuates this philosophy during Muldrow's conversation with the American ascetic. As Ernest Suarez rightly deduces, "Dickey uses the scene in that Muldrow encounters the American monk to distinguish between Muldrow's naturalistic impulses and the monk's Zen Buddhism" (Suarez, "'Real God, Roll'" 9). Beneath Muldrow's "naturalistic" drive—his attempt to take on attributes that will enable him to survive in Japan—rests his epicurean sensibility, which is apparent in his emphasis on the use and function of physical matter. After he kills the Japanese swordsman, Muldrow remarks, "You're a good one. . . . You sure are. I can use you" (*TS* 175), and indeed he does utilize him materially, splintering his forearm and gathering the boney needles for the purpose of sewing his Arctic outfit.

Drawing on his epicurean worldview, Muldrow discounts the American monk's philosophy because it rationalizes things into abstractions for which he has no use or interest. After the ascetic's psychological interpretation of dreams and temporality, Muldrow thinks, "I had never heard any kind of talk like this, and I tried to head it off. Not that it bothered me, but I couldn't find any way to connect with it, or get interested in it" (*TS* 195). The monastery's rock garden functions as the epitome of such abstract uselessness, symbolizing the monks' fabricated relationship with nature. As an artificial human construction of the natural world, the rock garden is, to Muldrow, as worthless as it is uninteresting. Whereas the monks repeatedly order nature into a time-honored, formulaic arrangement, Muldrow wishes to know and assume the identity of the natural world as it truly is. While Zen practitioners flirt with the void for the purpose of enlightenment (*kensho* or *satori*, the apprehension of the authentic self), Muldrow appreciates the importance of nothingness in relationships between natural manifestations. When, for example, he muses upon the shared qualities of clouds and icebergs, he concludes, "There was no reason for them to be like they were, and have the shapes that they did, except that that was the way they happened to be, for nothing" (*TS* 18). For Muldrow, nothingness is an integral part of understanding the natural world and its places rather than an abstract tool in the quest for an essence of the inner self.

Muldrow's contempt for the monk's impractical acquired knowledge, as opposed to his own experience-based, epicurean understanding, is substantiated later when he thinks back on their conversation:

> I thought of something I should have said to him when he was coming at me with all that religious stuff he had learned how to say. This would have been good, I thought: when he said something like, God is everywhere there is, God is in the snow, I should have come back at him and said, No, the snow is in the snow. That would have settled his hash, and it made me feel better when I realized I could have said it. (*TS* 217)

Elsewhere, Dickey himself has endorsed Muldrow's nonreligious material-based mentality, asserting, "The human being does not address or learn how to live with, to love and to use, by getting away from the immediate reality of the things of this world but by diving into them" (Dickey, Foreword x). Muldrow's allusion to snow and Dickey's emphasis on exploring "the immediate reality of things" also suggest Hegel's characterization of nature as frozen and nonspiritual:

> In Nature, . . . in theological language, we have the Divine Idea momentarily excluded from the Divine Love: everywhere it shows anticipations and vestiges of intelligence, but in a frozen, petrified form, in which God may be said to be dead. Nature, in short, is the raw material of self-conscious Spirit, and being raw, it is, in its immediate form, the exact antithesis of anything spiritual. (Findlay 272–73)

Recognizing snow for what it is—a minuscule manifestation of raw nature—Muldrow resists the monk's spiritual imposition of a divine entity upon it. For Muldrow, Dickey, and Hegel, spirituality is something humans bring to and imprint upon nature. Thus, Muldrow cannot help but abjure spiritual claims to universal enlightenment. As Richard Jefferies, one of Dickey's favorite writers, maintains, "By no course of reasoning, however tortuous, can nature and the universe be fitted to the mind.

Nor can the mind be fitted to the cosmos" (Jefferies 49). When Muldrow compares icebergs and clouds, he is glad that they are the way they are "for nothing"; abstractions only threaten to misdirect him from the natural essence he seeks to know and become.

Dickey used Peter Matthiessen's collection of journals, *Nine-Headed Dragon River*, for background on Zazen, monastic practices, and the Japanese landscape. Matthiessen's diaries constitute an introduction to Zazen from an American's perspective, and Dickey likely drew on the "I" of Matthiessen's writings as a model for the American monk in *To the White Sea*. The Zazen aim—"a silent training directed toward unification of body, mind, and spirit with the universal consciousness sometimes referred to as Oneness, Zen Mind, Buddha-nature" (Matthiessen 14)—superficially appears to suggest the embodiment of what Muldrow ultimately attempts to achieve. Yet, his goal is to assume the being of a physical place rather than bond with a transcendent spirit, a significant distinction. Furthermore, the monastery Muldrow visits strongly resembles Matthiessen's description of Kennin-ji, a traditional Rinzai training center in Kyoto with several stone gardens, where "seven days a week, as in the old days, thirty-one monks arise at 4:00 A.M. for zazen. . . . In the afternoon the monks perform their monastery duties, followed by zazen until near midnight" (172). The nocturnal ascetics Muldrow encounters wandering in the fog appear to be functioning on a similar ritualistic schedule. In addition to Kennin-ji, Dickey drew on Mathiessen's discussions of Zen time for the American monk's conversation with Muldrow. Matthiessen's citation of Dogen Zenji, a thirteenth-century Soto master, in regard to "Being-Time"—the understanding that different beings and states exhibit varying interpretations of temporality—suggests the ascetic's discourse on dream time and real time. Finally, Matthiessen's book makes references to the island of Hokkaido and the native inhabitants whom he calls "the remnant aborigines, or 'Hairy Ainu,' tall, blue-eyed, bearded hunter-gatherers, at one time considered a relict population of the early Cro-Magnon" (236). The tribe to which Muldrow refers as "the little bearded people, the bear people" (*TS* 261) are probably based on the Ainu, although he makes no mention of their blue eyes or the fact that they are taller than the average Japanese person is.

Beyond the sequence involving the American monk, Muldrow's epicureanism is present in his compulsive itemizing of equipment, which takes place at frequent intervals in the book. To be sure, equipment is critical in the Arctic, where a person cannot survive outside for long without the necessary tools (and the skill to use them) to provide mobility, food, and warmth. However, Muldrow's fondness for his equipment, which Dickey claimed he took from George Orwell, goes beyond the simple idea of material preparation. In his notes for the novel, Dickey contends that Muldrow's things have a "talismatic quality," exemplified by their associations with aspects of nature. For example, in addition to appreciating his knife's flexibility, Muldrow is interested in the way it captures and reflects light. He is fascinated by the manner in which it can manipulate light; not only possessing the pliable capacity to curve around a bone when plunged into someone, the blade can also "bend" light, giving Muldrow a certain control of and use for nature's illuminating element. Angling his knife toward a candle inside a Japanese home, he "catches" the flame on the blade and explains with satisfaction, "That was my mark" (*TS* 82).

In addition to his fondness for objects like the knife and compass, which gives him pleasure through its adherence to the northern magnetic pull, Muldrow enjoys appropriating physical aspects of the challenging opponents he conquers. Hoping to gain some of the power of his most worthy adversaries, he takes some physical part of them as a way of internalizing their essence. In addition to the aforementioned bone splinters of the skilled Japanese swordsman, Muldrow uses the skins of the goats that gore him with their horns. He is ecstatic when the bear women present him with a shirt and pair of pants made from the hides: "These were the hides I had skinned off the goats in the woods, and I can tell you I was plenty grateful, because I wanted to have that kind of vitality and fire pass into me. I had already eaten a lot of the goats, and now to wear them, too, would be luck beyond the best of luck" (*TS* 251). Dickey's interest in the talismanic effect of Muldrow's possessions is underscored by the fact that he read William Humphrey's short nonfiction work *The Spawning Run* in the hopes of finding a way to exhibit the "fishing mystique" in Muldrow. Humphrey's first-person narrator goes into great detail in cataloguing his gear and fishing techniques as if the gear itself is essential to understanding the fish. Similarly, based on his background, Muldrow believes that the proper comprehension and mastery of an adversary or environment is partly contingent on having the appropriate implements.

In addition to its focus on gear, Humphrey's *The Spawning Run* is a literal and symbolic meditation on instinctual homecoming, in terms of both salmon and humans, and just as salmon return, through very formidable obstacles, to mate and die in their native streams, so does Muldrow work his way north to the environment of his youth, the native habitat in which a defining transformation awaits him. Muldrow struggles to articulate the underpinnings of his migration, confessing, "North was north, and it would stay that way. And there was the pull of something else to go with it: that other thing that was not called north but was at the same place, the thing nobody could say" (*TS* 39). Scientifically, Muldrow's journey north is the embodiment of what biologist Hermann Schöne calls "goal orientation," a term which "includes all orientation behaviors that lead the animal to a previously determined place, near or far away. To reach distant or hidden goals an animal must employ orientation mechanisms whose spatial references are not directly associated with the goal" (Schöne 14). In Muldrow's case, the unrelated mechanisms are those necessary in negotiating the diverse environments through which he passes during his trek toward the "goal environment." Although Muldrow cannot express goal orientation as the "something else" he feels tugging at him, he recognizes aspects of it in various things. At the end of the decapitation scene with the old woman, Dickey wanted to emphasize Muldrow's "definite reluctance to leave the water-wheel: the connection of the wheel and the water, the never-ending quality of it, touches something in him; some primitive thing" (Dickey, Unpublished notes for *To the White Sea* 22). Although Muldrow cannot fully grasp it, the wheel's motion of eternal return suggests his own migration, which is also a return to his beginnings, through the cycle of elements, and constituting—in its relation to the point of origin and return—the circle of life.

Muldrow's place-based migratory impulse, his goal orientation, is also animalistic in its absorption of different creatures' characteristics for the purpose of increasing its effectiveness. This is something with which Dickey had experimented in his poetry. In his introduction to *The Achievement of James Dickey*, an early collection of Dickey's poems, Laurence Lieberman makes the observation:

> In the earlier poems, Dickey supposed he could give up his human self to the animal realm. The human/animal encounter in the last poem of the series, "Encounter in the Cage Country," has become a medium through which his human limitations can be transcended,

> but in going beyond his human condition, he no longer transforms into a new, wholly other being; instead, he intensifies and deepens the human self by adding animal powers to it. (Lieberman 21)

In addition to its similarities with some of Dickey's poetry, Muldrow's belief that animal traits are bound to his own human existence is a powerful Eskimo conviction. In *Arctic Dreams* Barry Lopez relates that Eskimos "have difficulty imagining themselves entirely removed from the world of animals. For many of them, to make this separation is analogous to cutting oneself off from light or water" (180). Drawing on Eskimo culture and his own poetic method, Dickey adds a compelling animalistic dimension to Muldrow's directional odyssey.

The main avenue by which Muldrow identifies with animals and their characteristics is dreaming. In his dream visions Muldrow exhibits a "totemic" relationship with creatures, in which the dream beast he imagines bestows its powers upon him. As Suarez holds, Muldrow's transformations are not abstract or philosophical: "instead each moment represents a transcendental attempt to attain skills that will enhance his power within the natural world" (Suarez, "'Real God, Roll'" 7). The alien systems through which Muldrow passes and the lack of animals he encounters on the main island of Honshu are responsible for the vivid immediacy of his dreams: "There was something about Japan that bothered me, now more than before. In all these woods, among the trees, under them, in them, and over them, there were not many birds, and I hadn't seen any animals at all. The ones in my head got stronger, though; stronger because of the absence of the others. Luck or not, I couldn't tell you" (*TS* 125). Muldrow's dream creatures are, in fact, fortunate for him since they strengthen his animalistic sensibility, unconsciously contributing in his practical need to survive.

Although Muldrow's dreams generally benefit him, they occasionally threaten to cloud his conscious perception of reality, resulting in dangerous situations. At one point he boasts, "I can hear as well as anything on two feet, and most of them on four. I can listen with any animal" (*TS* 115). However, Muldrow is both envious and embarrassed when he realizes the senescent swordsman can hear better, as well as move more quickly, than he. Indeed, his underestimation of the elderly man's auditory ability and darting swordsmanship nearly costs him his life. Muldrow's miscalculation with the swordsman makes the reader dubious when he later maintains, "I could outthink any animal or bird that lived in the cold, by thinking more like he did than he could do. All I had to do was get there" (*TS* 214). Becoming overly enamored of his *Umwelt*, Muldrow occasionally allows his dreams to become seductive abstract panaceas instead of life-enhancing catalysts. While plummeting to earth earlier in the novel, Muldrow becomes lost in the dreamlike sensation of bodily flight and comes to believe "that a man ought to be able to fly without an airplane" (*TS* 26). Almost simultaneously he realizes, "But that was dangerous: I could have held on to the notion too long," and he returns to his epicurean mind-set in time to activate his chute (*TS* 26).

While Muldrow's dream visions have an element of danger, more often than not they are beneficial to and symbolic of his practical challenges. For example, the recurring image of deer heads, introduced at the conclusion of the train ride, which Muldrow calls "Deer Herd for Infinity," suggests his northward journey (*TS* 145). Just as the entire herd gazes into eternity, so Muldrow concentrates all his energy and focus in one direction, toward a goal that is singular yet vague. The arrangement of Muldrow's unconscious world is suggestive of Paul Valéry's comments on the practicality of dreams:

> Man is the separate animal, the curious living creature that is opposed to all others and rises above all others by his . . . *dreams!*—by the intensity, succession, and diversity of his *dreams!*—by their extraordinary effects, which may sometimes even modify his nature, and not his nature only, but that surrounding nature which he tirelessly endeavors to subjugate to his dreams. (Valéry 29)

In addition to applying the positive elements of his dreams to his practical actions, allowing them to shape him in the process, Muldrow permits his reveries to define and shape the environment around him. As a result, the landscape Muldrow perceives, filtered through his dreams and his *Umwelt*, is drastically different from that which is visible to most humans. Shaped by him and reflected through him, the land is something he ultimately wishes to be the same as himself—a place in which he might hide to the extent that he *becomes* the place.

* * *

In a letter to his editor, Mark Jaffe, Dickey summarized his novel as follows:

> Drawing at least partly on his upbringing in northern Alaska, on the Arctic Circle side of the Brooks Range, he [Muldrow] has an instinctive knowledge and mastery of camouflage, the use of color to make himself either invisible or the next thing to it. The sections of the novel are divided into episodes dealing with the color spectrum, beginning with red—the fire-bombing raid on Tokyo—and ending in white, as Muldrow reaches the northern tip of Hokkaido and sees the icebergs in the water, fulfilling what he has told someone in the first section of the novel: "For me, the ocean is not the ocean unless it's got ice in it." (Bruccoli and Baughman 454)

Dickey's comments on camouflage and "the color spectrum" reveal both Muldrow's place-based interpretation of landscape and the text's underlying symbolic structure. At one point Dickey had even thought to entitle different sections of the book using the names of various colors, and early manuscripts demonstrate this practice. The black section of the novel, which also includes red, pertains to the burning and smoking descriptions of Tokyo. These colors then give way to orange as Muldrow leaves the city and dawn breaks on the Japanese countryside. Next, yellow, the balance of the roads and the countryside as he journeys north, becomes the dominant color, reflected further in the yellow glimmer of light on the knife blade. Dickey asserted that brown "centers around a grove or forest of trees, with pine needles on the ground. Everything brown" (Dickey, Unpublished notes 21). This section, in which Muldrow colors his hand the same color as the landscape, overlaps with blue, the sequence at the lake where he rests and begins to "conceive of Japan as his domain."

The symbolic sequence of colors concludes with white, which, drawing on his upbringing, Muldrow feels is the best color for camouflage. He says of his youth in Alaska: "I got to know what lived up there in the snow, and how they lived. Some of the animals, and birds, live by being able to hide, and the others live by being able to find 'em. But being hard to see, to make out, is part of it on both sides" (*TS* 16). Although Muldrow likens himself to both predator and prey, he has a special affinity for aggressive animals like the wolverine and hawk. Describing one of his poems, "Fog Envelopes the Animals," Dickey recounts the joy invisibility brings to the predator:

> "Fog Envelops the Animals" is about hunting. In the poem, fog rolls up and envelops the protagonist. . . . He feels himself become invisible. We all want to be invisible, at least part of the time, but most especially the hunter does. . . . In this case, the hunter being exactly the same color as the fog, has total concealment. As long as he can see enough to shoot, but the animals can't see him, he's in heaven. (Dickey, *Self-Interviews* 111)

Muldrow exhibits a similar feeling in his preferred method of killing, which brings his oblivious antagonist directly to him. Capitalizing on the blindness of the swordsman, Muldrow explains, "I led him with sound, he came in, he came onto my knife. I held it for him, just so" (*TS* 175). In the snow-covered expanse of an Arctic environment, Muldrow feels that his invisibility and camouflage come closest to reaching their potentials; in perfect harmony with his surroundings, he revels in silence, whiteness, and hunting.

Although Muldrow often speaks of camouflage in mystical, inhuman expressions, his merging also operates in terms of other human beings. During the chaos of the firebombing raid on Tokyo, he endeavors to blend in with the panic-stricken Japanese masses: "Through the blasts of smoke I got into the crowd, making the turn to be in their direction and slowing down to their pace, which was a kind of fast shuffle" (*TS* 44). Seeking to lose himself in the moving multitudes, he discards his efficient running for the herdlike shuffle of the terrified crowd. Using his mind instead of his legs, Muldrow later assumes the mental perspective of a Japanese soldier who is trying to kill him, anticipating his opponent's course of action. After having used his predatory cunning to dispatch two other servicemen, Muldrow pauses: "I changed my mind around and thought with him" (*TS* 202), thinking with his antagonist in order to survive, merging with the other for the purpose of its annihilation.

In addition to Muldrow's method of mind-merging, he is also significantly transformed by his immediate surroundings, influenced mentally by the camouflage he takes on from his various environments. Rubbing soot into his face during the bombing of Tokyo, he feels a change taking place: "As the color of my face disappeared and went to another color, there was something inside me that changed, too. It moved, and then sat still. In my mind there was a shape I couldn't exactly make out, but it seemed to be in a crouch, pulled up into itself and ready, and that was the feeling I got from the soot, the stronger the more I put on" (*TS* 47). Putting on a physical aspect of his immediate environment triggers a response from deep inside Muldrow's consciousness. In addition to its general suggestion of his predatory nature, "the shape" inside him is strongly suggestive of what Eskimos call the *angakoq*, a being of immense power and ardor, whom Barry Lopez characterizes as "an intermediary of darkness" (217). The *angakoq* possesses the gift of *qaumaneq*, explains Lopez:

> The inexplicable searchlight that enables him to see in the dark, literally and metaphorically. He reaches for the throat of darkness; that is the primitive, as primitive as an explosion of blood. Out hunting, in the welter of gore, of impetuous shooting, that heady mixture of joy and violence, sometimes it is possible for an outsider to feel the edge of the primitive. Unbridled, it is frightening. It also defeats starvation. And in its enthusiasm for the concrete events of life, it can defeat what weighs against the heart and soul. (217–18)

In the face of seemingly insurmountable odds, Muldrow summons the *angakoq*, which banishes his trepidation and accentuates his predatory confidence as he crouches in the shadows of burning buildings, waiting for the right victim. Further suggestive of the *angakoq*'s presence, although Muldrow's black face makes him resemble the soot-smeared Japanese civilians, he identifies not with them but with something, not someone, less distinct: "I was not like them, I say again; like something else" (*TS* 47).

Muldrow's successful use of camouflage in and around Tokyo helps him to arrive at his conscious strategy for reaching Hokkaido. After fleeing from some civilian men and hiding behind a wall, he thinks of the lynx and muses at great length on the prospect of surviving through his utilization of color:

> You need the color of the place you're in. Even in the big rush of good feeling, when the colors came over me and I felt like I could be any of them, any time of the day or night: when I felt like I could lie down in green or yellow, in purple or red, in the moonlight or the sunrise, and I could stay until I got ready to get up and go on, and nobody would know, or fall out of any of them, like a hawk: fall on somebody's back, or right into his face like a blaze of light flashing

> through him, or doing anything I wanted, I knew that it was only part of the truth, only part of the truth that would be, from here on. There would be lots of colors between me here and the snow fields there, between me and the ocean and the bergs, and there was not any way I could take advantage of everything between the place I was now—this wall—and where I was trying to get to. But there would be long stretches—there were bound to be long stretches—where the color was more or less the same, and if that was true, I could find some way to tap in on it, take advantage of it, make it work for me. If there were colors in Japan, if there were colors in the world, I could go with them, be what they were. I could, damn it: I sure could. When I came on a long stretch of color—stayed in it for a day, maybe—I would try to make the best way to do it for the next day. (*TS* 72–73)

Having already instinctually exercised his gift for concealment, Muldrow rationalizes it as a long-term practice of survival, a progressive method that can both deliver him to Hokkaido and bring him closer to the transformation he seeks.

As a result of Muldrow's oblique statements and allusions, his specific understanding of camouflage—as well as what it leads to—remains partially buried. Indeed, his philosophy of camouflage takes him to the other side of visibility, and he even evokes a ghost when speaking about it:

> To be invisible and still know what was going on, that was something. I wondered what it would be like to be a ghost. When I started thinking about camouflage, like I say, I knew what I wanted to do—no, what I *had* to do. It was going to be the way. . . . There ought to be places between me and the mountains and the snow fields where I could more or less pick the colors, and take them on, at least in some way. If I took my time—and I had plenty of it—I should be able to fit the color of some of my situations—hillsides, fields, woods—and tune to them by color. Maybe this wouldn't always work, and maybe I wouldn't always be able to do it, but I planned to try. It was worth it, worth a lot. It might be worth everything. (*TS* 101)

Muldrow's assertions that he "*has*" to practice concealment and that it "might be worth everything" point to the defining metamorphosis toward which he is gravitating. Like the migratory impulse of the salmon,

Muldrow's drive becomes something he lacks the power to alter: an unavoidable destiny he does not and cannot resist.

Muldrow's transition puts him beyond human existence and more fully into the place that surrounds him. Dickey explains:

> Muldrow wants to achieve the perfect camouflage. He believes that the perfect camouflage will enable him to cease to exist and merge with the landscape. The only thing that will give him away is his eyes. When he closes them, he thinks he can become the place. He is covered with his own blood and swan feathers when he goes out into the snow and attempts to become a landscape of snow and cold and desolation, an environment that he's always loved so much. Perhaps he's killed. It may be that death itself is the perfect camouflage. I'll leave that for the reader. (Suarez, "An Interview" 130)

Although the speeding bullets complicate the exact nature of Muldrow's ultimate fate, he fully believes that his shift into a place has the power to save him, transferring his essence to a nonhuman area of existence:

> From watching the animals and birds up on the muskeg, on the tundra, and on the Brooks, I've always believed that if camouflage is good enough, if it is right *exactly*, the bird or the animal will not just be invisible, it won't be there. When the rattlesnake did something so that my eyes—which can see what the others can't—couldn't pick it up, I knew I was right. My hand on the bare place on the slope, there in Japan, was like that. Like that or just about, it was almost somewhere else, or just not. (*TS* 112)

At the conclusion of the novel, when Muldrow feels a bullet pass through him without touching him, we are witness either to the surreal impressions of a dying man or to the moment of metamorphosis in which Muldrow sheds his humanity and assumes the identity of his surroundings, literally becoming "somewhere else" or "just not." Corresponding, in Dickey's notes for a proposed screenplay for *To the White Sea*, he portrayed Muldrow's would-be killers as not knowing "where he is. They don't know what's happened. What has happened is that he's a place. One of the posse picks up Muldrow's red knife out of the snow and looks at it uncomprehendingly, and then they go on walking around, as the camera pulls back, and that's the end" (Dickey, Unpublished notes).

Muldrow's final transformation, whether into death or a place, also rescues him from the barren solipsism of his human existence. No longer constituting a destructive and alienated self, Muldrow becomes part of the "all" that constitutes a natural environment. Such a shift suggests David Abram's use of Edmund Husserl's defense of phenomenology against the accusation of solipsism: "The field of appearances, while still a thoroughly subjective realm, was now seen to be inhabited by *multiple* subjectivities; the phenomenal field was no longer the isolated haunt of a solitary ego, but a collective landscape, constituted by other experiencing subjects as well as by oneself" (Abram ix). Constituting a connective part of a collective place, Muldrow rejoices at being "everywhere in it" (*TS* 275). Furthermore, Abram maintains that the premise of his philosophical and ecological book, *The Spell of the Sensuous*, asserts that "we are human only in contact, and conviviality, with what is not human" (37), and Muldrow appears to establish the ultimate "contact," to the point that his human form no longer exists.

Although Muldrow's final transformation marks the literal death of his human existence, there are hints of his departure from the human world throughout the novel. While riding on the train and imagining various animals, he recounts, "The chute had saved my life, but this was better—better, believe me, there are better things than life" (*TS* 144). Meditating upon the qualities of inhuman creatures, Muldrow belittles the importance of his own mortal existence, for, in becoming an inhuman place, he feels that he will have achieved a higher level of being. As Sartre says, "Let no one reproach us with capriciously creating a being of this kind; when by a further movement of thought the being and absolute absence of this totality are hypostasized as transcendence beyond the world, it takes on the name of God" (Sartre 171–72). Having moved "beyond" the human world and into the planet's very essence, Muldrow becomes part of the inhuman order of things, which many people identify as God. And losing his human life along the way is a small price to pay since "One who lives the life of the universe cannot be much concerned for his own" (Santayana 56).

In addition to dream animals, the most powerful expressions of Muldrow's inhumanism are linked to manifestations of ice. At one point Dickey had even thought to use an epigraph concerning icebergs from *Arctic Dreams*: "I looked up at the icebergs. They so embodied the land. Austere. Implacable. Harsh but not antagonistic. Creatures of pale light" (224–25). Like the icebergs, Muldrow wishes to "embody the land," and his cold, inhuman harshness is part of what makes that possible. Although he is responsible for many deaths, Muldrow does not kill in inimical rage but rather revels in his own existence; solitary and white, he, too, is a creature of pale light. Muldrow's inhumanism is also captured in another manifestation of ice. While paddling from Honshu to Hokkaido, he remembers witnessing the pure blue heart of a calving glacier:

> I had seen it, and would see it again, the real pure thing, the pure color. Believe me when I tell you that when the glacier calves off there is something that you don't get with every day. . . . Well, where I was heading I couldn't get enough of remembering it, the pure blue: the pure more-than-blue. . . . It was the most intense, and the most pure, it was—well, you could say—secret, the best of it, the heart of ice, the heart you never had any idea was there, and when you saw it, knew had to be there. (*TS* 231–32)

In *Arctic Dreams*, Barry Lopez speaks of a Lakota woman, Elaine Jahner, who holds that the religion of hunting peoples relies on the idea that "a spiritual landscape exists within the physical landscape . . . occasionally one sees something fleeting in the land, a moment when line, color, and movement intensify and something sacred is revealed, leading one to believe that there is another realm of reality corresponding to the physical one but different" (245). In the icebergs and the blue heart of the glacier, Muldrow glimpses cold, inhuman embodiments of the natural world that promise another reality. His identification with them simultaneously reminds him of something in himself and increases his desire to become part of their natural essence.

* * *

After departing the company of the bearded bear people, Muldrow exclaims, "I felt young, young and on top of the whole situation, to go on up north, to go *into* it" (*TS* 157), and the final step of his inhuman evolution centers around his connection with an old hermit's great birds. More than his imaginary dream creatures, the flying predators demonstrate the bestial abilities and visionary perception he wishes to attain: "I began to transfer my feelings—or soul, or spirit, or whatever you want to call it—to them, because they did more than any other creatures for the wish I had that was most like me: not only the need to attack but to fall on something from above" (*TS* 265). However, more than their diving attacks, Muldrow admires their vision, which fascinates him because it is superior to that of any human. He reflects: "The hawk's view, which was beyond any man's. It was being able to see what you don't. It was being able to see into the snowbank, into the stone. To see beyond what any human, any man who has ever been born, could see. Like I tell you, out of the snowdrift, into the snowdrift, into the stone" (*TS* 271). Nietzsche conceives of average people as being "deeply immersed in illusion and dream images; their eyes glance only over the surface of things and see 'forms'; their sensation nowhere leads to truth, but contents itself with receiving stimuli and, as it were, with playing a game of touch on the back of things" (Nietzsche 175). Muldrow admires the hawks because they see beyond surfaces and *into* the hearts of things. Possessing an inhuman visionary power, the birds apprehend the essence in all things, something Muldrow achieves only rarely, as when he glimpses the heart of the calving glacier.

Having arrived at the inhuman sensibility necessary for his transformation, Muldrow waits for the appropriate time: "All the time I'd been in Japan, all the time I'd been living, this seemed to be the truth of the thing: you can get to the perfect blend if you know exactly how to do it, and if the time is right" (*TS* 272). Reaching the northern tip of Hokkaido and developing his understanding of the birds, he has nothing left to accomplish as a human being. In a letter to Richard Roth, Dickey explained that in the film version he envisioned Muldrow disappearing amid a heavy gust of snow while the Japanese posse fires at him (Bruccoli and Baughman 509). Like the speaker in "Fog Envelopes the Animals," Muldrow feels that "Soundlessly whiteness is eating / My visible self alive. / I shall enter this world like the dead, / Floating through tree trunks on currents / And streams of untouchable pureness" (*The Whole Motion* 80). Although he may literally be killed by the bullets, Muldrow believes with Lucretius that "The minds of living things and the light fabric of their spirits are neither birthless nor deathless" (Lucretius 108). Dead or transformed, he feels himself flowing out of his human existence and into the grand being of another—of a place. Whether or not the metamorphosis actually takes place, Muldrow's *Umwelt* can only believe that it has; in his dream of reality, it is real enough.

II

A Matter of Context

Region and Place

2

One Writer's Place

The South of George Garrett

> Place is not located in a pre-given space, after the manner of physical technological space. The latter unfolds itself only through the reigning of places of a region.
>
> Martin Heidegger, "Art and Space"

Well-worn and much-maligned, the interdisciplinary concept known as globalization generally espouses the vision of a borderless world dominated by multinationals and markets, vanguards of a homogenized culture shaped by Western values and a grand narrative of reason. However, beneath this imagined oneness reside a number of lingering, though perhaps doomed, systems and paradoxical elements. For example, the concept of nationalism continues to present itself as a complex sociopolitical phenomenon, constantly in formation, deformation, and reformation in response to various other catalysts of change. The dominant state form over the last five centuries or so, the nation-state emerged on a broad historical canvas out of dramatic processes of social change that incorporated empires, city-states, tribes, and feudal lords. Often taking the defensive in light of its tenuous mutability, the nation-state usually is portrayed by globalization proponents in terms of its narrowness, selfishness, and exclusiveness. Delving deeper, beyond nationalism, we spy the stubborn, familiar phenomenon of regionalism, nearer to each of us though sometimes more difficult to perceive. Often depicted by globalization thinkers as a smaller, meaner, more nostalgic form of nationalism, regionalism perpetuates a collective set of visions and values aimed at the establishment of a local system, formal or informal, within a specific geographical area. Yet, for all its backward provincialism, the regional context finds itself attracting increasing recognition from observers of international relations, international political economies, and international development, as well as by governments and other stakeholders in civil society and the private sector. Increasingly, economic and cultural leaders find themselves searching for regional solutions to the problems and challenges presented by national and global forces. As a result, much energy is now being devoted to studying how regional processes relate to globalization, including how regional trade arrangements may be stumbling blocks or stepping stones to ever-increasing free trade and whether regional integration, economic as well as cultural, can be understood as a way of negotiating nationalism and globalization or as a way of creating a social buffer against these forces' potentially disturbing effects.

As strange as it might seem, these issues and revelations are not particularly new or unrecognized in the literature of the American South, a regional genre of writing long conversant with the pressures and complexities of national and, increasingly, international discourses and economies. After all, with the notable exceptions of university presses and marvels such as Algonquin Books, it is to the large (inter)national presses and the still-dominant literary region of the Northeast that southern writers continue to turn, and often move into, in the hopes of garnering publication and reputation. This long-standing diasporic intellectual trend—lamented by writers as far apart in chronology and sensibility as William Gilmore Simms and Lee Smith—also manifests itself on the international level as witnessed by Faulkner conferences in China and the odd phenomenon of Christine Chaufour-Verheyen's work of criticism *William Styron: Le 7e jour* appearing in France as a mass-market paperback and outselling hosts of novels.

* * *

Although many writers have commented knowledgeably on the shifting place of southern literature in national and international literary contexts, the single figure who invested the most time and ink examining the tension between southern writers and the national publishing scene over the past half century was George Garrett, who, up to his death in 2008, ranked as one of the region's few remaining distinguished men of letters. Editor, translator, dramatist/scriptwriter, Poet Laureate of Virginia, award-winning fiction writer, teacher, and mentor, and wide-ranging reviewer and essayist (whose work regularly appeared in the *Virginia Quarterly Review* and *Sewanee Review*), Garrett—by turns donning the armor of poetry, prose, or spoken rhetoric (his father was an admirably hard-nosed and uncompromising lawyer)—consistently waded headlong into the issues at hand, be they aesthetic, historical, social, economic, political, or otherwise. Over the years, the South and the publishing dilemma for southern writers remained particular and constant points of interest: from his first two published essays in 1957, dealing respectively with the work of Faulkner and Garrett's Georgia relative Harry Stillwell Edwards, to his 2003 collection of essays and reviews pertaining to the South, *Southern Excursions*. In fact, Garrett's critical facility as a scholarly essayist and reviewer was noticed nearly as quickly by observers as were his gifts in fiction and poetry. Writing in 1963 the Faulkner scholar James Meriwether asserted, "No examination of Garrett's literary accomplishment is complete without mention of his critical writing, which has produced two of the best articles ever written on Faulkner" (29). The ensuing years have borne out Meriwether's declaration, and there might have been more scholarly work had he not directed his energies elsewhere. A notebook entry dated January 29, 1965, finds Garrett expressing an intention to write a critical study entitled "The Southern Past: A Literary Image"; two years later he told an interviewer that he hoped to "write a short critical book on certain aspects of recent southern fiction" ("Writer-in-Residence" 1). Yet, for all the scholarly enthusiasm, during this period Garrett's most celebrated literary achievement, the historical opus *Death of the Fox*, also beckoned, and one would be foolish to argue that his time would have been better spent on literary criticism. In fact, Garrett's fiction and criticism are not so far apart as one might suspect. Just as his historical Elizabethan novels interact with vast stores of scholarly knowledge in making unique philosophical statements about the nature of human history, so do his fictional southern narratives subtly complement his critical essays on the southern literary genre, together delineating an idea, as well as a practice, of the regional form.

In order to articulate Garrett's conception of southern literature and its relation to the rest of the country and the world, one first must attempt to understand him as both a southerner and a writer. In 2003 Garrett recounted to me the following anecdote:

> In the 1930s I used to visit my grandfather, who lived in a place called Naples, North Carolina, which doesn't exist anymore, I'm told. It was between Asheville and Hendersonville. All around there

> were developments that never got off the ground: street lamps and sidewalks without houses or buildings. That was the norm growing up: that you would see things that came to nothing. Very surreal. I didn't even know what a development was. I would get on my bike and go out in the woods and suddenly come upon an area with driveways, sidewalks, beautiful street lamps, and sometimes an old abandoned hotel. I thought, naturally, as a child does, that's the way the world is: it's full of abandoned places and buildings. Then everything changed radically and I began to feel, as many others do, the need to preserve some memory of that earlier version of place. (Garrett, Interview)

Struck by the haunting image of a world full of empty, abandoned places, the young Garrett initially glimpsed writing as a means of immutable historical preservation, an endeavor he would later identify as definitively southern. More than thirty years before our conversation, he had written, "Change and decay have always been primary subjects in southern literature. Because it is characteristic of the southern writer (especially in prose fiction) that he feels compelled to capture in words and describe things as they are before they crumble and vanish forever" (Garrett, "The South" 33). At the heart of this sensibility are both a critique and an embrace of the inevitability of change, the future ever abandoning an unrealized present. Though less polemical and more detached, the approach vaguely echoes the earlier perspectives of the Agrarians, and, in fact, Garrett specifically evoked the pastoral South in the early 1960s, remarking, "You can hardly find a Southern writer who does not love the land he writes of. . . . [It] sings lyrically in their work . . . even the cities and suburbia and the new industry cannot efface the almost instinctive affection for the land—for there is too much of it and it is too strong. It triumphs over our best intentions" (Meriwether 31). Such an outlook, voiced early in Garrett's career, attempts, perhaps a little stubbornly, to recognize and confer with a prior southern tradition of land-based literature, even as the inevitable, encroaching dark cloud of industrialization threatens to alter it forever.

At their worst, such aesthetic philosophies of preservation flirt with a kind of implacable, sentimental romanticism, denying the inevitable changes at hand while wistfully memorializing a way of life and *Umwelt* now gone with the wind. Yet, Garrett defends the objectivity of his approach: "I think there's not so much a sense of nostalgia as there is something akin to the urge to fill a photograph album before everything has changed." (Garrett, Interview). Although this attitude is noble, its practicality presents formidable difficulties to the artist. Pictures, as professional photographers can attest, do not always accurately capture objects. The image-shaping eye of the photographer and the person who views the picture conspire—not unlike the author and the reader—to create an object and its meaning in a new way. Likewise, exploring and portraying history—what Eliot called its "cunning passages" and "contrived corridors" ("Gerontion" 20)—is not so easy as it might seem, the historian and the reader bringing their respective interpretive agendas to so-called factual events. However, a masterful renderer of historical fiction like Garrett recognizes and welcomes this danger. Writing about the Civil War in his essay "Under Two Flags," he concludes, "In spite of growing and towering mountains, huge slag piles of factual history and many kinds and forms of poetry and fiction, and even the wonders of television, it is still very difficult to imagine the Civil War accurately and honestly." In fact, one might argue that the numerous layers of conflicting interpretation and representation only serve to cloud the immediacy of the event, with the latest scholarly contributions resembling—to extend Garrett's metaphor—a gratuitous sprinkling of pebbles on an already enormous mountain of rock.

Confronted with the equally perilous dangers of nostalgia and numerous, disparate historical theories, serious writers of historical fiction often are left to draw on their own histories and experiences as means of interpreting and portraying the human element of antiquated events, a technique traditionally suited to southern writers. In a 1958 review of Robert Penn Warren's *Promises,* Garrett notes, "The South, his as well as ours, is haunted by its ghosts, benign or malevolent, but omnipresent. History, personal or public, is always here and now. . . . For the Southerner, rooted in his living history, time is an intricate network, an ever-spinning web" ("Review" 106–7). Living in their own times, yet irrevocably anchored to earlier ones, Garrett's and Warren's southerners roam, whether they wish to or not, "out of history into history and the awful responsibility of time." Whether dealing with the recent dynamics of racial and sexual conflicts or the more distant legacy of the war of 1861–65, most southern writers still employ some measure of generational inheritance in their narratives. In Garrett's own early military vignette "How the Last War Ended," the final section of his 1957 story "Comic Strip," the protagonist Captain G.

tells his unidentified captor, "I know what it's like to be defeated. . . . I am a Southerner," thereby invoking the bequeathed shadow of a lost cause described by C. Vann Woodward and many others (*King of the Mountain* 99). Yet, for all its complexity and psychological baggage, the lingering specter of the past is not without its artistic advantages. Perhaps most notably, it infects objects and places with useful characteristics and narratives. As Garrett explains, "Precisely because I *am* a southerner, I believe that places are enchanted. Rich with spirits. All houses, sooner or later, are haunted" (*Southern Excursions* 105), the aesthetic implications of which were summarized best by the scholar William Robinson: "Garrett is a Southern writer and *the* subject of the Southern imagination is history" ("Imagining" 35).

Accompanying history, particularly southern history, is the common and sometimes unavoidable phenomena of guilt, which in the South most often is associated with race and the legacy of slavery. In his notebooks for the novel *The King of Babylon Shall Not Come Against You*, Garrett admits, "[S]ince it deals with the South and some Southerners during the late 1960s and now, it likewise has to deal with various kinds of racism among other things." Demonstrating a much earlier interest in racial conflict, Garrett's notebooks from the 1950s include an untitled fictional account of a lynching in a small southern town. More than forty years later, a similar episode would appear in the title story of the 1998 collection *Bad Man Blues*, reworked into a fable narrated by the African American lawyer Willie Gary, a character from *King of Babylon*. However, just as Gary's lynching anecdote serves as a single episode in a much larger narrative, so does Garrett's historical view of the South include racial conflicts while weaving them into an enormous tapestry containing numerous other historical catalysts. Including race under the general moniker of southern history, reviewer Adam Mazmanian suggested that the protagonist of *King of Babylon*, Billy Tone, is concerned "not with the crimes he studies but with the South itself and with the accumulated psychic debt of history" (176). Mazmanian's linking of personal crimes to the great currents of history is all the more significant since it concurs with an earlier, more encompassing observation from Fred Chappell: "Garrett's vision of civilization as the relentless sacrifice of individual personality for the sake of order and continuance is deeply tragic" ("Fictional" 74). Built upon the tension between isolated historical phenomena like guilt and racism, and the impersonal, interweaving historical forces beyond any individual's control, Garrett's historical fiction of the South documents the local joys and agonies of citizens even as it simultaneously, and often a little reluctantly, abstracts them into the vacuous realm of human history, small footnotes in an enormous, multivolume, ongoing drama.

* * *

In admirably attempting to propel southern history and literature beyond reductive polemical and regional contexts and into a tragic human universality, southern writers like Garrett inevitably encounter a new set of difficulties. As William Robinson has summarized, "One of the problems about trying to write about southern politics or anything set in the South is that there are so many clichés and conventions that people expect or look for to identify, besides the fact that it takes place in a certain place and has a certain dialect and quality of language" ("George Garrett" 84). In addition to combating one's own temptations to memorialize or critique a given southern tradition, southern writers also must account for the sometimes-debilitating expectations of their readers. With a hint of irony, Garrett observes, "The southern novel has gradually become a genre, every bit as formulaic as science fiction, the thriller, the historical romance, or the old-fashioned western. . . . The southern novel advances through a minefield of habitual gestures and conventions, edging closer and closer to the pure and simple status of irrepressible cliché" (*Southern Excursions* 167). Established to the point that both writers and readers entertain a common expectation of specific tropes and rules, most contemporary southern literature, to Garrett's thinking, runs the risk of forsaking immediacy and relevance for the mastery of a long-established, though now less culturally-applicable, form.

If much contemporary southern literature conspires to constitute a collective cliché, how then may its more useful and unique narratives be identified? One solution is to read for language as much, if not more, than content. Garrett notes, "The prose fiction of the South has an enormous range as compared to the prose fiction of other regions of the country. Even at his most literary, the Southern fiction writer doesn't go too long on a high tone. Even Miss Eudora loves to drop into the colloquial. They love variety of speech, from public rhetoric to the rhetoric of movies and the pop culture" (Israel 44). The scope of convincing voices, whether rendered by Faulkner and Erskine Caldwell or Alice Walker and Dorothy Allison, has long been a strength of southern literature, and this dynamic informs narrative relationships between southerners and nonsoutherners as much as it does purely regional ones. For example, in Garrett's short story "A Hard Row to Hoe," the narrator describes his friend Bill, a Princeton undergraduate from Georgia, as "a Southerner with a rich amusing accent and idiom that gave whatever he happened to be saying a strangeness which made people listen" (*King of the Mountain* 103). Possessing an unusual, compelling voice in a foreign setting, Bill captivates his Princeton acquaintances with the peculiar sound and method of his storytelling as much as for the stories themselves. And among southerners, a writer's use or rejection of certain types of southern voices sometimes may lead to assumptions about his or her own personality or societal views. As Garrett humorously notes in "Don't Try and Sell Me No Pink Flamingos," his introduction to *White Trash: An Anthology of Contemporary Southern Poets*, "Some southern writers would rather die slowly and badly than admit to a touch of trash. They will go to great lengths to deny there's any such (of a) thing as a Cracker in their gene pool or a Redneck in the woodpile" (xi). Of course, the voices in Garrett's own southern narratives are both inclusive and unpredictable, with the working-class southerner often appearing as a prominent figure. In his unpublished 1950s poem "The South," a kind of experimental montage of southern voice and identity, Garrett writes, "The South is a pinch-faced, deep eyed sharecropper / Face to face with poverty and death for life" (Garrett, George Garrett Papers). Later, Garrett would articulate several different voices and points of view, nearly all of them lower- or working-class, in the 1965 novel *Do, Lord, Remember Me*, the depth and richness of which have been summarized by R.H.W. Dillard:

> The South of *Do, Lord, Remember Me* is, like Chaucer's England, a confused landscape in which religion and sex, honesty and petty evil, the haunting dream of purity and the fallen world of lies are so subtly interwoven that no one can judge another or even himself or herself, and in which the most serious of religious pilgrimages is at once an occasion for true religious feeling and unrestrained bawdiness. (*Understanding George Garrett* 86–87)

Just as Chaucer jumped from disparate personality to personality amid the dramatic action of a religious journey, so Garrett leaps among his odd assortment of characters, deeply embracing each individual while using them collectively to perambulate toward central philosophical aspects of existence.

Although language and narrative technique function as the potentially liberating and self-defining implements of many southern writers, there remains much that makes them uneasy about their aesthetic decisions and the genre in which they are attempting to participate. Beyond specific literary conventions, many—perhaps too many—of southern literature's achievements and current expectations still are traced to the work of Faulkner. As Garrett notes, this is a fact to which writers readily must resign themselves: "It is impossible for any Southern writer aware of his place and people and aware of his own literary tradition *not* to be influenced by the towering energy and example of Faulkner. Those who pretend otherwise (and there are a number) are either trying to fool themselves or us or both at once" ("Foote's *Civil War*" 86). For Garrett, the southern writer who refuses to confront Faulkner is practicing an ill-advised conceit and playing a dangerous game. Yet, unlike many writers, Garrett does not view Faulkner as a potentially abusive literary father or menacing intellectual shadow. Instead, Faulkner's work stands as a kind of rich resource, a vein to be mined with great reward. He explains at length:

> Faulkner's work offers consolation and direction to the contemporary Southern writer. It offers a challenge as well: the writer is dared to divorce himself from easy habits of thought which are prevalent in the overall culture. Dared, by that towering example, to cultivate his art without regard to present systems of praise or blame and, indeed, without embarrassed or inhibiting reverence for the immediate past, the past which includes the achievement of William Faulkner, of Thomas Wolfe, of all of the Fugitives and other masters. By example, he demonstrates that the Southern past is not dead or disposable and cannot be ignored. It remains a resource to be wisely *used.* (*Sorrows* 213)

Secure in the ideas behind his own work and convinced of the value of southern literature's cumulative achievement, Garrett heartily recommends Faulkner as an exemplar of aesthetic integrity and for his unique ability to make relevant and alive his particular southern past.

Faulkner's mark on Garrett's work is glimpsed most readily in his numerous narratives involving the Florida Singletrees, who, appearing over the course of several stories and novels, call to mind Faulkner's recurring Mississippi families. Mark Royale, the protagonist of Garrett's first novel, *The Finished Man*, originally was a Singletree before Garrett decided to shift the name to his mother's side of the family. Later, Garrett intended to use a character named Angus Singletree as the protagonist for his novel *Which Ones Are the Enemy?* Other Singletrees include Raymond ("Bread from Stones"), Cortney and TeeJay ("A Game of Catch"), and—despite his last name—Fergus McCree ("Man Without a Fig Leaf"). Revisiting the Singletrees and their fictional Florida community of Paradise Springs enabled Garrett to build a small imaginative world that grew with each new narrative while also establishing an interesting intertextual historical continuity across his writings. Garrett also embraced and used Faulkner, rather than ignoring him, by giving at least two of his southern protagonists some knowledge of Faulkner's work. For example, in one section of the *Finished Man* Garrett has Mike Royale imitate Faulkner's narrative style to demonstrate his character's familiarity with the author. Yet, this playful reference only served to confuse and anger reviewers. As Garrett accurately summarizes, *The Finished Man* "was praised, for the wrong reasons, by one crowd of Southerners and damned and savaged by the Fugitive point men, also for the wrong reasons" ("George Garrett," *The Fugitives* 24). Baffled by Garrett's unusual, playful references to Faulkner, some reviewers attacked him for unimaginative imitation while others, equally wrong, lauded what they perceived to be straightforward thematic applications of southern literature's most popular and relevant writer. However, Garrett's use of Faulkner hardly is essential to his achievement and almost always appears more whimsical than vital. For example, in "A Hard Row to Hoe" Bill humorously critiques Faulkner in passing: "Why, that man's characters are much too civilized. Where I come from Erskine Caldwell characters are fine ladies and gentlemen" (*King of the Mountain* 104). Later, when the story turns serious, Bill tells an aristocratic southern friend, "You can't be yourselves and you won't allow anybody else to be either" (*King* 108). Over the years, critics have attacked other writers, southern and nonsouthern, for perceived imitations of Faulkner—Cormac McCarthy, Ernest Gaines, Reynolds Price, to name but a few—to the point that one might apply Bill's advice to reviewers of southern fiction. Ingrained with Faulkner's legacy, which inevitably intersects with the experiences of other southern writers, and with a formulaic set of expectations for southern literature, critics rarely afford writers the opportunity to wrestle or play with the master, choosing instead to guard assiduously his hallowed ground.

Citing his versatility and openness, Madison Smartt Bell has suggested that Garrett actually "has influenced more writers than Faulkner," an assertion that is difficult to dismiss given Garrett's long years of teaching and his scores of successful students, including Bell, who now are published writers (Bell, Novel Panel). To be sure, Garrett plunged into literary scenarios involving southerners that likely never entered Faulkner's mind. For example, in an untitled play from his notebooks, Garrett planned to have all his characters, including a Singletree, appear as ghosts in a graveyard. Slightly more grounded, though still unconventional, Garrett's short story "Bread from Stones" follows Raymond Singletree, a well-bred, habitually impoverished southerner who infrequently strikes it rich by serving as a companion for mature wealthy women. Although a story concerning a male escort from the South certainly is not traditional, near the beginning it contains a line that might have come from one of Faulkner's characters: "[I]t is all right to be southern and poor if your ancestors were southern and rich" (*Cold Ground* 81). Drawing on the vagaries of southern wealth, class, and identity, the story's opening passages call to mind the Faulkner character Quentin Compson. Like Quentin, Raymond, the "black sheep" of his family, desperately and futilely attempts to escape his southern history. However, the disparate and equally unpromising avenues of liberation he follows separate the story from Faulkner's work. For example, at one point Raymond invites self-parody, hosting a mock square dance for his love interest's wealthy northeast acquaintances. Part of Raymond's problem is that he is drunk on appearances, a remnant of his aristocratic upbringing. Lacking wealth, he nonetheless desires the appearance of it and seems to believe that by denigrating his southern heritage he may somehow escape his past and embrace a new image. Yet, as his wealthy female benefactor confides to Raymond's visiting brother, "what he really desires is some little sign of approval from that crummy Tobacco Road family of his" (*Cold Ground* 96). For all his posturing, Raymond cannot desert the importance of his southern values even though they are mocked and disowned both by his friends and by himself.

* * *

The wealthy northeasterners in "Bread from Stones," half-serious observers of Raymond's mocked southern background, continue to appear in the literary world today as national readers and publishers who expect to encounter a specific constructed image of the South that is consistent with their preconceived cultural notions of a region they know little about. As Garrett explains, not without some bitterness:

> [T]he history, nature, and character of the South (thus of all southern traditions, including the literary) have been so distorted and clouded by an accumulation of misinformation as to require major rehabilitation before we can think or talk sensibly about the subject. For more than a century since the South was defeated in our most savage and destructive war and subsequently treated (that is, mistreated) worse than any enemy the United States has ever battled, for more than a century the victors have written the history of the South, and the revisionists have also continuously modified that history. (*Southern Excursions* 46)

Entertaining sometimes drastically different images of the region, (inter)national observers and southerners periodically still find it difficult to locate common points of cultural and historical agreement by which to communicate and move forward. For nation-state Americans, the South usually is critiqued in a way that most contemporary southerners find offensive and/or outdated. Too often southerners still find themselves attempting to explain or apologize for cultural and historical issues that reach back to the Civil War and beyond, a phenomenon that has been noted and criticized by Garrett: "I, too, must bear my burden of contemporary guilt like a student's obligatory backpack. But I flatly refuse to add to it one ounce, one feather's weight, of *historical* guilt for anything. I am not guilty of or for the actions of anyone but myself" (*Whistling in the Dark* 38). Some of Garrett's characters are less certain; in *The Finished Man* the theme is played out between Mike Royale and his wife: "[S]he was from New England and different enough to find his ways and assumptions a little strange. And in the mirror of her eyes he had felt compelled to justify not only himself, but also his whole region, its past, its faults and follies as well as its virtues. . . . Like many a Southerner he loved and hated his history just as he loved and hated himself" (178). Confronted with his wife's New England background, Mike, a lawyer by profession, feels as if his own culture constantly is on trial. Yet, the ambivalent nature of his region makes it impossible to defend in rational terms; he is both proud and ashamed to be a southerner, and the duality is never successfully resolved. It is hardly surprising that their relationship ends in divorce.

Significant in Mike's dialogue with his wife is the fact that his culture, never his wife's, is the one on trial. A northeasterner by birth, Mike's wife functions as an agent of the dominant, culture-enforcing region of the nation-state. Spilling over into the literary world, an almost identical relationship exists between most southern writers and the people who publish their books. Garrett recounts:

> Ever since the Civil War, the southern writers who had any kind of national ambitions or aspirations, or the writers who worked in special forms—the drama, for example—whose principle centers of commerce and appreciation are elsewhere, have been forced to live up to an alien image of what the southern writer is supposed to be and to say; and, behind that, the subject itself, the truth presented in approved and certified southern literature, must conform to an outsider's image. (*Southern Excursions* 4)

Once again, Garrett's critical observation also finds expression in his fiction. In "Man Without a Fig Leaf" Fergus McCree, originally bearing the name Angus Singletree, is described by his Jewish New York friend, Sam, as a "crazy southerner with a taste for elegance and no money to support it" (*Cold Mountain* 52) and, in an earlier unpublished dramatic version, as "a malcontent, gifted, ambiguously mad." Throughout the story, Fergus repeatedly takes it upon himself to speak for his region while lamenting the debilitating ways in which it has kept him from succeeding as a writer in the culture of New York. Well-meaning and sympathetic, Sam, in the unpublished version, playfully tells Fergus that he looks like "the walking, decaying corpse of the Deep South. You're all covered with ringworm and hookworm. You're pellagra-ridden, illiterate and thoroughly corncobbed. If I looked like you I'd join the Ku Klux Klan just to have a chance to hide my face behind a sheet." Although Sam is joking with his friend, there is more truth in his jest than he suspects, and Fergus does not laugh. Though he would have Sam think otherwise, Fergus genuinely is troubled and hindered by the negative aspects of his region and their unavoidable connection to his tenuous identity and dysfunctional life.

Whereas Sam means well and wishes to help Fergus, his aid repeatedly takes the form of condescension, a relationship that symbolically translates into the literary world. As Garrett notes, "They (the Other, Yankees and such, as they say) do still take us Southerners, the men and the women alike, to be at best a kind of literary junior varsity" ("Literary Ladies of Dixie"163). Concerned with the vast (inter)national literary stage, the American literary establishment allows southern writers their own provincial bush league. Of course, the irony in this relationship is that southern writers consistently transcend the limitations of regional categorization by writing memorable novels that take place in national, international, and historical milieus. In an address to the Women's Club of Richmond, Virginia, Garrett noted two contemporary regional novels of New York City and Washington, D.C., written by southerners: Tom Wolfe's *The Bonfire of the Vanities* (1987) and Garrett Epps's *The Floating Island* (1985). Ignoring authors' southern roots when it is convenient, the national establishment never hesitates to claim and assimilate those talented writers whose work does not espouse a strong southern regional interest. Thus, Tom Wolfe, who lives in New York and whose work is national in flavor, generally is not referred to as a southern writer, but Cormac McCarthy, with his collection of undeniably southern and southwestern material, is. Categorized and shaped by the ambivalent rules of a national literary establishment that is itself anchored to a very small region and cast of players, southern writers—even the best-selling, award-winning ones—discover, sometimes painfully, that their reputations and identities ultimately are out of their hands.

Not content to weather silently the ongoing colonization of southern literature, Garrett continually referenced the problem in essays and readings, while also stubbornly refusing to conform his creative work to the rules and expectations of the national publishing scene. In this practice he is not alone. Citing writers such as R.H.W. Dillard, Lewis Nordan, Barry Hannah, and Jim Grimsley, Garrett notes, "All these people have worked away from and played with the expectations of audiences and publishers of what a good Southern novel is supposed to be" (Garrett, Interview). Infusing the genre of southern writing with nontraditional subject matter and parody—from violent, sex-crazed Confederate officers to unprecedented, courageous homosexuals—such writers strive to reinvent the form for various new aesthetic and philosophical purposes. One of the single most ingenuous examples of playing upon traditional southern tropes appears in R.H.W. Dillard's title piece from a short story collection coedited by Garrett, *That's What I Like (about the South)*, in which each section is preceded by a phrase—"family bonds," "local tradition," etc.—from the book's tongue-in-cheek introductory essay on what constitutes southern fiction. Consciously building a fictional narrative around the traditional formulaic variables of southern literature, Dillard skillfully appraises the genre while toying with the expectations of readers and conventional publishers.

Bearing Dillard's short story in mind, it is significant to note that *That's What I Like (about the South)* is the publication of a southern university press rather than a northeast/(inter)national one. Although its contents convey something new and innovative with regard to the established regional genre, the book's publisher, residing and predominantly marketing within the same region, ensured that its revelations probably would not reach the national readers who likely would benefit from them the most. As things stand then, the most groundbreaking southern writing is likely to remain well below the radar of the (inter)national literary establishment; as a result, a significant regional subjectivity will no doubt remain generally unrecognized by the cultural commissars of the greater nation-state. However, as Garrett's criticism and fiction keep telling and showing us, this state of affairs is nothing new and, for all its inauspiciousness, is not something that should cause aspiring southern writers to despair. In the summer of 2003 Garrett told me, "Right now the commercial world is not real interested in southern points of view but that's not very meaningful. We have such a strong tradition, I suspect it'll just go on" (Garrett, Interview). Continuing to evolve and articulate itself in spite of national forces that threaten to misinterpret or, worse, ignore it, southern writing carries on much as it has, fueled by the small, dedicated regional presses and periodicals that provide its largely regional readership. Having done more than his share over the past half century to document and critique the South's ambivalent literary identity in this national context, Garrett made his own forecast of southern literary endurance all the more possible and likely.

3

Representing Urban Appalachia

Fred Chappell's *The Gaudy Place*

> Place is that, which is the same in different moments to different existent things, when their relations of co-existence with certain other existents, which are supposed to continue fixed from one of those moments to the other, agree entirely together.
>
> Bertrand Russell, *A Critical Exposition of the Philosophy of Leibniz*

> The spirit of the place is poetic, as is the spirit of any place when you come closer to the heart of it. I can't think of any book of real worth, except maybe Dante's *Inferno*, that says, underneath, "This is a horrible, lousy place, nobody should live here, and the people are dumb" [laughs]. On the other hand, every book that deals with place is also a criticism of place, but not simply a wholesale thrashing.
>
> Fred Chappell, Interview with the author

On the dust jacket of the first edition of Fred Chappell's fourth novel, *The Gaudy Place* (1973), is a bare room, naked except for a table and two empty chairs. On the table sits a napkin dispenser, a bottle of whiskey, a tumbler (empty except for two large cubes of ice), and an ashtray containing two crushed-out fags and one burning low. A single door stands at the far wall, the light beyond the glass panes inked in the same rich golden hue as Chappell's name. Is this scene the Ace or Juanita's Place, Gimlet Street bars where the boy-hustler Arkie works his two-bit cons? The Big Bunny, another seedy dive where Oxic informs Clemmie he no longer can afford to pimp her? The Brass Rail, a swank, new, carpeted downtown establishment where Ted Pape makes his upwardly mobile political maneuverings? The back room of some elitist country club where the aristocratic Zebulon Johns Mackie bullies city leaders into submitting to his crooked business schemes? Probably it is all of these places, for it is the collective scene(s) of the book itself.

The Gaudy Place essentially is a meditation on place (the small fictional Appalachian city of Braceboro, North Carolina), which separates it conceptually from Chappell's first three novels. To be sure, milieu is important when considering those earlier novels, especially since they share, with some varied and notable exceptions, very similar rural western North Carolina settings. However, Chappell's interests during the compositions of those books lay more in working out the psycho-philosophical complexities of his young male protagonists than in relating an authentic sense of culture and community. In *The Gaudy Place*, as is the case in novels such as Ivo Andric's *The Bridge on the Drina* and Sherwood Anderson's *Winesburg, Ohio*, the book's setting also serves as its dominant character, with the various personalities contributing distinct aspects and avenues of interpretation to the collective identity of Braceboro. Like Mary Lee Settle's *Blood Tie*, the book frequently switches characters and perspectives, which, in turn, episodically construct the small Appalachian municipality that serves as both the novel's backdrop and its central subject, defining and defined by the people and objects that exist in its space.

Using locale or place as its guiding point of inquiry, this chapter reads Chappell's novel as a place-based social text that critiques its setting through cross-section and narrative-advancing representations of its socioeconomically disparate denizens. After presenting significant details of the novel's composition, early reviews, and structural qualities, I move into a largely theoretical meditation on place, underscoring its significance in southern Appalachian literature, how it is specifically portrayed in terms of urban milieus, and the way in which convincing characterization is essential to its construction. The consideration of characterization leads quite logically into an examination of the book's major characters in terms of the various subenvironments in which they function—how individuals operate in their immediate place, which in turn affects seemingly unrelated events and, in fact, the entire city itself. Finally, I argue that *The Gaudy Place*, with its interest in a small, closed society, marks a career-changing authorial shift from an existential, philosophical, and intellectually disciplined mode of prose expression in his first three novels to a more humane, comic, and community-based style of writing—paving the way for the more approachable Appalachia-based Kirkman stories

Chappell would begin writing in the 1970s and that would appear as four novels in the 1980s and 1990s.

* * *

Chappell maintains that the original germ for *The Gaudy Place* arose in the late 1960s out of the most unlikely and disparate of elements, most notably satire, civil rights, and societal violence:

> My wife and I belonged to CORE, you remember that, the Congress of Racial Equality, one of the first civil rights groups? It was a corrupt group in the town we were active in [Durham, North Carolina]. It was a corrupt political group. It really didn't do that much. That's why it died, I'm sure. There's no CORE now, at least as far as I know. And I thought, I'm going to do a long satire about civil rights and how corrupt sometimes it is at the beginning, though the great organizations like SNCC, NAACP, those are fine. But then, Mr. King, Martin Luther King, was assassinated while we were in Italy. And you couldn't write any satire on civil rights anymore. It would break your heart to think about writing something like that. So I got taken with the notion of how a violent act occurs. And this new novel is about a guy getting shot through the collarbone—not a terribly violent act, you know, no death, but violent enough. I wanted to follow it from the very beginning, the full act itself. How it came about. (Graham 41)

Having originally intended to write a bitter fictional satire of Durham's fraudulent CORE chapter, Chappell felt compelled to alter his plans after the tragedy of King's death, which he believed effectively rendered any such critique politically inappropriate. King's passing, along with Robert Kennedy's assassination and the general violence of the late 1960s, persuaded Chappell to redirect his attention from the corrupt nature of a supposedly idealistic organization to the societal essence and causes of individual violent acts. Interestingly, Chappell's shift in intellectual focus mirrored the general cultural movement of the 1960s from abstract youthful idealism to visceral violence—from Woodstock to Altamont, from genuine drug experimentation to narcotic addiction and junkies, from nonviolent protest to the Black Panthers and outright insurrection. Witnessing the riots in Detroit and Watts and other forms of urban unrest, Chappell also became interested in the way violence could be produced, often unintentionally, by the various socioeconomic participants in an urban society. This society-based line of thinking led him into a new realm of aesthetic and philosophical possibilities that excited him:

> When I came to write *The Gaudy Place* I was tired of writing little novels that take place in one immediate family, with a limited cast of characters. I'd never had the opportunity to write at length because of the pressures, of work, school, and my other commitments. I wanted to try to draw the street society of Asheville as I knew it in the mid-1950s. I wanted to try to draw it from *A* to *Z*, from [the characters] Arkie to Zebulon, as somebody has pointed out. I just wanted to write that kind of novel and to show that all the classes are intertwined, that they affect one another's destinies. It's kind of a mechanical way to do it, but it was fun, both because I got to use a broader canvas, and I got to use some observations that I really hadn't had an opportunity to use before. And I got to employ some humor for the first time. It's the only one of my novels that doesn't take place on the farm. (Palmer 405)

Taking as his model a small urban milieu (Asheville, North Carolina), utilizing the dynamics of its "street society," and generously employing levity and humor, Chappell found himself applying materials and methods radically different from the more meditative and overtly intellectual techniques which had informed the compositions of his first three books.

Ironically, Chappell wrote most of his comic and community-based Appalachian novel in Italy on the backs of the galley proofs for the largely despairing and solipsistic *Dagon*. When *The Gaudy Place* was published, Chappell's shift to a lighter, more readily accessible tone generally seemed to surprise and please critics, several of whom previously had appeared to suffer through *It Is Time, Lord* (1963), *The Inkling* (1965), and *Dagon* (1968), ignoring, misreading, and/or condemning the dense intertextual and philosophical structures at the centers of those works. As opposed to the first three novels, reviewers seemed to grasp Chappell's moderate ambitions for *The Gaudy Place* and were generally laudatory of his attempt, praising the novel's clear, witty writing style and its convincingly accurate construction of a small urban milieu. Critics literally applauded the book's tight readability with comments such as, "This delightful little novel is a series of character studies connected by an unpretentious plot" (Review of *The Gaudy Place*, *New Republic* 30). However modest they may have regarded the book in terms of its conceptual aims, reviewers were generally complimentary in regard to the effectiveness with which Chappell fulfilled his intentions.

The only major problem early critics found in Chappell's fourth novel stemmed from its organization and point-of-view. As Jonathan Yardley noted in the *New York Times Book Review*, "If there is a serious problem to *The Gaudy Place*, it is structural" (Yardley 36). Yardley's remark seems to have been extraordinarily perceptive since Chappell himself claims he was never comfortable with the book's organization: "Now the structure of the book—ponderous job that it is—is all mine, as far as I know. I'm not very satisfied with it" (Interview with the author). Chappell's shifting narratives and sudden transition to the first person in the book's final section seemed unnatural and contrived to some critics, several of whom believed the technique came across as a little too distracting or technically cute. Sammy Staggs, for example, lamented in *Library Journal* that Chappell suffers from a "showy craftsmanship, which calls attention to itself so often that one finally wants to shout 'Plot! Point-of-view!'" (Staggs 563). Staggs's concern, hyperbolic as it is, was shared by Chappell in slightly more deliberate and articulate terms:

> I feel ambivalent about that novel. I like some things about it. I like the first—I forget how many parts it has now—but I like all the parts except the last part. The last part does not quite work; it's not quite successful. But I was real proud of the first three or four parts. . . . But it needs—it only has one last chapter. It needs two more last chapters. And the last chapter switches over to first person; it all should have been in third person for the novel to work better. It's just that I discovered, as I was writing along, that if I shifted to first person in the last chapter, I wouldn't have to write one of the sections. I could cut it down. But it makes a sudden shift of point-of-view that is not really quite smooth or artistic, I'm afraid. (Palumbo 168–69)

Attempting to shorten the book, bringing about its conclusion without lengthening the narrative, Chappell moved to first person in the final section, which slightly disrupts the novel's structural rhythm. However, the book's overall formative composition remains a lively and original technique for developing largely mundane characters without allowing the text itself to become mundane. This observation was shared by at least one initial reviewer, who praised Chappell for successfully rendering his periodically bland street people "without duplicating the despairing banality of their lives" (Review of *The Gaudy Place*, *Kirkus Reviews* 17). On a decidedly smaller scale, Chappell's task was not unlike that of John Dos Passos in *Manhattan Transfer* and *USA*: to create a largely urban sense of place in compelling aesthetic terms through a convincing and realistic portrayal of less than ideal characters. Attempting simultaneously to introduce and develop characters, advance a story, and construct a vivid sense of place, Chappell arrived at a promising structure that, in the end, he was required to bend, perhaps a little surreptitiously, in order to make it succeed.

* * *

Putting aside *The Gaudy Place*'s specific structural issues and how they interact with the book's setting, it is essential to establish how Chappell conceptualizes a purely general sense of place in art and writing. Speaking of portraying Appalachia, he maintains:

> The spirit of the place is poetic, as is the spirit of any place when you come closer to the heart of it. I can't think of any book of real worth, except maybe Dante's *Inferno*, that says, underneath, 'This is a horrible, lousy place, nobody should live here, and the people are dumb' [laughs]. On the other hand, every book that deals with place is also a criticism of place, but not simply a wholesale thrashing. (Interview with the author)

In composing his fourth novel, Chappell was more interested in the accurate representation of a place through interesting aesthetic means, as opposed to polemical social criticism or the sentimental romanticizing of a specific community. With its focus on the street life of Braceboro and the corruption of its various leaders, *The Gaudy Place* is not unlike some of the more notable work of Hermann Broch, who in books such as *Die Schlafwandler* (*The Sleepwalkers*, 1932) and *Die Schuldlosen* (*The Guiltless*, 1950), chronicled the depravity and decadence of German life in the decades leading up to the Third Reich. Broch, gifted in demonstrating how noble impulses are almost always sullied and warped by unconscious depravity, often portrays corruption without changing a narrative's tone, which further enhances its power. Broch believed that art which is not capable of reproducing the totality of a defined world is not really art, and such an aesthetic conceptualization is applicable to *The Gaudy Place*, in which Chappell presents a nondiscriminatory, unifying vision of contradictory moral, economic, and social types, which results in a successful totalizing vision of a specific place. Just as A.'s and Zacharias's rambling conversation covers everything from *A* to *Z* in Broch's *Die Schuldlosen*, so *The Gaudy Place* offers a wide-ranging construction of place literally "from A(rkie) to Z(ebulon Johns Mackie)" (Dillard, "Letters" 13).

Broch entertained the conviction, borrowed from Oswald Spengler, that history progresses in cycles of disintegrating and reintegrating value systems. Such a perspective is useful in considering the history of Appalachia as a place and the impact its development has had on its traditional cultural norms. As Ernest Lee notes in his introduction to an anthology of Appalachian writing, *Discovering Place*, "[The] struggle to feel a sense of place is a major one for writers who have lived or are living in the Appalachian region, an area of the country that has experienced profound changes . . ." (xi). When Lee speaks of "profound changes," he suggests the presence, beginning in the mid- to late twentieth century, of interstate highways, large industries (such as the menacing Canton, North Carolina, paper mill that haunts several of Chappell's narratives), and the general economic hegemony that grasps the rest of the country in the form of corporate-owned drive-thrus, strip malls, and super chain stores. In *The Gaudy Place* Chappell moves from a more traditional, rural Appalachian background to an Appalachian city in the initial stages of being affected by the transition of which Lee speaks—a place in which traditional values are disintegrating while new immigrant variables, such as Oxie/Theodorik Paparikis/Ted Pape, are in the process of being integrated.

In her essay "Place in Fiction," Eudora Welty explains, "For the artist to be unwilling to move, mentally or spiritually or physically, out of the familiar is a sign that spiritual timidity or poverty or decay has come upon him; for what is familiar will then have turned into all that is tyrannical" (qtd. in Brinkmeyer vii). Moving "out of the familiar" rural Appalachian landscape and into a more uncharted urban one, Chappell faced the challenge of conquering and portraying an entirely new sense of place. Furthermore, in choosing Asheville, North Carolina, as his model, he was working with a setting that already had been etched memorably into the American literary imagination. As Frederick Turner asserts in his preface to *Spirit of Place*, "Thanks to our writers we also have a national literary landscape, places made special, if not sacred, because they have been the inspiration of literature" (Turner x). Synonymous with Thomas Wolfe as much as Dublin is commensurate with Joyce, Asheville carries with it a "literary landscape" and a legacy that Chappell had either to confront or to ignore. Because Appalachia, rural and urban, had changed greatly since Wolfe's time, Chappell was able to choose the latter path. Furthermore, Wolfe's Asheville was constructed in relation to the fictional Gant family and especially the youthful and dreamy Eugene of *Look Homeward, Angel*, which allowed Wolfe to write in the wistful, poetic, and occasionally sprawling prose he so admired. Although Chappell's Lin Harper has certain naive and idealistic similarities with Eugene, the novel as a whole, both in its compact stylistic tone and street-based subject matter, is a vastly different work from Wolfe's, opening up previously neglected aspects of Asheville in a distinctly contemporary format. Anaïs Nin commented in the late 1960s: "It is a curious anomaly that we listen to jazz, we look at modern paintings, we live in modern houses of modern design, we travel in jet planes, yet we continue to read novels written in a tempo and style which is not of our time and not related to any of these influences" (Nin 29). With its episodic, multiple narratives and use of street diction, *The Gaudy Place* brings Asheville up to date in a manner of which Nin would have approved. Although Wolfe and Chappell address the same geographic area, due to their respective times and divergent aesthetic intentions, they actually describe two very distinct places.

In an early study of American city fiction, Blanche Gelfant makes the obvious but important generalization, "Behind the rise of the modern city novel has been the awareness—always growing stronger and more clearly articulated—that city life is distinctive and that it offers the writer peculiarly modern material and demands of him literary expression in a modern idiom" (Gelfant 3). Beneath Gelfant's focus on the city is the assertion that place in general shapes aesthetic technique, which is true of Chappell's novels. In the first three books, and especially the second and third, the isolated pastoral landscapes are conducive to meditation and reflection. Beyond associations between family members, human relationships are largely deemphasized in favor of the protagonists' interior psychological and philosophical monologues. In *The Gaudy Place* relationships and dialogue are constant and fundamental to the novel, especially as they begin to overlap and interact in unforeseen ways toward the book's conclusion. Chappell's fourth novel is also "faster" than the first three, the urban pace of life causing events and action to unfold at a quicker, sparser, more literal pace. Time is also important in the book in a different sense. In their introduction to *Literary Landscapes of the British Isles*, David Daiches and John Flower remark, "It would surely be a needless puritanism that would deny to readers the satisfactions and insights provided by topographical aids to reading and especially by linking place with time so as to understand more clearly the total ambience within which a writer's imagination moved" (1). With the exception of Andrew Harper's brief academic regional history (*GP* 150–53) and Zebulon Johns Mackie's pompous amateur genealogical studies, less importance is placed on time-related aspects of place such as memory and history in *The Gaudy Place*. Unlike the reflective protagonists of Chappell's first three books, the characters in the fourth novel are generally forward looking, searching for the right con, deal, or general course of action to improve their various stations in life. Even the self-proclaimed backward-looking Mackie boasts that he studies and likes history, "even though there didn't seem much a feller could *do* with it," subordinating his interest in the past in order to become a corrupt, real-estate-developing civic leader instead (*GP* 155).

As Robert Brinkmeyer maintains, the movement away from memory and historical introspection is a postmodern quality of contemporary southern literature:

> In part because of the of the influence of developments in postmodern literature—a literature, broadly speaking, celebrating imaginative free play rather than memory—Southern writers have more and more been striking out on their own, moving away from the "imaginative" shape of "classic" Southern literature that is so secure in regional place, history, and memory. (Brinkmeyer 26)

Although Chappell does not forsake "regional place"—in his case, North Carolina—in any of his novels, *The Gaudy Place* does portray a different western North Carolina environment, an urban one, and does so without invoking history and memory as major themes. Instead of employing the meditative and often traumatic histories and memories of what Brinkmeyer calls "'classic' Southern literature," Chappell reveals place through the largely spontaneous and visceral manner in which his characters function in their environment. In listing his key elements for considering place, Leonard Lutwack includes "place in its literalness, a character's response to this place in both its concreteness and its symbolical relation to his life, and an important action transpiring in this place. This is a proper use of place in a measure not too meager to do justice to the importance of place in narrative not so concrete as to overwhelm with fact the imaginative power in the art of fiction" (Lutwack 26). In pointing out the significance of "a character's response" to place, Lutwack underscores the defining importance of the independent variables existing in the same space that constitutes a place. Along similar lines, Bertrand Russell paraphrases Leibniz when he puts forth the definition that serves as the epigraph for this chapter: "*Place* is that, which is the same in different moments to different existent things, when their relations of co-existence with certain other existents, which are supposed to continue fixed from one of those moments to the other, agree entirely together" (Russell 252). Throwing different "existent things," in this case different characters, into an environment that is the same for all of them, Chappell, drawing on the roots of the naturalistic novel, constructs a drama in which place and its variables/characters mutually work together in order to define each other.

Although characters in the book both shape place and are defined by it, Braceboro constitutes a setting in which people are unable to map clearly in their minds either their own positions or the urban totality in which they find themselves. Yet, it is upon this very tension and ambiguity that the novel bases much of its literary drama and humor. Concentrating on urban aspects with literary potentialities, James Machor describes his book *Pastoral Cities* as "a study of a conception of America's urban environment that has played an important role in our culture and literature. I have called this conception urban pastoralism" (Machor xi). In the interesting way in which its environment is conceptualized as revealing and being revealed by truths about its characters and human nature, *The Gaudy Place* would seem to constitute one of Machor's works of "urban pastoralism." However, any substantial conclusions regarding the relationships between characters and place remain speculative and elusive, since ultimately, at least in terms of perception, Braceboro constitutes a different place for every character. As Gerd Hurm argues in *Fragmented Urban Images: The American City in Modern Fiction from Stephen Crane to Thomas Pynchon*, "The social and literary modes emerging in the modern city cannot be reduced to single causes and deterministic relationships" (326). In *The Gaudy Place* a static set of environmental conditions has varying effects on characters, while characters construct and define the same place in erratically different terms. Out of this complex matrix emerges a place producing divergent characters, characters perceiving different places, and a novel of varied and conflicting perspectives and faces.

* * *

Richard Gray begins his book *Southern Aberrations: Writers of the American South* with the blunt, yet accurate, observation, "All relationships with place are difficult, but some are more difficult than others" (Gray ix). The most difficult and satisfying aspect of *The Gaudy Place* for Chappell was the successful and convincing construction of Gimlet Street and its seedy inhabitants as an original urban environment. He remarks:

> I drew, I think I was the first person to draw, the street people of the New South. The whole first three chapters are about street people, the people who live and make their living by their wits on the street. One's just a two-bit hustler, a kid that I knew and admired—this really takes place on Lexington Avenue in Asheville in the late fifties—and a prostitute. I used to see bunches of them and interviewed them in a couple of bars on Lexington Avenue. And I knew a bail bondsman who had made his way off the street and had landed a little bit of a semi-legitimate business. I just kind of went up the ladder of society in that novel. (Palumbo 168–69)

Chappell's interest in multi-/cross-class relationships is genuine and evident in other works, such as his unpublished and undated short story "The Little Wedding," involving a wealthy man's temporary marriage to a prostitute. *The Gaudy Place* embraces this class theme on a much larger scale, introducing a cast of characters, each generally higher in social standing than the previous individual, and providing a number of conflicting narratives that eventually merge into a single story.

At the bottom of Chappell's social and narrative ladders are the hustlers and whores of Gimlet Street, and he begins the novel with a character so far down the ladder that he hardly exists in society's eyes: Arkie (James Parker McClellan). Chappell underscores Arkie's lack of societal presence on the book's first page by having the omnipresent barfly Teach mock his lack of public documentation: "You got a driver's license? . . . You got a social security number? . . . Birth certificate? . . . And no school records and no vaccination scars and no doctor's records and no dentist's records. I guess you don't even have a mailing address" (*GP* 3). By all societal measures, Arkie is not a real person, utterly invisible to the organized governments administering his city and state. However, in response to Teach's premise that he does not exist, Arkie stubbornly maintains, "I do though," and in the context of Gimlet Street's loose, undocumented society he does function as a kind of human plankton or parasite, scurrying about at the bottom of the economic food chain, living off other people's crumbs—a dime here, a quarter there (*GP* 4). His grand life's ambition, to replace Oxie as Clemmie's pimp, serves as a humorous point of transition between his own paltry socioeconomic status and Oxie's, the successful Gimlet Street mover and shaker having passed on to more lucrative and socially acceptable downtown cons and manipulations.

Arkie's street-hustling characteristics align him with memorable impoverished fictional juveniles such as Charles Dickens's Oliver Twist and Horatio Alger's Ragged Dick, and his name suggests the word *archetype*. In fact, Chappell maintains that Arkie grew out of a very specific literary source:

> Sometimes you can't tell what's a literary inspiration and what comes from what you observe, because sometimes those two are very similar. There's a wonderful novel called *Don Sequndo Sombra* about a street hustler and how he makes his way in the world. I must have read that when we were visiting Italy, I'm not quite sure. At any rate, that novel seemed to me to have a lot of energy and a lot of affection for its waif, and I admired the ingenuity of the poor characters, how they made a living in the city in the novel. I had some knowledge of how that worked in Asheville, North Carolina, and so that novel kind of gave me the idea for how to do it. (Interview with the author)

Chappell based Arkie on Ricardo Güiraldes's memorable fourteen-year-old *gaucho* Fabio Cáceres, and just as Fabio leaves his trivial, streetwise existence behind him to become a nomadic *gaucho in rural Argentina*, so Arkie constantly looks for ways to improve his condition and, at the novel's conclusion, implies that he is fleeing Braceboro ("Fuck the law, I'm going down to ARKANSAS!"), presumably to lead a wandering life resembling Fabio's (*GP* 177).

Despite the fact that he lacks any substantial knowledge of the way larger business and society function, Arkie possesses a sleazy cleverness that enables him to make a living and even accumulate a small savings from working the streets. Furthermore, although uneducated, he has an extraordinarily quick mind and excellent memory. For instance, the narrator reveals that Arkie "could jabber it [the gambling odds] off like a radio announcer, faster than they could take it down, and never a mistake. He could carry policy numbers too, all in his head like that" (*GP* 7–8). In addition to his intelligence, Arkie is also uncommonly perceptive, astonishing Oxie with his prophetic prediction that Oxie will stop pimping Clemmie and constantly keeping his ears open in the bars and on the streets, hungrily digesting any information that might be useful to him. Arkie might well boast, like the narrator of Chappell's poem "Page," "But I'm no featherwit, as soon you'd see, / Were you my master. For I have a clever / Way with secrets, how to weasel them out" (*Castle Tzingal* 10). When he "weasels out" the fact that Oxie is likely to cut Clemmie loose, Arkie surprises the hardened hustler and earns Clemmie's respect.

Although he lacks any formal education, Arkie succeeds in making money and predicting events because he is so thoroughly a product of the place in which he functions. Like the cockroach or the rat, he thrives at the bottom of the food chain while the larger animals work each other over and wear each other down. The name of his environment, "gimlet," is defined as a small tool with a crew tip for boring holes, as well as a type of cocktail. It is a perfect moniker for Arkie's section of Braceboro, where alcohol flows freely, and one is constantly either screwing others or being screwed in a ceaseless struggle to survive. Chappell emphasizes Arkie's suitability for this urban jungle in a number of ways. For instance, he records Arkie's seemingly unnatural hatred of sunlight and the smells of vegetables and earth at the farmer's market: "Arkie rubbed his nose with his wrist, not caring for the smells of vegetables and jonquils and fresh earth. The sunlight seemed worse. When he cut the corner of Rance Avenue he was in the shadow of the buildings and he felt a lot better" (*GP* 13–14). Chappell effectively couples Arkie's dislike for the life-giving sun and traditionally pleasing organic matter with his love of cool, hard concrete; when he ducks out of the sunlight he is not only thankful for the dark coolness but also for the reassuring nearness of the synthetic buildings themselves. Chappell extends this condition as the day comes to an end: "He began to feel better as the sun got lower," underscoring Arkie's nocturnal predisposition (*GP* 25). While most boys his age are preparing for bed, Arkie is licking his lips and making his rounds, hunting for inebriated johns to hustle.

Young and still developing, Arkie is formed by the place in which he functions, which allows him to recognize patterns in his environment, enabling him, in turn, to make accurate predictions regarding future events. Chappell effectively uses Arkie's prophetic capacity in order to foreshadow various incidents in the novel. In addition to his aforementioned prediction of Clemmie's rejection by Oxie, Arkie believes that Oxie does not know Gimlet anymore: "[H]e don't know this territory near as good as I do. Got too many other things on his mind" (*GP* 29). Arkie intuitively senses Oxie's borderline existence between Gimlet Street and downtown politics, between the hulking pimp Oxie and the suave bondsman Ted Pape, and believes that Oxie's juggling of these two spheres has lessened his knowledge of the former. Chappell also has Arkie foreshadow the introduction of Linn Harper when he describes Arkie playing Space Patrol pinball (*GP* 30). Arkie's ability to win money at Space Patrol sets him off against his youthful opposite, Linn, who reads *Galactic Patrol* and contemplates cosmic ideals. Whereas Arkie plays the game for the very literal and practical purpose of winning money from opponents, Linn reads a book with an almost identical title in order to revel in abstractions and later purposefully performs a materialistic act of theft for something he does not want or need (chicken feed) as a humorously absurd philosophical exercise.

Arkie also foreshadows his own criminal actions at the end of the novel and suggests an earlier version of the book when he performs his endearing dance while singing, "I'm going down to Arkansas!" (*GP* 26, 30). At the book's conclusion the song implies that Arkie will be fleeing Braceboro, yet he has been singing it throughout the novel, insinuating that his unplanned departure has been inevitable all along. In fact, in an earlier version of *The Gaudy Place* Chappell had arranged for Arkie to leave Braceboro much sooner:

> I wanted to write a picaresque novel and it was the one I was working on that became *The Gaudy Place*. I think I had written the first chapter of *The Gaudy Place* and I thought it would be great for Arkie to take off and get out of there, bum around the country. Then, as I was pondering this, the design of *The Gaudy Place*—how it really could be a very tight story and a very wry one—came to me, so I went in that direction. I really would like to write a picaresque

> novel. I enjoy reading them, but I guess I'll never have much chance to do it. Two of my favorite novels are *Don Quixote* and a novel by Thornton Wilder called *Heaven's My Destination* and, of course, *Huckleberry Finn*. I love the spirit of the picaresque. (Interview with the author)

Resisting the temptation to transform Arkie into a picaresque waif, Chappell kept him scurrying around the cage that is Braceboro rather than turning him loose on the rest of the country. However, if Arkie is a rat, he is an uncommonly adept one, knowing his way around the maze and how to work both it and its other inhabitants to his own, albeit small, advantage.

As the speaker of Chappell's poem "The Peaceable Kingdom of Emerald Windows" summarizes, "But then we-all is a primitive sort / Of animule," this perspective effectively describes the instinct- and material-based existences of the people who live and work on Gimlet Street (*Earthsleep* 15). If Arkie is a kind of parasitic predatory rodent, living off others, his slow-witted love interest, Clemmie, resembles an exploited herd animal. A victim of and slave to her environment, she lacks the proper skills to survive on her own. By turns naive, paranoid, and feeble-minded, Clemmie, both humorously and poignantly, demonstrates—through her own darkly ironic, ignorant actions—that she really does need a pimp to look after her. Nowhere is her ineptitude more in evidence than when she hands over one hundred dollars to Teach for safekeeping (*GP* 34, 55). A weak-willed alcoholic, Teach promptly spends all but a few dollars on drinks. Although she is generally unhappy and unsatisfied with her life on Gimlet Street, Clemmie cannot conceive of any alternative kind of existence. When Arkie tells her that Oxie is climbing out of Gimlet Street, she wonders, "What did you climb *to*, though, if you left Gimlet?" (*GP* 33). Like Arkie, Clemmie is a product of the environment in which she functions; yet, unlike her diminutive admirer, she lacks the ability to manipulate her environment to her own ends, helplessly allowing it to shape her destiny instead.

Relatively early in the book Teach is reading the futuristic science-fiction novel *Galactic Patrol*, in which the protagonist, Kim Kinnison, tries to survive inside a hostile alien base (*GP* 35–36). The plot of *Galactic Patrol* comments on *The Gaudy Place* in general in the way it follows an individual's attempt to endure in a closed unfamiliar system. Although this theme is applicable to several of the novel's characters, it seems to have particular resonance for Oxie/Ted Pape, who is trying to move into the exclusive alien system of downtown politics from his familiar roots on Gimlet Street. Pape is fearful of going back to Gimlet ("A man could work his way up from Gimlet Street once in his life but he could never do it twice"), fearful of becoming Oxie again (*GP* 102). He has escaped the cage or been granted a furlough and does not want to be thrown back into it. Ironically, his semi-legitimate job involves getting people out of jail.

Pape's fear of returning to Gimlet Street humanizes his character but also results in several humorous incidents. For instance, in the nouveau riche tradition, he equates outward image with success: "His carefully resplendent appearance, for example, was for him no luxury but grinding necessity" (*GP* 102). The theme reappears a couple of pages later when the woman he sleeps with corrects his grammar (*GP* 104). In the tradition of John Gay's *The Beggar's Opera*, *The Gaudy Place* uses Oxie/Pape to portray, often comically, trashy people imitating their supposed socioeconomic betters while, as we shall see, their so-called betters dabble in trash themselves. The humorous quality of Pape's attempted ascension of the class ladder is intensified by the utter seriousness with which he toils up it. Practical and methodical, he plods through the best-selling *How to Win Friends and Influence People* (*GP* 41) despite the fact that he can barely read, and perhaps the funniest scene in the book involves the nearly illiterate Pape searching in vain for a newspaper at the city library (*GP* 124). Yet, for all of Pape's comic superficiality and illiteracy, he is neither shallow nor ignorant. In fact, his inability to read aids him in recalling Linn Harper's face from an obscure newspaper article; not having words to distract him, he remembers the picture. Oxie also measures his practical knowledge favorably against Freene Sluder, a college-educated local of decent social standing who lacks common sense (*GP* 107).

If Pape is unsure of himself in his downtown dealings and in the Harper home on Wedgewood Drive (*GP* 140), he is precisely the reverse when he returns to Gimlet Street as Oxie, a place where people respect his accomplishments and influence. Clemmie underscores his high status when she muses, "Any dumb john could work hard. Luck was part of Oxie's class" (*GP* 38). Oxie's success is based on his ability to know his environment; like Arkie he is a product of Gimlet Street and knows it the way Zebulon Johns Mackie understands downtown politics: "He knew every inch of it, every wall, corner and door. . . . He knew the graffiti painted on the bricks and the weeds that sprang up in the gravel-strewn alleys. And he knew the faces; especially he knew the faces. He knew everything" (*GP* 108). Like Arkie, Oxie uses his perceptive wits in order to prosper, and Chappell unites the two hustlers in a number of ways. In addition to the obvious similarity of their names, when Clemmie mentions Arkie to Oxie, Oxie visualizes him nostalgically: "The picture of him stayed in Oxie's head because when he saw him he couldn't help but remembering the way he himself had come along" (*GP* 116). The narrator also juxtaposes descriptions of the hustlers, especially "everybody knows Arkie" and "Everybody knows Oxie" (*GP* 24, 126). Oxie evokes the novel's title when he thinks of Gimlet as a "feverish gaudy place," yet it is a place that reflects and is reflected by him, a place that has produced him and of which he is master (*GP* 134).

* * *

After recounting the everyday existences of Arkie and Clemmie, the novel undergoes a dramatic shift in terms of tone and subject. With the chapter entitled "Ignominy of a Skylark," the book segues from the visceral hustling themes of Gimlet to the formless adolescent and academic idealism of Linn Harper's nerdy adolescent boys club (*GP* 61). In contrast to the uncensored reality of the first two chapters, the Skylark section portrays a failed attempt to apply a "code of behavior" to practical conditions, namely as a result of the organization's humorous virgin naïveté with regard to genuine adult experience (*GP* 61). Since the group's founding, membership has shrunk from nine to three as the boys have matured hormonally and developed strong interests in sports, girls, and James Bond. Yet, the club toils on led by its idealistic leader and aspiring intellectual, Linn Harper, who, like Wolfe's Eugene Gant in *Look Homeward, Angel*, seeks dreamy solace from the mundane reality of Asheville, North Carolina, in books and ideas. Unlike Eugene, however, Linn's interest in literature is a result of his heavy science-fiction reading (*GP* 62–65), which allows him to make a connection between physical science and the universe as being "a gaudy place in which we live" (*GP* 64). Linn's conception of a "gaudy place," with its focus on science, space, universality, and abstract thought, stands in direct opposition to Oxie's, which absorbs only the literal characteristics of life on Gimlet.

Despite his fascination with idealism, Linn's days of pure abstraction are numbered. As the narrator relates, "For ours is an age in which, even among the innocents, idealism cannot long endure" (*GP* 66). Ironically, it is the Skylarks' very idealization of philosophy that leads to their ridiculous attempt to apply it practically and results in its inevitable rejection. Just as the reader chuckles while Ted Pape illiterately stumbles about the local library, so Chappell pokes fun at Linn as he tries to reason his way toward a practical theory of existence without the benefit of any real life experiences. In the mountain cabin of Terry Burge's father—an isolated, pastoral setting where, as in William Golding's *Lord of the Flies*, the juveniles make their own immature and unrealistic rules—the Skylarks challenge Linn to apply Camus's fictional representation of a gratuitous criminal act (*GP* 75–76). The absurdity of the idea's conception is matched by the humor with which Chappell renders the act of the square clean-cut boy awkwardly attempting to pilfer a bag of chicken feed. The comedy reaches its height when one of the arresting officers accuses Linn of being a dope-fiend, completely shocking him since he is ignorant of the fact that such people exist (*GP* 82). As opposed to Arkie's effective street smarts, Linn's intelligence is abstract and ultimately useless in the practical sense: "Yet for all his reputation for brains he'd been unable to steal twenty-five pounds of chicken feed" (*GP* 84). Like George Brush in one of Chappell's favorite picaresque novels, Thornton Wilder's *Heaven's My Destination*, Linn applies his idealism and naïveté to everyday people, only to have them end up either misunderstanding or disliking him.

The inability of Linn's background and worldview to handle practical situations dawns on him while in jail: "[H]e didn't live like this, he had never even imagined the possibility of living like this" (*GP* 91–92). Like the aliens in one of his science fiction books, who "believe in an ancient legend which says that their race arose as a result of immigrants from another galaxy," Linn constitutes an immigrant in unknown territory (*GP* 145–46). Interestingly, his father, Andrew Harper, finds himself in similar immigrant circumstances when he moves his family to western North Carolina and learns about the history of his wife's family, the Mackies. Figuring out on his own the involvement of Zebulon Johns Mackie in local political corruption, Andrew initially is resistant when Katherine suggests that they let Mackie get Linn out of jail. Yet, Andrew is forced to compromise his idealism when he realizes he lacks the ability to function effectively in the downtown Braceboro environment. As Katherine says, "You don't know any of those people down there" (*GP* 149).

Although Linn and Andrew are united by their common idealism ("an abstract double allegiance to an idea of justice"), Andrew has no practical choice but to submit to Mackie's authority (*GP* 139). A product of class and privilege, Mackie has the inherent ability to manipulate the events of downtown Braceboro to his advantage. Furthermore, as a successful politician, he also is capable of swaying people purely as a result of his formidable charisma and powerful personality. For example, he coerces a less-than-enthusiastic Andrew into undertaking a history of Bunker County, a purely narcissistic exercise since, as Mackie maintains, "A lot of it I don't even have to look up. Part of our Family history, you know" (*GP* 156). Mackie's historical browbeating of Andrew foreshadows the political bullying he employs in illegally making money from the city (*GP* 159). When he finally encounters Pape, he speaks down to him "with a distant, almost cold, reserve," the same manner in which Oxie condescendingly addresses his Gimlet Street acquaintances (*GP* 176). Chappell purposefully makes this connection since he is trying to demonstrate that, rather than being morally or socially superior, Mackie constitutes only a larger, older, more powerful and socially acceptable thug, one who opportunistically pimps and cons his way about city hall. Even the appearance and sound of his name associates him with the tactics of the Gimlet Street crowd (Mackie, Arkie, Clemmie, Oxie). With grim irony, Chappell illustrates how little difference there is after all between people from seemingly distant points on Braceboro's socioeconomic ladder.

* * *

At the conclusion of *The Gaudy Place* nearly everyone is displaced from the environments in which they best function: Arkie is jumping town, the seemingly invulnerable Mackie lies bleeding in a parking lot, Oxie perhaps has overreached his ambitions, and Andrew Harper laughs at it all while his son sits in a jail cell. The rich golden light of freedom and possibility shining just outside the door on the book's dust jacket seems an almost laughably distant thing for everyone except perhaps the highway-bound Arkie—an ironic twist since he is the perpetrator of the book's central violent act. Yet it is crucial to acknowledge that the reader *can* laugh along with Andrew at the book's ugly company and their comedy of errors. Mackie's wound is superficial, Oxie will keep striving upward, and Linn will walk out of his cell a more mature young man. Chappell's first three novels have debilitating traumas and body counts, flirting with madness and destroying lives; *The Gaudy Place* also interrogates existence but does so with humor and forgiveness—the characters have futures and life will go on. In this way one recognizes the book's importance as a transition between Chappell's first three novels and the Appalachian Kirkman narratives he began writing in the 1970s, a relationship he unknowingly underscores himself when describing the composition of *I Am One of You Forever*:

> I had been engaged for many years in writing a very dark, experimental kind of fiction, which everybody else called Southern Gothic. Except for a novel called *The Gaudy Place*, in which I tried to write a very detailed, realistic novel, these were kind of symbolic novels of heavy philosophical import, and then when I switched over to poetry I didn't need to write things quite so heavy as that any more, it seemed to me. I wanted to lighten up a little bit, and write a book that people might enjoy reading, a book that might sell some copies for a change. (Palumbo 167)

Between *Dagon* (1968) and *The Gaudy Place* (1973), Chappell published his first book of poetry, *The World Between the Eyes* (1971), which he felt allowed him to "lighten up a little bit" in his fiction. Seen in this manner, the golden light on the novel's cover might have more to do with the book's author than its characters. Forsaking the brooding existentialism of the first three books and escaping, opening a door, into another way of writing novels—emphasizing such elements as place, humor, and storytelling—Chappell passed into a new stage of novel-writing which would light the way for his output in the ensuing decades.

4

The Truths of William Hoffman's Southern Appalachian Places

The Critics' and His Own

I. The Critics'

> Each truth was a composite of a great many vague thoughts. All about in the world were the truths and they were all beautiful.
>
> Sherwood Anderson, *Winesburg, Ohio*

James Dickey liked to declare, "The true consciousness of the race is in the hands of the liars," by which he meant "the artists" with their powerful capacities to invent and/or fabricate resonant archetypal artifacts that at once transcend and speak for a given cultural moment. It is an assertion that proceeds from the old controversial idea of aesthetically produced truths. Getting the dialogue going in earnest, the philosopher Kant denied that art could possess truth in general, only to complicate his argument by offering that indeed it did contain something ineffable which lay somewhere beyond or between experience and reason. Schiller and others later would take up the banner. Closer to our own time, in the twentieth century Hans-Georg Gadamer, wandering away from Kant's position yet still dependent upon it, offered, "The work of art is the expression of a truth that cannot be reduced to what its creator actually thought in it" (95). By this time, the author had been dragged more into the equation, albeit as an ironic and peculiar kind of somnambulist variable that knows not what it does. And even now, as the philosophers and critics carry on the debate, the truths mysteriously continue to spring forth from the artists, be they earnest prophets, unconscious mediums, or outright liars.

Ever since his days studying classical languages as an undergraduate World War II veteran at Hampden-Sydney College in Virginia during the late 1940s, William Hoffman entertained a powerful fascination, an insistent compulsion, for the truth of the powerfully constructed image and the memorably wrought word. The underpinnings of his vividly realized novels and stories, though sometimes autobiographical, seem almost to erase the presence of the authorial self altogether in allowing a work's visceral material and action to evolve toward an end that seems not so much brought about as made to appear naturally inevitable. Ironically, however, Hoffman asserted that his idea of artistic destination in his work comes from perhaps American literature's most notorious and gifted prevaricator, Poe, and his famous, albeit somewhat dubious, essay "The Philosophy of Composition"—that instructions-included formula for literary invention that may or may not actually have worked for Poe. Complicating matters further, not unlike Kant had for the philosophers who followed him, Hoffman informed a number of literary acquaintances and interviewers—sometimes joking, sometimes not—that his epitaph should read, "He didn't cheat," a reference to his claim that none of his novels or stories ever proceeded from or were fueled by a consciously forced inclination or disingenuous gimmick. That a body of work of such constant and astonishing integrity should be built in part upon what may be one of literary history's most bogus compositional theories underscores for me both the suspect value and effect of artistic theory in general and the ongoing, unexplainable presence of the aesthetic ineffable—that strange shadow region (perhaps a making-cave, perhaps not) which lies somewhere between the talented artist, with all her well-meaning theories and conscious intentions, and the myriad unlooked-for truths of her achievement.

* * *

William Hoffman's fourteenth and final published novel, *Lies* (2005), published precisely fifty years after his first, *The Trumpet Unblown*, marked a return to the primarily literary concerns of his earlier extended prose fiction, following a trilogy of more commercially oriented mystery novels: *Tidewater Blood* (1998), *Blood and Guile* (2000), and *Wild Thorn* (2002). Whereas buried formulas of circumstance lie at the operative heart of the trilogy, *Lies* is more concerned with the philosophically self-reflexive, wholly irrational mysteries of the buried and invented life: how, against a powerfully imagined backdrop of place, over the course of an existence, one adopts or is made into the identity or identities by which one comes to be known.

Like several of Hoffman's earlier short stories and novels—most notably *A Place for My Head* (1960), *A Walk to the River* (1972), and *Godfires* (1985)—much of *Lies* takes place in a fictional projection of southside Virginia, a section of the state Hoffman lived in and wrote about now for more than half a century. Completely at home in this rural milieu, which he conveyed with unobtrusive skill, Hoffman unravels slowly and steadily the solid, yet finely nuanced, elements of character and story for which he is most known and celebrated, both as a novelist and as one of our best living practitioners of the short story form.

The protagonist of *Lies*, Wayland Garnett, suffers from what might be termed a late-life crisis. A product of the Depression and World War II, Wayland returns to the southside Virginia county where he was raised for the purpose of confronting and putting to rest the demons of poverty and social inferiority that constantly plagued him as a boy. Although his journey is made in earnest, he remains unsure as to what he is really searching for. Now a highly successful Florida businessman, Wayland marvels how he overcame a distant childhood of rural want to nibble "Brie and cold-broiled shrimp" at his daughter's Agnes Scott graduation while "tuxedoed musicians played Schubert's 'Trout Quintet' under candy-striped tents" (52). Wayland knows he isn't "the same person who had left Howell County, Virginia, some forty years ago," yet the manner in which he conceptualizes his progress and success is flawed: they are subjected to a material rather than spiritual assessment, which, though he does not know it, informs the very root of his need to return (36). Minus his childhood deprivations, Wayland might dwell more on the qualities of love and devotion he both practices and receives, but instead he lies about his violent, poverty-stricken past and celebrates his Mediterranean-style four-bedroom house, his big boat, and his membership at a country club "with two eighteen-hole courses, an Olympic-size pool, and a ballroom lighted by a dozen chandeliers" (69). For all the richness of his years and experiences, he remains marked and dominated by the corporeal absences of his youth, an old man still very much in the process of coming to terms with himself and running out of time to do it.

On a conceptual and cultural level, a significant measure of the book's value lies in its preoccupation with various connections between the Depression, World War II, and modern America as experienced by an author and narrator who have lived through these events and times but remain uncertain of their collective meaning. In a number of very real and brutal ways, the suffering concomitant with Depression-era rural Virginia forges and hones Wayland into the figure who is able to tolerate and function amid the savagery of modern warfare. For instance, Wayland likens the stench of deceased German soldiers laid out in a ditch to "dead cattle and hogs killed in the flood and left unburied" (184). Later, when he fires a round into a fleeing Wehrmacht infantryman, he considers the man's blood trail the way he would a "deer he's tracked and killed back in Howell County" (196). In the wake of an engagement, when he discovers small pieces of shrapnel embedded in his skin, Wayland "pinches out seeds of it as he might have Howell County ticks" (208). Psychologically, whether he realizes it or not, Wayland makes sense of the chaotic sufferings of war by comparing them to the less brutal, though physically punishing and almost equally senseless, dynamics of life and death in his rural upbringing, a process that enables him to relate and understand his considerable wartime trauma.

In 2005, as part of its *Voices of the South* series, Louisiana State University Press reissued another World War II Hoffman novel, *Yancey's War* (1967), a book that masterfully and hilariously filters the maddening qualities of conflict and military life through satire. However, with that notable exception, Hoffman's staggeringly realized view of war, as it appears across some of his most memorable novels and short stories, remains one of life-defining suffering and struggle. A medical corpsman in the 91st Evacuation Hospital during the Normandy Invasion, Hoffman witnessed firsthand some of the worst injuries modern warfare can inflict, recording much of that experience in his powerful first novel, *The Trumpet Unblown* (1955). Some of the grim, unflinching beauty of that prose is recaptured in *Lies* via Wayland's wartime reflections. When a grenade explodes near his shallow foxhole, he "feels the squish and smells the stink of his asshole letting go. He becomes wailing, cringing flesh nosed into defying earth" (186). Later, near a burning farmhouse, Wayland comes upon a dead heifer that has been riddled with small arms fire by drunken German soldiers, discovering, upon closer inspection, that "bullets have splattered the udder, causing milk and blood to fuse" (205).

Though such passages may weigh heavily and unpleasantly on the minds of some readers, Hoffman records them not for shock value's sake but rather to give his accounts an authentic immediacy, portrayed as they are by one who has lived them. And there are occasional glimmers of happiness, islands of joy, rendered just as vividly as the carnage that surrounds them. When, for instance, Wayland's unit meets up with a contingent of the Red Army along the Elbe, Hoffman skillfully captures the ecstatic union of American and Russian soldiers: "Unauthorized celebrations erupt. Wayland and a husky Russian private armed with a rifle dance and kiss. She smells of sweat, cordite, and onions. They drink vodka from her canteen as soldiers fall laughing and whooping into the river" (219).

If *Lies* has a possible seed for readerly frustration, it may be its difficulty in crafting and establishing smooth transitions and connections between and across its various time periods and disparate milieus: 1930s southside Virginia, 1940s Western Europe, modern America. However, this occasional disconnectedness also functions as an accurate and perhaps necessary narrative composite of Wayland, who is arduously seeking to reconcile the poor country boy with the combat veteran and wealthy businessman across bewildering chasms of time and experience. Whatever rough edges the book's episodes possess ultimately reinforce the various jagged wounds to Wayland's character. However, reliving and reflecting upon the traumas of the past over the course of his journey, Wayland learns and reconciles much, though he decides that some falsehoods are, after all, sometimes worth the effort of cultivating and sustaining. And wisdom is the reward of the reader who accompanies Wayland's reminiscences and discoveries over the course of the book. A subtle portrait of a generation, rendered by one of its finest writers, *Lies*, for all its fictions, is a book possessed of many truths.

* * *

Its substantial chronology and wide-ranging themes notwithstanding, *Lies* only barely reflects the substantial complexity of Hoffman's collective fictional concerns established over more than a half century of writing. Unfortunately, nearly all of his books up through the mid-1990s are out of print, which means interested readers will need to contact their local libraries or haunt the aisles and Internet sites of used-book stores if they wish to peruse them. Fortunately, a skilled and detailed scholarly assessment of Hoffman's literary achievement up though the late 1990s exists in the form of *The Fictional World of William Hoffman* (2000), a broad yet penetrating collection of essays edited by former Longwood University professor William Frank. However, little criticism beyond individual book reviews has appeared since this noteworthy publication. In his introduction to the collection, George Core notably asserts that the achievement of Hoffman's fiction has "seldom been equaled and only rarely exceeded," while also labeling Hoffman's neglect "on the critical front" as "both mysterious and unfortunate" (Core 1, 8). Despite the strength and value of the essays in *Fictional World*, the climate of puzzling critical neglect continues today unchanged.

What manner of questions and considerations might change that? What are the apparent strengths of Hoffman's overall oeuvre and what might remain to be said about them? In an undergraduate course I teach on contemporary southern writers, Hoffman's short stories often have a powerful and inspirational effect on students, particularly those who are aspiring writers (as opposed to aspiring literary critics). They frequently marvel at the visual and psychological range of what Hoffman is able to achieve while employing minimal materials and fictional conventions. Moreover, they delight in (and sometimes are stumped by) the fact that his approach almost always is standard and traditional while the end product—the collective achievement of a given story—typically is not.

At the beginning of an essay on Hoffman's short fiction, originally appearing in the *Sewanee Review* and later reprinted in *Fictional World*, Fred Chappell reacts not unlike the students. He says of Hoffman's tales, "They are lean but strong, moving with quick grace from point to point, and when they conclude, the figure they have shaped is a memorable and pleasing one" ("Taking Measure" 16). Chappell also speculates convincingly upon Hoffman's general lack of variation, offering, "He rarely writes what we could call an 'experimental' story; he probably feels no need, being so expert in the art of straightforward narrative" (10). To Chappell's fitting observations I would add that the paragraphs of Hoffman's short fiction typically are notable for their brevity, while the spare yet deft prose style contained within them keeps the authorial self thoroughly reigned in and affords a startling resonance to the archetypal and natural forces contained within the pages. The end product of this combination is a kind of brilliance that is as seamless as it is subtle and indirect. Indeed, its profound naturalness, expertly rendered with such standard materials, appears to blunt the academic critical endeavor to a significant degree. Instead, what often emerges among literary commentators is a sincere appreciation largely bereft of traceable variables. Case in point: reviewing Hoffman's third collection of stories, *Follow Me Home* (1994), at its time of publication, the vigorous reader and reviewer Robert Buffington glowingly declared, "He is the best pure storyteller I have read in these two years" but did not elaborate at much length on what in fact made Hoffman the best (236). Considering *Follow Me Home* among the hundreds of other titles he had perused, Buffington simply recognized that it was superlative.

Beyond the difficulties associated with formally oriented academic considerations of Hoffman's fiction, there is much that is tantalizing, promising, and largely unexamined in terms of its range of subject matter and the concepts and philosophies that surround it. In *Fictional World*, both George Garrett and William Frank comment at length on Hoffman's war fiction, with the former contributor unreservedly offering that Hoffman's military novels are "at the highest rank of the American fiction coming out of World War II" (88). Appearing across several novels and a number of short stories, Hoffman's war-related narratives excel in reflecting the social alienation, psychological trauma, and moral ambiguity that generally define the best military writing. Setting this work more fully alongside that of other contemporary vet scribblers such as Tim O'Brien would seem not only appropriate, but also potentially valuable.

A lesser-known early novel of Hoffman's likely demands equal attention. *A Place for My Head* (1960) unfolds in the midst of a racially charged representation of late 1950s Farmville, Virginia, the town in which Hoffman lived and worked during the tumultuous years of *Brown v. Board of Education*. The book's white lawyer protagonist, Angus McCloud, elects to represent an African American man, Edwin Trent, whose children have been killed in an auto accident involving a wealthy white driver. Though McCloud wins the case against long odds, he discovers to his disbelief that his client as well as a number of influential African American leaders actually had wanted him to lose for various political reasons. A vivid and occasionally disturbing reflection of that complex era, McCloud is a conflicted character: like most white citizens of that time and place, he supports segregation in the schools but, unlike most, believes he has a moral duty to provide legal counsel for African Americans, even when pressured by intimidating and potentially violent local whites to desist and drop the case. The ongoing public and scholarly interest in *Brown v. Board* and the recent appearance of novels such as Dennis McFarland's *Prince Edward* (2004), much of which takes place in a less convincingly rendered Farmville of the same period, conspire to make a new edition of Hoffman's book appear both highly relevant and long overdue.

Near the conclusion of his wonderfully titled essay "Mary Poppins's

Mouth" in *Fictional World*, Dabney Stuart perceptively points out that Hoffman's novel *A Death of Dreams* (1973) provocatively bridges his preferred settings of southside Virginia and southeastern West Virginia coal country, a region in which Hoffman spent his childhood and from which his ancestors hail. Like the Farmville of *A Place for My Head*, Hoffman's West Virginia settings often are mired by terrible local upheavals of a political nature, and in both environments Hoffman notably excels in providing believable composites of the disparate forces and players at work. For example, his first definitively West Virginia narrative, *The Dark Mountains* (1963), anticipates the coal novels of Denise Giardina in its balanced characterizations of both everyday miners and the despotic owners who employ as well as govern them. Hoffman also succeeds in creating conflict in the reader by relating the poverty-stricken starvation-tinged beginnings of the novel's owner-protagonist, James MacGlauglin, who eventually rises to become the wealthy operator of a successful coal camp. As Hoffman pointed out to me in the interview featured in this chapter, "Now you might not think of a coal-mining tycoon like James MacGlauglin as an underdog, but he was when he was a penniless immigrant and he was again when it came to fighting the United States government." A proverbial robber baron MacGlauglin may turn out to be, yet his origins are humble and his empire self-made. It is a tribute to the power and complexity of Hoffman's characterization that we continue to sympathize with him a little even as his mining operation comes to resemble a dehumanizing fiefdom.

Among other things, *The Dark Mountains* led to an invitation from legendary West Virginia editor Jim Comstock for Hoffman to come write for the *West Virginia Hillbilly*, a peculiar and arresting publication offering unique commentary on both mountain culture and national events. Although Hoffman would not return to dwell in West Virginia in person, he would visit the state imaginatively in his 1990 novel *Furors Die*, as well as periodically over the course of his more recent mystery trilogy. Martha Cook and Jeanne Nostrandt offer finely nuanced readings of *The Dark Mountains* and *Furors Die* respectively in *Fictional World*, yet more remains to be observed through a number of promising interpretive lenses and in comparison to the substantial body of contemporary fiction dealing with similar subject matter. That these novels are both out of print and generally unknown among contemporary readers of West Virginia coal narratives and Appalachian literature in general is particularly lamentable and seems to me another clear and notable symptom of what Core earlier described as Hoffman's "mysterious and unfortunate" neglect.

* * *

The philosopher Heidegger thought truth was already there; Nietzsche believed it to be something that was actively made up. Both thinkers often are feared and/or willfully misinterpreted, but it is the latter writer, with his occasionally musical language and outrageous declarations, who had more of the artist about him. For the artist the rapture of the creative impulse ultimately trumps reason. The philosopher's often tin-eared premise and inference give way to the artist's siren voice, which might say any number of things but usually speaks with a sound resembling the timbre of Keats: "I mean Negative Capability, that is when man is capable of being in uncertainties, Mysteries, doubts, without any irritable reaching after fact and reason." Philosophers and contemporary literary critics often scoff at this sort of passage, as well as the irrationality of creations such as, "Beauty is truth, truth beauty." Yet Keats was not chiefly interested in being logical or rational, though some scholars have had the presumption to reckon him a philosopher. Nevertheless, it is hard to fathom that he ever would accept a mantle such as "speculative epistemologist" over that of "poet." Likewise, Hoffman's best work, the most evocative truths of his fiction, often, like life, are of a conflicted nature—difficult to talk about critically, as if arriving to us from a place we might never have predicted, that remains perhaps traceless, yet is always made to feel resonant and right. With so much work behind him, the truths of his fiction appear to have rendered his own theories and intentions, well-meaning or suspect as they may have been, irrelevant. And it is to our enduring advantage that he possessed the courage to allow the truths to have their way. He didn't cheat.

II. His Own

The following interview with Hoffman took place in August 2001 at his home in Charlotte Court House, Virginia; he passed away in the nearby town of Farmville in 2009.

* * *

CLABOUGH: Who were your literary influences early on, when you were first publishing short stories, before the first two novels came out? Hemingway was an obvious stylistic and thematic source—who else?

HOFFMAN: I went through a progression that drew me into writing, and the first writer that really lit my fire was Thomas Wolfe. For a while I couldn't seem to read anyone else and I read everything he wrote. He really got me going. It took me a long time to get into William Faulkner. I would say I next read Hemingway, largely because I was over in Italy [during World War II] and I bought a very cheap copy of one of his short story collections. Then I began to read his novels. This was a golden age of writing for a reader. Of course, I also got into Fitzgerald very deeply. Later on, I admired Robert Penn Warren a lot, especially *All the King's Men*. I read these people while I was branching out and trying to find my own way of writing, my own voice. I don't keep up with current writers as much as I should. I do like Cormac McCarthy, for example, and there are certain books I like by some of the people I know. I like George Garrett's books and some by Fred Chappell, but I think by the time I got to those people I was pretty much set in the way I write. And I think what those early writers taught me was not so much a sense of style, I had to find my own style, but what I hoped would be a sense of integrity in what I was doing. And I was always conscious of this very fine writing that sort of set a benchmark on what I was trying to create myself.

CLABOUGH: Has the kind of writing you admire changed over the years?

HOFFMAN: Yes, it has somewhat. It changed, of course, when I got into William Faulkner by reading a story of his called "A Rose for Emily." That made me see what he was really doing and the depth of his writing, all the various levels and whatnot. In fact, I was so taken with that story that when I taught at Hampden-Sydney I had my freshmen read it, and we took up three classes on it. In fact, there are people today I taught in the 1950s who see me and say, "A Rose for Emily" [laughter]. I still like Thomas Wolfe, but he reads a lot differently now than when I was a young man.

CLABOUGH: *Days in the Yellow Leaf* (1958) was the first novel you wrote, but *The Trumpet Unblown* was published three years before it. How did that come about?

HOFFMAN: It came about this way as far as I can tell. I had an agent up there [New York City] who was just starting out, and she sent *Days in the Yellow Leaf* around to two or three places and the last place she sent it to was Doubleday, and there was an editor there who turned the book down but wrote me a very encouraging letter. I submitted *The Trumpet Unblown* to the same editor a month later, and he accepted it, also agreeing to publish *Days in the Yellow Leaf* later on. That's how it happened.

CLABOUGH: Although *Days in the Yellow Leaf* was your first book, it seems to begin chronologically where *The Trumpet Unblown* ends. Both books take their titles from the poetry of Lord Byron, and the respective protagonists, Tyree Shelby and Tod Young, are drained and largely apathetic as a result of their war experiences. Shelby goes through the war and is unable to connect with anyone afterward, and in *Days in the Yellow Leaf*, Tod seeks refuge from the gaudy postwar economic prosperity with his hard-luck veteran buddies.

HOFFMAN: I think there's a continuity of subject matter there. Certainly, that's the idea. It was this frame of mind I was in when I came back from the war, and the first thing I had to write about was the trouble I had working my way back into civilized life. That's the thing a young writer would normally go to and that's what I did. And that was more important to me at that time than the actual war itself. The first two novels are autobiographical to a certain extent. As I progressed, I was finally able to break away from the autobiographical stuff, but in the early days I was very much tied to the war. And I'm still. . . . when people consider time they might mention A.D. or B.C., but when I think of history it's almost automatic: I say, "Was this before or after World War II?" That was such a strong experience for me that sometimes I feel like I'm living on one side of the divide, and everyone who wasn't there is on the other.

CLABOUGH: I've heard the so-called brutality of your first couple novels made you kind of unpopular in certain administrative circles on the campus of Hampden-Sydney College.

HOFFMAN: Well, I doubt if teachers today really know what it was like to teach at a place like Hampden-Sydney back then. The power of the president and the board was just overwhelming. The teachers had no union or whatever you might call it—they were kind of academic slaves to a certain extent. So when *The Trumpet Unblown* came out, some of my colleagues got a little nervous about being around me because nothing had come down from the president's office. Just to digress, there's an anecdote that goes with this. There was this prestigious visiting historian from the University of Virginia with the actual name Thomas Jefferson Wertenbaker. As the name might suggest, he and his wife were very courtly and genteel and correct. They were sitting in their parlor one evening, he was doing some work, and his wife was reading my book. All of a sudden she let out a loud gasp, and Dr. Wertenbaker asked her what was wrong. She looked at him and said, "Is there a Mrs. Hoffman?" [laughter]. But anyway, I received in my mailbox a notice to come see the president, and I thought to myself that this might be pretty lively. The president was a Presbyterian minister of the severe old order, and, yet, he had a side to him that was very progressive. I had no advanced degree when I was hired, and the terms of the contract were such that I could only teach for two years, after which I had to get a degree. So here I was going to the president's office, having been there almost three years and with a controversial book just come out. I went in there and he stood for me and shook my hand and then he said, "Bill, I haven't read your book, but I notice it's getting a lot of attention. We're going to waive the rule that you have to go to graduate school." As soon as word got around that people weren't going to be smeared or polluted by being around me, everything was fine and smooth as can be.

CLABOUGH: Violent acts often seem to be of great symbolic importance, even in several of your nonwar narratives. Fred Chappell remarks that in your work "the violence brings to sharp focus truths that go generally unremarked in the course of daily events" ["Taking Measure" 23]. Do you agree with that?

HOFFMAN: I guess back when I first started writing I was considered by reviewers to be a pretty violent writer. I admit I was somewhat surprised by it since I was only portraying my experiences. It seems to me in light of today's fiction, I'm not a very violent writer. I mean some of the recent writers I've read are really violent, perhaps excessively so. Now I do believe that life is violent. It's violent and it's tragic: that's my experience with it. If someone finds something symbolic or revealing in that, I'll take credit for it, but I don't sit down and write up violent acts in order to reveal character, even though violence often does reveal character—that's just a given.

CLABOUGH: George Garrett asserts that your two wartime novels, *The Trumpet Unblown* and *Yancey's War* (1966), belong "at the highest rank of the American fiction coming out of World War II" ["A Life without End" 88]. In addition to the Hemingway influence, to what extent were those books indebted to other war fiction?

HOFFMAN: I'm trying to think of the war novels I'd read. Of course, the one I like as well as any of them is *All Quiet on the Western Front*. Around the time I was writing I read Irwin Shaw and James Jones. I remember reading *From Here to Eternity* at Virginia Beach and becoming so engrossed I got a bad sunburn.

CLABOUGH: World War II, especially in American popular culture, is lionized as the "Good War." Even supposedly realistic films like *Saving Private Ryan* portray "good" American soldiers combating "evil" Germans. However, *The Trumpet Unblown* vividly portrays the rape, abuse, and exploitation of German people by American servicemen. Do you think that dynamic might inform the book's relative anonymity?

HOFFMAN: I don't know. What I said to myself about war at certain moments while I was there was, "No war is worth this." I'm not a pacifist, to show you how contradictory that may sound. I was anxious to get to war; I couldn't wait to get there. I wouldn't trade the experience of war for anything, even though I think it's the most terrible thing to happen to me. I guess what it came down to in *The Trumpet Unblown* was that everyone became a sort of animal, or at least a lower form of human being, and exploitation was the name of the game. You were being exploited by the army and what was going on, so you did it too. War does irrational things to people.

CLABOUGH: Reviewers of *Yancey's War* compared it to Joseph Heller's *Catch-22* (1961), yet several of the events and figures in Heller's book seem drawn from scenes and characters in *The Trumpet Unblown*. Is there any connection?

HOFFMAN: Well, I think there is a connection. I think there are specific scenes in books like *MASH* and *Catch-22* that come directly from *The Trumpet Unblown*. I'm not talking about military actions, which repeat themselves in most war novels, but in comic situations that I invented and were later mimicked in more popular war narratives.

CLABOUGH: Your fourth novel, *The Dark Mountains* (1963), is the epic story of the MacLauglin family. Twenty-seven years later, MacLauglin descendants appear in *Furors Die* (1990). What is the relationship between those two books?

HOFFMAN: That whole sequence comes from my great-grandfather, who came from Scotland and made his fortune in the coal business. He was very much like James MacLauglin, very powerful, everyone felt a sort of aura around him. I remember people had a natural tendency to take off their hats when they talked to him. The book follows him and his descendants. Even though my father was a coal miner, I knew very little about mining and actually went back to West Virginia while I was teaching at Hampden-Sydney. I drove back roads and talked to mining people. A lot of them were very reluctant to talk to you, but I learned a lot about their lives and mining. Anyway, only half of *The Dark Mountains* was ever printed. It was twice as long as the published version. I sent it to Doubleday, and they wanted to conclude the book with James MacLauglin's death. So there was this kind of lingering, amputated part of the book hovering around, and I used material from that to flesh out part of *Furors Die*. What I had in that book was the so-called thinning of the blood, the old strong MacLauglin blood was running out. Now I'm going to switch to something you don't know. I have a book coming out soon [*Wild Thorn*] in which another generation of MacLauglins appear. It takes place in the mansion James MacLauglin built in *The Dark Mountains*.

CLABOUGH: Your first two novels deal with men who have been beaten down and drained by their war experiences. In books like *A Place for My Head* (1960), *A Walk to the River* (1973), and *Godfires* (1985), your protagonists are older "dead men," men with talent and responsibility who have somehow underachieved and lost in life. What interests you about these kinds of characters?

HOFFMAN: It seems to me I've always kind of come down on the side of men who didn't quite make it, and I've wondered in these later years if it was sort of an egotistical thing, that I felt I was a failure too. I didn't really think of myself that way at the time when I was writing those books. But I've almost always been on the side of the underdog. Now you might not think of a coal-mining tycoon like James MacLauglin as an underdog, but he was when he was a penniless immigrant and he was again when it came to fighting the United States government. I just feel more real affection for those kinds of people, who I think are tragic people. And of course there's the struggle for equality by the black community when all the schools were closing in *A Place for My Head*. It was just a damn hysteria in that town [Farmville, Virginia], and it was good material. I could use it.

CLABOUGH: The protagonist in *A Death of Dreams* (1973), Guy Dion, is sent to a Richmond-area substance abuse/mental rehabilitation clinic for therapy. Angus McCloud visits an almost identical facility in *A Place for My Head*. In the stories "Dancer" and "The Secret Garden" (*Follow Me Home*), the female protagonists are threatened with being institutionalized. What interests you about that kind of milieu?

HOFFMAN: That's an easy one to answer. My mother all of her life was in and out of places like that, and her life ended in a place like that. When I was just a very small boy, we would take these trips to see her wherever she would be. She went to a number of places, some very genteel, others not so nice. Sometimes she became so out of it, she couldn't really function. . . . she ended up undergoing a lobotomy. By the way, I'm very fond of Ken Kesey's book [*One Flew Over the Cuckoo's Nest*] for his treatment of that subject. I was very moved. When my grandmother died, I looked after my mother and saw that she was being cared for. At times she could come out for a while, she would be alright, but then she would have to go back. So naturally this has been with me my whole life, and it gets transformed in fiction. But that story of mine, "The Secret Garden" . . . that is my mother. And it's one of my favorite stories because I think I really put it all together there. I like that it's about the best I can do, and it's about her.

CLABOUGH: *The Land That Drank the Rain* (1982) strikes me as a biblical allegory, the title itself coming from a passage in the book of Hebrews (6:1–9).

HOFFMAN: Yes, it is consciously allegorical; it's a little bit different from anything else I ever did. It's essentially a religious book, and the great sin that Claytor is guilty of is a sin of the flesh. And it takes a great sacrificial act upon his part, the shedding of his own blood, to be redeemed. In the process he also saves the young man he's befriended.

CLABOUGH: Your two most recent collections of short stories, *Follow Me Home* and *Doors* (1999), contain several powerful first-person narratives by female characters. How do you go about writing from a woman's perspective?

HOFFMAN: I don't particularly find it hard or difficult. You know I have an odd thing that happens to me, and I don't know how to explain it. Sometimes when I take a shower somebody's name will pop into my head, male or female, and for just an instant I feel I'm that person and I see their face right in front of me. It's a spooky thing. Sometimes, too, when I've been writing hard in the morning I'll come out of my office, and for a moment of two I'll have a conflict as to just who I really am. I don't know whether that's a gift or a curse. So maybe that's why it's not hard for me to imagine a female character. I guess *empathize* is the best word for it.

CLABOUGH: The protagonists of "Night Sport" (*Follow Me Home*), "Landings" (*Doors*), and *Tidewater Blood* (1998) are bitter war veterans who in some ways resemble Tyree Shelby and Tod Young. However, their war was the Vietnam War. How do they differ from the World War II veterans in your earlier fiction?

HOFFMAN: I really feel that war is a timeless universal. The only thing that changes are the cultural conditions and the outer accoutrements: tactics, technology, uniforms, and so on. But the central truth of it is the same in all wars. The reason I use Vietnam now is the immediacy it has for readers, but the essence of war doesn't change.

CLABOUGH: The suspenseful mystery narratives *Tidewater Blood* and *Blood and Guile* (2000) have brought you to the attention of a new readership. However, *Godfires* (1985) was probably your first true mystery novel. These books stand out, structurally and stylistically, from your earlier material. Did you use a different approach in writing them?

HOFFMAN: I think *Godfires* is the best of those types of books. When I wrote *Tidewater Blood* I never thought of it as a mystery novel. Then the publisher and critics started calling it a suspense novel, and of course I try to have suspense in every book. So I wasn't really trying to target a specific audience, but that's the way the publisher pitched it. I didn't care so long as they were trying to sell the book. So the response kind of blindsided me. But when I wrote the sequel, I was very aware of the mystery dynamic. Part of the reason for doing that is that I'm getting to the age where it's harder for me to come up with new material to write about. I still enjoy writing, and by writing in this style I'm finally making a little bit of money.

CLABOUGH: *Tidewater Blood* and *Blood and Guile* take place in and around the fictional setting of King County with overlapping characters. Do you plan to write more King County mysteries?

HOFFMAN: Yes, there'll be one more, the one that's coming out next year [*Wild Thorn*]. I don't know after that. I've got one more novel out there that I wrote during the period between *Tidewater Blood* and *Blood and Guile*, which is more of a standard literary novel, but its fate is yet to be decided. One of these days soon I'll have to go down there and sit at the desk, and face the terror of the blank page. I don't have any idea what I'll do, but I'll do something.

5

Southern Appalachian Montage

Reviewing Books across Regions (A Collection)

This chapter functions as a concluding microcosm—a subregion, if you will—of this section on region and place. In addition to bringing to light some deserving twenty-first-century writers this book otherwise would not address, the compressed book-review format of these pieces forces my interpretive hand in places, demanding I make judgments and declarations which likely would remain more nuanced and considered in the more leisurely, extended essay context. Each review also reflects, to varying extents, the literary landscape during the particular year in which its book appeared. The organization of the chapter has the individual reviews drifting from southern regional contexts into mixed southern Appalachian accounts, before concluding with two reviews that are purely Appalachian in their concerns. As a final note, it is perhaps worth pointing out that these reviews appeared respectively in periodicals dedicated to specific regions, thus directing their compositions as well as the editorial hands that further shaped them. In this way, authorship, editorship, and audience become variables in regional context, all shaping the ways in which ever-arriving new books are interpreted and presented.

(Re)Discovering Guy Owen: The 40th Anniversary Edition of *Journey for Joedel*

Journey for Joedel, by Guy Owen. Winston-Salem: Press 53, 2010.

Guy Owen fits into that tragic class of writer whose high quality work never quite achieved the readership or critical recognition it deserved and thus has languished out of print for decades, left to be read mostly by waning contemporaries, former students, and a handful of younger oddball indiscriminate readers such as myself. It is a phenomenon particularly common for southern writers—a fact lamented by scribblers as far back as Poe and William Gilmore Simms—as demonstrated by their being largely shut out of northeastern commercial publishing circles for a couple centuries or so. Even now, it seems a great many southern hamlets and remote counties can boast an unfairly out-of-print and critically neglected scribbler or two. (Where I live in Virginia, for example, it's William Hoffman, who wrote a half dozen astonishingly good novels, most of them published in the 1950s and 1960s, and some short stories which stand among the finest by twentieth-century southern writers.)

The undeserved relative anonymity of Owen and his work in current literary and academic discourse makes a biographical capsule necessary. Born in Clarkton, North Carolina, in 1925, Owen performed both his undergraduate and graduate work at the University of North Carolina at Chapel Hill. His first book, *Cape Fear Country* (1958), was a collection of poems, and early on in his career, he was predominantly a poet, producing three volumes over a decade period during the 1950s and 1960s.

Owen's prolific editorial work, some would contend, is of greater value than his writing. He founded the *Southern Poetry Review* under a different title at Stetson University in 1958 and edited the magazine for nearly two decades with minimal assistance and funding, publishing such versifiers of note as A. R. Ammons, Doris Betts, Fred Chappell, James Dickey, Donald Justice, and David Madden, among many others. He also edited or coedited eight books, two of which are particularly recommended to readers possessed of an interest in North Carolina's literary tradition: *North Carolina Poetry* (1970) and, especially, *Contemporary Poetry of North Carolina* (1977).

Given North Carolina's current vigorous literary community, it is perhaps difficult for younger readers and writers to imagine a time when reading groups, workshops, and publishing venues were not readily available in manifold forms across the state. Yet these things did not manifest themselves of their own accord; rather, they were built slowly atop a sturdy foundation established by the arduous, groundbreaking literary labors performed long ago by Owen and his kind. He taught and edited across genres most everywhere in the state where one might have dared do so back then—Chapel Hill, Davidson College, Elon University, UNC Greensboro, North Carolina State University, Appalachian State University, etc.—and everywhere he went, he was an advocate for literary culture during an era when North Carolina desperately needed such champions.

Ms. Dorothy Owen, Press 53 editor Kevin Watson, cover artist Benita VanWinkle, writer Sally Buckner, and the Press 53 staff are to be commended for bringing back into print the novel *Journey for Joedel* in a special fortieth-anniversary edition significantly more attractive in design and presentation than the original version generated by the New York commercial publisher Crown in 1970. The book was Owen's third novel and is easily deemed his finest by readers of my acquaintance who are familiar with his work. This is not to discredit, by the way, his three other works of fiction, which might all cheerfully be characterized as part of the Mordechai Jones franchise: the rambling adventures of a fun-loving, ribald, southern picaro introduced to thousands through George C. Scott's portrayal in the still-funny 1967 film *Ballad of the Flim-Flam Man*, directed by Irvin Kershner (who would go on to greater fame working on *The Empire Strikes Back* and Sean Connery's final Bond film, *Never Say Never Again*).

Many elements—too many to mention or examine here—conspire to make *Journey for Joedel* Owen's best book and an exceptional novel by most any critical measure. The protagonist and plot are fundamentally of interest: a part-Indian teenage son of a tobacco sharecropper faced with the challenges of coming of age in a Depression-era community possessed of no relevant category for his identity. Sharp of mind, Joedel attracts the affection of a white female classmate only to be called a nigger and to endure the harsh severing of their bond. Yet Joedel is not without his supporters, and the manner in which he deals with his adversities is as remarkable as Owen's overall presentation of the then-unprecedented subject matter.

Like most high quality works of literature, *Journey for Joedel* remains relevant today, not only for its archetypal triumphs in verisimilitude and human tenderness (specific qualities of the book praised by Robert Penn Warren and Walker Percy following its initial publication) but also for its historical value in faithfully rendering ecological and cultural dynamics now mostly lost to us. Indeed, ecocritics and readers interested in agricultural history will encounter no better work of fiction, to my knowledge, on the function of dark leaf tobacco in early-twentieth-century southern life. Just as William Hoffman's out-of-print novel *The Dark Mountains* constitutes the best fictional rendering of coal's story in West Virginia from its earliest beginnings, so *Journey for Joedel* authoritatively presents the many ramifications of tobacco on a specific landscape, people, and culture of a specific time. And just as Hoffman's also out-of-print *A Place for My Head* records the ethnic strife and political complexity surrounding the closing of the schools in Prince Edward County following *Brown v. Board of Education*, so Owen's novel deftly and unpolemically examines the challenges of a biracial child in a community largely unaccepting of such persons. These and other dynamics surely will lead scholars, writers, and general readers to identify and appreciate a number of items instructive and useful to their various interests and purposes.

A final contextual consideration for Owen and his novel in light of the current publishing landscape. In the wake of the unfortunate demise of LSU Press's *Voices of the South* series and the ongoing general tenuousness of the literary publishing scene, Press 53's acquisition and reintroduction of outstanding out-of-print southern titles (including three fine, previously out-of-print novels by John Ehle) is all the more significant and vital to the literary community at large (and particularly, I think, to the younger writers in it), which surely will benefit from renewed or initial exposure, as the case may be, to such long-overlooked classics. That *Journey for Joedel* is counted among the initial crop of such reissues constitutes a well-deserved distinction for the book, a tribute to the legacy of the hardworking man of letters who produced it, and a delight to those readers who encountered it for the first time during circumstances they likely still can recall on account of the pleasure the book gave them. Welcome back, Mr. Owen.

Review of *Double Vision*

Double Vision, by George Garrett. Tuscaloosa: University of Alabama Press, 2004.

The postmodernist literary landscape is littered with metanarratives, novels and stories that in their cute, self-absorbed manner celebrate the self-reflexive challenges and issues of the writer and his craft. Although often clever and dexterous, this kind of writing almost always fails to accomplish anything new, an irony since the writer usually believes she is involved in the latest, cutting-edge literary fashion, pushing the boundaries through her own application of an "innovative" (in fact, it already seems tired and old) formula.

Double Vision, the ninth novel by award-winning novelist and Virginia Poet Laureate George Garrett, flirts with metafiction. However, there are a number of elements that make this book genuinely inventive and fresh. For starters, the novel is not so much a work of metafiction as meta-metafiction; that is, it is "about" metafiction, ambitiously questioning the form in a straightforward, even visceral, manner and tackling the big philosophical question of what is to be gained from it. Two epigraphs at the beginning—"Anything processed by memory is fiction" (Wright Morris) and "I would prefer fact" (V. S. Naipaul)—meet the issue head on. In this insinuated context, we initially encounter a fictional representation of a convalescing George Garrett (Garrett himself battled a prolonged illness), who is attempting to flesh out a partially autobiographical character named Frank Toomer for a new novel. However, even as this Garrett figure cracks the door to the composition process and his own life, he issues interpretive warnings to the reader, characterizing, for example, a literary interview as "a couple of people kidding each other to the outer limits of probability and then joining together to kid the readers, if any" (11). If this is the attitude of Garrett/Frank and *Double Vision*, who/what in the book do we trust? Where do our sympathies lie? And what, if anything, is at stake?

Although such episodes and issues of interpretive ambiguity may frustrate some readers, they generate provocative questions and ultimately point to the heart of the book and its concern with the uneasy union of fact and fiction. Since the novel literally is preoccupied with doubling (characters and events), one must don a pair of funny glasses and read it from a kind of dual perspective, relegating certain phenomena to the arena of verisimilitude and others to the realm of joyous imaginative creativity. Indeed, one of the book's most impressive achievements is that Garrett successfully performs these abstract exercises while, unlike so many postmodern novelists, also convincing us to care genuinely for his characters. Adding to the book's immediacy is its subtle preoccupation with the decline and passing of the southern writers of Garrett's generation: those who began their careers after World War II and lived to see the world and the literary scene change radically, sometimes to the point of passing them by. Garrett partially explores this theme through his moving portrayal of Aubrey Carver, who is based in part on the writer Peter Taylor, Garrett's next-door neighbor in Charlottesville for many years. Charged with writing a review of a recent biography on Carver/Taylor, Frank/Garrett contemplates the life of his close contemporary in the context of his own mortality and literary legacy. Here again, we are not only charged with additional doubling, but also with some dizzying and often dazzling interactions between fact and fiction; for example, the "real" Garrett really has published a review of *Peter Taylor* by Hubert McAlexander (a "real" biography and biographer), but Frank never reviews Carver's biography.

The novel concludes with a chapter and postscript that center around a book (doubling again) that Frank is writing in his head: part of a historical novel about Robert Greene, the Elizabethan writer who is remembered nowadays for having had the audacity to criticize Shakespeare. And as Garrett describes Greene, one recognizes his comparative concerns with the literary careers of Peter Taylor and himself. Having written a contemporary narrative that meditates at times on the nature of literary legacies, Garrett tacks on a historical account of an Elizabethan writer at the end, as if to demonstrate and contextualize the timeless, universal quality of his own self-reflexive authorial concerns. It also works as a kind of symbolic promise to his readers: in spite of illness and everything he will/is continue(ing) to write.

People familiar with Garrett's earlier work will recognize *Double Vision* as his most conceptually ambitious novel to date, and it will humble many readers (such as myself) who believed they had developed a rough understanding of his fictional concerns. Complex, deep, and multimirrored like a funhouse, the book is not for everyone and likely will confuse a number of general readers. However, there are enough genuine hard-earned tears, suffering, and laughter here to make the novel a fine read for even the most literal-minded person. And for those interested in postmodern fiction and the literary life, *Double Vision* constitutes an indispensable text, generating a number of innovative assumptions about how writers live, perform their craft, and portray/manipulate their existence through the act of composition. The book's concluding sentence speaks to these very concerns: a quote from Thomas Nash about Robert Greene that reads, "No leaf he wrote on but was like a burning glass to set on fire all his readers" (175). Like Greene's leaves, the pages of Garrett's novel burn with a brilliance that blinds and perplexes but also enlightens and delights. A book that makes numerous demands, it is possessed of just as many rewards, all of which conspire to make *Double Vision* well worth the effort of reading.

Mystery and History in 1980 North Carolina: Lynn York's *Piano Teacher*

The Piano Teacher, by Lynn York. New York: Plume, 2004.

The literary mystery narrative has a long and distinguished history, reaching back to Poe and finding powerful expression in the work of Joseph Conrad, W. Somerset Maugham, and Daphne du Maurier, among many others, as well as—more recently and closer to home—novels such as William Hoffman's memorable *Tidewater Blood*, published by Algonquin in 1998. Constituting a kind of subcategory in the genre are a number of books that abstract their literary whodunit concerns into historical milieus. Umberto Eco's *Name of the Rose* surely is one of the most popular exemplars, but other gifted literary novelists have made forays into this area as well; for example, George Garrett's two 1990s novels, *Entered from the Sun* and *The King of Babylon Shall Not Come Against You*, transport hard-broiled detective elements into Elizabethan England and the 1960s American South, respectively, with innovative and entertaining results.

Whether it consciously intends to or not, Lynn York's first novel, *The Piano Teacher*, participates in this tradition, employing a deft literary style in slowly unraveling a murder mystery set in the fictional Swan's Knob, North Carolina, of 1980. Although a classic mystery plot generates most of the narrative's events and surface themes, regional place and history conspire to fuel the book's more compelling and unique conceptual agendas. Beyond dealing with the provincial everyday events of Swan's Knob, the late-middle-aged protagonist, Wilma Mabry, struggles to make sense of the lives of her daughter, Sarah, and son-in-law, Harper—children of the late sixties who have been leading slightly bohemian lives in New Mexico while trying to raise their daughter, Starling. When the family descends on Wilma's house, followed shortly by the arrival of Sarah's Native American lover, Jonah Branch, a number of events and themes begin to emerge that subtly reflect and examine the culture and era of the small North Carolina town.

Early in the book, Wilma recognizes what makes Harper compelling to Sarah and wanting in her own estimation: "He had a kind of charm that worked on just about everyone at first, although Miss Wilma figured that his apparently overwhelming sex appeal was reserved for those of another generation. Harper was no taller than the average woman really, though she had to admit he had a beautiful, soul-searching kind of face" (40). Diminutive and sensitive looking, Harper holds no attraction for Wilma, yet she is successfully able to imagine how younger women view him. What makes Wilma especially wise and astute—and different from her fellow townspeople—is that she recognizes generational and cultural differences and accepts them, even when they fly in the face of her own culturally shaped preferences. Instead, it is the younger folks, led by Harper, who come off as inflexible and occasionally bigoted. At the local bar, Harper plays pool with a man who reminds him of "someone out of that *Deliverance* movie" (51). For him, Swan's Knob "had little to offer a global wanderer unless he needed a grilled cheese sandwich or the kind of serviceable shoes old ladies wore" (47). Yet, for all of Harper's professed worldliness and cosmopolitan pomp, he is a failure both as a husband and a father. Hiding behind a thin veneer of intellectual and artistic sophistication is a cowardly, selfish, amoral, petty man. As Wilma says of Harper's creed, "Everything was situational, no right, no wrong, no do it this way. Too many decisions, and this was where it got you" (137).

Teetering between Harper's philosophy and her small-town roots is Sarah, seduced by the former but slowly beginning to recognize the value of the latter. Near the beginning of the book, the narrator explains, "Now that she had left the high desert and come home, Sarah could feel all the parched tissues in her body slowly absorbing the moisture that lurked in the mountain air and in the soil, and she felt for the first time in weeks like a being that belonged on the earth" (31). The central event in the narrative for Sarah is her brief western flight to the mountains, an episode that may appear meaningless to many readers but is, in fact, a classic motif in American literature, from *Huckleberry Finn* to *All the King's Men*. American protagonists journey west in search of a tameless frontier, an environment of natural freedom in which the process of reflecting upon and molding one's life becomes possible. Heading for Fancy Gap, Virginia, Sarah hopes to "find the right atmosphere for thinking, an ancient and clear air to sort the whole thing out" (83).

What makes York's use of the western flight motif interesting and memorable is the way in which she plays Sarah's assumptions about mountain culture against the historical development of Appalachia. Succumbing to romantic stereotypes, Sarah half-wishes "to drive into some lost Appalachian civilization where people said 'holler' and 'settee' and played old-timey instruments on unpainted porches" (96). However, after running out of gas, she instead finds herself spending the afternoon in a couple's tidy summer home/mountain getaway. Implicit here is recognition of western North Carolina's gradual transition from perceived cultural backwater to trendy recreation spot—an area where, depending on the season, one is just as likely to encounter an out-of-state banker/cyclist or an amateur trout fisherman as a local farmer.

York's measured use of Appalachia, coupled with her adept representation of small-town southern life in Swan's Knob, conspire to make her novel a significant historical evocation of western North Carolina circa 1980. As such, it is hardly surprising that the book attracted the praise of Lee Smith in the form of a generous cover blurb. However, it is important to remind ourselves that what appeared in the work of Smith and, say, Bobbie Ann Mason as contemporary cultural narrative and critique in the early 1980s is delivered here through the medium of historical fiction. The explorations of occasional southern bigotry and sexism that stirred interest and admiration among readers of these two established female writers may be confronted in York's book with a certain amount of abstraction and indulgence. The reader smiles ever so slightly at the shock the town endures when Sarah's Native American love interest, Jonah, arrives, for this reaction is so far from us now—and getting further all the time—that the local mores of a quarter century ago may appear vaguely foreign, especially to younger readers. One wonders then if the book's social apparatus would work in the present; who would the cultural "other" be? Perhaps an immigrant or homosexual figure, but even these veins are more or less well tapped in contemporary southern fiction. No, the "wronged other figure" who informs, to different extents, the ongoing value of books such as *Light in August* and *To Kill a Mockingbird* seems destined to appear with more frequency in historical southern fiction than in contemporary narratives, which probably constitutes a favorable development for southern culture as a whole.

Its well-wrought mystery narrative notwithstanding, *The Piano Teacher's* most enduring achievement clearly is wedded to its historical cultural observations. In fact, the narrator evokes the agenda of literary naturalism when she remarks, "Sarah could no longer remember exactly what she expected to accomplish by coming back to Swan's Knob. It was like she had brought home some small science experiment that proved lethal when the general population was exposed" (168). Caught up in a social equation that takes as its variables the slippery vagaries of time, place, race, and culture, the novel's characters grope about, uncertain of a future that is already our past. That York renders the complexity of their dilemmas with immediacy and innovation makes her achievement all the more remarkable, and her book well worth reading and thinking about.

Two Views of the Mountains: Appalachian Literature at a Crossroads

A West Virginia Trilogy, by Victor Depta. Ashland, Ky.: Blair Mountain Press, 2004.
My Old True Love, by Sheila Kay Adams. Chapel Hill: Algonquin, 2004.

Stereotypes and authenticity often find themselves at odds in literature, particularly in minority discourses. Time and again, regional and/or ethnic writers strive to present visceral, experience-derived milieus and figures, only to watch them morph, gradually or suddenly, as the case may be, into recognizable clichés and types. Although their failures often are gross and unfortunate, such writers deserve a generous measure of our sympathy for their courageous attempts to afford legitimacy to their much-maligned characters and regions at the risk of opening both to further ridicule and caricature.

Victor Depta, a native of the West Virginia coalfields near Logan, has tread this dangerous path across a number of books of poetry and fiction, and his most recent offering, *A West Virginia Trilogy*, manages to capture both its potential pitfalls and considerable rewards. Although the coalfields of West Virginia constitute a region of Appalachia, the culture and ravaged industrial economies of these areas make them drastically different from the agrarian-based pastoral settings of most Appalachian literature. Narratives set in mining communities often simply do not fit the interpretive frameworks of Appalachian literary scholars. As a result, much of this literature is either undervalued or ignored (the best coal-mining novel I know of, William Hoffman's *The Dark Mountains*, has been out of print for over forty years).

Given the despairing economic and historical legacy under which they labor, it is difficult for writers from and in the coalfields not to employ an overt political agenda in their work. Denise Giardina, for example, has supplemented her novels with community activism and even a campaign for the governorship of West Virginia. Depta, by contrast, generally keeps polemics and protest at arm's length, preferring instead to tap the underpinnings of vivid interpersonal and communal interactions outside the workplace or union hall. Having authored several books of poetry, Depta is at his best articulating the subtle nuances of the senses, as well as capably rendering regional dialogue between his characters. Although he is usually responsible and sometimes memorable in his descriptions, Depta occasionally delivers a hyperbolic phrase or image for which the reader is wholly unprepared, such as Ruby's summary of her sexual relationship with her feeble-minded uncle: "It occurred to her vaguely that she was doing it with her uncle, but the thought was vague because Franklin was only four years older than she was, because he wasn't a man, really, but a moron, and because she was revenging herself on William" (110). Such passages often appear just when the reader is growing comfortable with Depta's linguistic flow and the rhythm of the novel, rasping like low-grit sandpaper over a baby's bottom. Beyond formalistic considerations, some of Depta's descriptions seem to work toward reinforcing a few of the more unfortunate stereotypes of West Virginia and Appalachia, a problematic phenomenon since Depta is describing his native region. This apparent lack of sympathy reveals itself most notably through the character of William, a World War II veteran who, like Depta and many others, returns to West Virginia after having escaped it via military service. At Vida's home William notes the obligatory

> scraggly lawn and ramshackle house, the sagging picnic table and rusted lawn chairs, the clutter of beer bottles and the slack-mouthed drunks, the squeals and guffaws. Except for a few steady ones like Jake, and he wasn't all that steady, the men had just enough foresight to shirk on the job, get to Riverton for a fifth, and lay hands on the nearest whore. The women cooked the millionth pan of cornbread and pot of beans, raised brats, nagged and bitched. And that was it, no real effort, no future, nothing to show for the labor. He felt as if he had walked into a swarm of gnats. (76)

What are we to make of such passages? Are they compliant, conscious renderings of overexaggerated regional stereotypes or the authentic recollections of a native son bent on telling the truth of his place, no matter how ugly?

In the end, I found myself drifting toward the latter scenario. Like Depta's narrative, life in the coalfields often is slow and uneventful, only to erupt with the shocking and immense violence of a mine disaster, flood, or other personal tragedy. In this sense, Depta's outbursts of sudden, violent action perhaps are appropriate. Another potential problem in the book also may be a byproduct of an accurate symbolic regional critique and therefore acceptable. Although Depta's descriptions are detailed, rarely do they provide grand vistas of or panoramic references to terrain or events. Depta's authorial eye remains pressed close to the action and people, locked in the home or hollow at hand. Intentional or not, this technique results in a kind of claustrophobic feeling which echoes the close-pressed sensory deprivation of a mine and the inability of hollow-dwellers to see over the next ridge or improve their prospects (they cannot "crib" the dark fortunes that descend upon them or forsake the innumerable mountains that isolate them from another life). And, in a sense, we as readers are trapped intimately and perhaps appropriately with Depta and his characters, an experience that is at once suffocating, odd, and engaging.

* * *

Sheila Kay Adams's mountain background couldn't be any more different from Depta's, nor could her rendering of it. The Carolina mountains of *My Old True Love* consist mostly of benign, agrarian, closely-knit families and communities in which people raise children and crops, and then sing about it. Adams, an Appalachian balladeer and oral historian, is at her best rendering the songs and dialogue of her region. Events and stories often are framed or introduced by the indented lyrics of a song, a kind of implicit intertextuality that links the fictional events of the book to a genuine historical cultural tradition. Fred Chappell employed a similar technique in certain portions of his Kirkman novels, but whereas Chappell put a number of other text-shaping aesthetic forms and philosophical principles to work, Adams uses the ballad as the dominant model for her storytelling, which is mostly episodic and apocryphal. As much as Depta brings the camera in on his characters and their day-to-day lives, Adams holds hers back, frequently skipping over days and months at a time. In addition, true to the method of most balladeers and oral storytellers, she is more likely to tell us about a character's sensual experiences than to evoke them. Whereas a poet like Depta conjures the stale sweat and rough curses of a drunken excursion, Adams reports it in a condensed panoramic style:

> Hackley had brought some liquor to the house and all three of them had been drinking. Larkin not as much, or at least that is what he said, although you can take that with a grain of salt. He could lay right in there with the best of them. For all of Hackley's bragging and swaggering he could never hold his liquor and wound up passing out. (83)

Missing here is the immediacy of experience that indelibly burns events in the reader's mind. In fact, most of the book's dramatic passion and violence—with the exception of the vividly wrought fever section in chapter 10—rest in the songs that are quoted. Lacking sufficient visceral detail in their doings, several of the characters from the novel's cast (and there are a lot of them) occasionally fail to take on enough life or color to fulfill successfully their functions.

Although Adams's episodic balladeer form sometimes eschews the bare bones of experience, it remains true both to what it is and what it is trying to achieve. This is a cleanly written novel, and there is a music to the language that carries us along to the next event/verse without our worrying too much about the details we may have been denied in a given scene. As much as Depta remains consistent in and dedicated to his intense, physical vision, Adams's voice does not waver or find itself singing out of tune or time as it evokes a powerful musical and cultural tradition across decades. Indeed, Adams is very adept at wedding the formal vehicle of her tale with the historical forces that must necessarily inform it. The peaceful, pre–Civil War prosperity of the area succumbs quite naturally to the harsh impact of the conflict on the Carolina mountains, before a sense of hard-earned resignation sets in at the outset of Reconstruction, providing hope and redemption for some and bitterness for others. Adams's handling of immense historical forces without sacrificing the intimate stories of her characters or making them seem wooden or contrived is a fine achievement that places her book in the company of the historical mountain fiction of Robert Morgan and Lee Smith.

The substantial differences between these two engaging novels may in fact suggest an incomplete but provocative microcosm of contemporary Appalachian literature, which seems to have arrived at a kind of crossroads. On the one hand is the ongoing need to record and express various cultural aspects of the agrarian mountain past: to generate new narratives about the songs and ways of our ancestors, an essential process of cultural legacy and transmission. The risk here, or seductive compulsion, has to do with writers unduly idealizing and mythologizing their culture and past, which in the end works as a disservice to them and their history, not to mention to uninitiated readers and outsiders who simply want to learn about the region. On the other hand is the desire to critique Appalachia with a hard, naked eye that finds itself having to negotiate the uglier cultural aspects of the area and the inevitable culpability of its people in these flaws. This proposition is much more dangerous than the former since it threatens to reinforce certain stereotypes while destabilizing and rearranging much of what has been established by those earlier writers and scholars whose work has represented Appalachia as a unique region with a rich culture worthy of national respect and sustained inquiry. Yet, this is a route that, sooner or later, will have to be taken with greater force, frequency, and detail. A writer like Robert Morgan, for example, treads this path from time to time with skill, celebrating the genuine cultural wealth of his North Carolina mountain people, while also unflinchingly reflecting their general ignorance of issues pertaining to disciplines such as medicine and law. Rarely is he overly sympathetic or condescending: his characters are merely people functioning within the historical conditions of their places and eras.

From time to time readers of Appalachian literature might also do well to remember James Dickey's response to the harsh attacks he endured for his portrayal of Georgia mountain culture in *Deliverance*: "Hill people are not subject to anything less than the rest of us are. There are good ones and bad ones" (Baughman 21). Writers like Dickey and Depta who delve deeply into the unpleasant dark side of southern mountain culture do so at great peril. Yet, their narratives must be confronted with as much openness and objectivity as possible if we are to continue to cultivate our understanding and appreciation of the region. In the meantime, we may safely continue to celebrate books such as Adams's—works that deftly and uniquely present a cultural mountain past and our connection to it in the present. Although their aims and rewards are quite different, Depta's and Adams's novels constitute valuable contributions to a regional genre still in the process of establishing and becoming itself.

Review of *Blood Kin*

Blood Kin, by Mark Powell. Knoxville: University of Tennessee Press, 2006.

Mark Powell's second novel, *Blood Kin*, delivers on many of the intriguing promises indirectly made over the course of his first, *Prodigals* (2002). The close natural imagery, acute historical detail, and prolonged mountain wandering that informed that debut book all are in evidence in the second, albeit cast on a larger canvas with a more fully realized, yet still evolving, sense of voice and idea. Whereas *Prodigals* focuses primarily on a single man on the run, *Blood Kin* boasts a number of singular characters trotting away from and veering toward—crisscrossing in the process—an assortment of pasts and fates.

Powell, consciously or unconsciously, spends the earliest part of the novel establishing its mountain credentials and its links to the Appalachian literary tradition. The character Bobby Thornton's comment, "Hard is all mountain folk know. If you living soft you must be town-raised," might easily appear in hundreds of mountain narratives (and no doubt has) (38). Yet, Powell nearly always saves the novel from clichés through his distinctive language and imagery. Even when they are very familiar, the book's action and objects are made new again through Powell's evocative presentations. And he is equally adept in giving us convincing familial discord, pillow talk, wartime action sequences, and barroom brawls. Often the gems are brief and appear in passing, such as his description of the hulking drunk, Shine Addis: "His eyes were bloodshot and held steady the promise of some future atrocity not yet realized" (100).

As Shine's description may suggest, the reader spends much of the novel borne along by Powell's vivid prose while waiting all the while for bad things to occur. When they do happen, we suffer a little in the process as a result of Powell's fully realized characters and unrelenting dramatic descriptions. The book's pains and joys center literally around three

Burden brothers, the women in their lives, and the rest of their family and friends. Yet much of its abstract philosophical connotation and value derives from the fact that nearly all the male characters, great and small, are connected by their wartime experiences in different eras, from the Great War up through Vietnam. The experience of war links them in all manner of ways across generations, while also making them challenged and all too often dysfunctional in their dealings with nonveterans. Of special interest, a number of Appalachian scholars and writers have pointed out that the effects of Vietnam on southern mountain culture really have not been imagined or dramatized fully. Powell evokes this remote and important theme vividly and convincingly, and all the conventions of the best postwar/vet writing are in attendance—physical and psychological suffering, disillusionment, alienation, apathy, narcotic solace—without coming across as clichés. Perhaps *Blood Kin*'s most appropriate southern literary precursor in this regard is Madison Smartt Bell's *Soldier's Joy* (1989), which deals with the readjustment of Vietnam veterans in Tennessee.

Mix together war flashbacks, witty dialogue, and eccentric folks in a mountain milieu, and it is not surprising for the grotesque to rear its ugly laughing head. Read the chapter-opening sentence, "Seven miles up the mountain from the Burdens' homeplace, old man Joseph Cory was keeping his daughter in an iron cage meant for gorillas," and we are well on our way, though such routes often prove problematic for mountain scholars chiefly interested in crying wolf at the first perceived stereotype (57). However, Powell fully understands the thin ice he is treading upon and winks to let us know by introducing in the scene a Rottweiler named Burt Reynolds. Indeed, the chapter's junkyard mountain setting strongly resembles the one in James Dickey's *Deliverance* in which the four Atlanta city boys encounter rural Georgia mountain people for the first time. Powell is not only aware of this connection but embraces it with irony and levity, flashing us a quick grin before bending back to the dramatic work at hand.

It should be remembered that at its best the grotesque is both darkly disturbing and comic, and Powell readily achieves a another formulation later in the book when he has Cory attempt to build a spaceship after his youngest daughter, Mary Anne, is gored to death by his bull while trying to run away from home. As he explains to one of the Burden boys, "When

Jesus comes back direct like, I don't plan on sitting still for it. I'm getting out. . . . He's real. I'll admit as much, like it or not. But when He comes I'm taking off and flying away right smart" (225). Insane? Probably, yet also very funny.

Blood Kin is not a perfect novel, though its weaknesses stem from unrealized potential rather than gross errors. It is a testament to Powell's craftsmanship that one must squint hard even to discern the weaknesses. Roy Burden's naive realization of land development (213) and his melee with the just-out-of-boot-camp super-idealistic Martin Staples (108–109), for example, constitute sequences that feel a bit worn and strained, though the episodes ultimately succeed in serving as parts of larger functions and purposes. Also, the descriptions in the second half of the novel generally are more spare. As with any book, some sections work better than others, yet there are no glaringly awkward progressions or shrill notes. Powell listens closely to the characters and landscape he has imagined, and little is lost when he translates what he has heard to us.

Perhaps most impressively, Powell vividly and painstakingly provides the right word of dialogue and last squeeze of sweat in just the right places while also never losing sight of the big picture. The story of the Burdens is a powerful and arresting one, yet it unfolds against a backdrop that cares nothing about them or any of us: "These mountains were old, riddled with hard, stone-eyed trilobites, older than the Rockies, older than anything Europe had to offer, and like all things old they were slouching, heaving forward, tired, no different from the men and women who grew old trying to beat or scratch a living out of them" (40). As one of Robert Morgan's short story titles proclaims, "The Mountains Won't Remember Us," yet they remain forever remembered by those they have shaped—a process, Powell would have us believe, that is still going on. Roy Burden feels it, despite the immense weight of his unhappiness, while scanning the peaks of the Blue Ridge and Appalachians: "It was the sense of something very old in the world, as if this were a holding ground, a place of last things, a sense of something here that would outlast him, and though he did not know its name, it comforted him" (40). In its evocation of its mountains and the people who dwell among them, *Blood Kin* comforts even as it disturbs. Its best parts, like all good literature, capture and reflect the paradoxes of existence, great and small.

Old Timey New: A Note on Appalachian Environmental Writing and the Work of Jim Minick

That corporate industrialism separates people, places, and products from their histories and cultures while also systematically destroying the environment is a fact some areas of the mainstream American media finally have come to recognize. Given that American thinkers and writers have been studying the problem now for over a century, the concession is long overdue. An unlikely and complex matrix of artistic, intellectual, political, and vulgar economic forces inform the contemporary commercialization of environmentalism, which one may witness readily on television screens, computer monitors, magazine pages, etc. Among writers of the American South, Wendell Berry came to inhabit the role of literary statesman for the phenomenon of local environmental and cultural destruction long before it was fashionable to do so. He now finds himself joined by scribblers from countless regions of the world who are seeking to maintain, or at least record with dignity, their places, cultures, and peoples as they struggle in the face of faceless massive multinational economies hungry for their resources and markets. In Appalachia, a number of memorable literary meditations that deal in some way with the byproducts of this sort of exploitation have arrived in the last couple of decades, taking as their focus air pollution, logging, tourism, water quality, dams, and that persistent old bugaboo, coal. Another generation of writers now grapples with the manifold problems of their region, and the best of their work will offer the joys and agonies of their localities while also teaching us how to notice similar dynamics in our own places, wherever we may be. In perceiving the local, the best regional literature serves as a lens for the world, affording an acuteness of vision both near and far.

* * *

Readers who had previously encountered Jim Minick's poems and nonfiction in various periodicals and newspapers were treated in 2005 to a compilation of his prose pieces entitled *Finding a Clear Path*. It is perhaps unusual for a writer who is primarily a poet to publish first a book of nonfiction, but the result has proven favorable for Minick's readers in that *Finding a Clear Path* situates him in a literary tradition of local environmental and subsistence concerns while also serving as a kind of compass for navigating his poetry. Thus Minick's 2008 collections of verse, *Burning*

Heaven and *Her Secret Song*, afford perspective to and further elaboration upon the place-based topics of *Finding a Clear Path.*

Minick's topical and lived-in region is an eastern locality of southwest Virginia, hilly and precariously rural but not so far west as to fall beneath the ever-lengthening shadow of coal. The final section of *Finding a Clear Path*, entitled "Following Myself Home," embodies the primary task Minick stakes for himself both in that book and in *Burning Heaven*: his self's recording of the everyday natural world surrounding his domicile. As a result one may read with profit the poem "Trying to Tell Time by Splitting Wood" alongside the wood-chopping prose piece "Hitting the Mark"; the lines of "The Bear to the Hunter" in conjunction with the essay "Health, Hunger, and Hunting"; the eight-poem verse section "Wings" with the eight-piece prose section "Flying"; and so on. These are companion books, siblings or friends on a journey toward the artistic identity of their maker and the nature of his lived-in place.

Yet Minick's imagination is not limited to his own place and time, and the collection *Her Secret Song* spans back into the lives of his ancestors, guided by the inspiring and sturdy example of his Aunt Ruth. This collection, different from Minick's other two books in focus and form, nonetheless is connected to them through its various portrayals of the natural world. Indeed, in placing his contemporary environmental concerns beside the rural practices of his ancestors, Minick establishes an important indirect association between current manifestations of organic and sustainable living and traditional methods of country subsistence often identified now as quaint.

Minick's work to date thus reflects an interesting and sometimes uneasy contemporary dialectical relationship between cutting-edge environmental concerns and rural folkways of the past. Undoubtedly, this dynamic likely goes all but unnoticed by individuals who have not lived or read about the historical part of the equation. By way of example, I will note that although I am a decade younger than Minick, my father was the tenth child of a Smoky Mountain farmer born in 1897. As a result, my family-based knowledge and associations place me closer to a male Appalachian in his sixties or seventies than a Generation Xer exiting his mid-thirties. I can recall many an occasion when a schoolmate responded with incomprehension, fear, or ridicule when I recounted to him or her my family's traditional methods of gardening, cutting wood, or managing varmints, to say nothing of my easy familiarity with guns, physical violence, and the cycle of life and death. Yet it slowly has become politically favorably—and, for some, downright *chic*—to embrace numerous elements of the rural methods so recently viewed as politically unacceptable or "backward." So it is not terribly uncommon to hear of soccer moms frequenting organic goat-milk stands and avowed pacifists beating on man-drums before taking up their shotguns to help bring balance to the local deer population and venison to their families' tables.

Ironies aside, these developments are favorable and perhaps necessary ones for American society. As contemporary sustainable practices become more familiar and their rural antecedents die off into matters of historical record, it is well we have writers like Minick to give indirect articulation to the deep connection between the two.

III

Looking Closer

A State of Place

6

"Out of Space, Out of Time"

The Virginia Novels of Julien Green

I have reached these lands but newly
From an ultimate dim Thule—
From a wild weird clime that lieth, sublime,
Out of SPACE—out of TIME.

Poe, "Dream-Land"

While his fiction remains strangely unfamiliar to most readers and scholars in the United States, Julien Green's work has garnered acclaim at one time or another from such celebrated European intellectuals as Hermann Hesse, Carl Jung, George Orwell, and Rainer Maria Rilke. Some of his books were translated by T. S. Eliot. And in his native France he attended Gertrude Stein's salon, was a close confidant of André Gide, and a friend to André Malraux and Jean Cocteau, among a very long and deep assortment of other twentieth-century literary Parisians. (Born in 1900, Green lived to the age of ninety-eight.)

Understanding what variables truly establish and erode literary reputations is a tricky and sometimes hopeless endeavor, especially when the context is confined to the space of a given nation or time. Having perused Green's output and nearly three-quarters of a century of critical reaction to it, the somewhat dizzy observer wonders if Green's long writing career very well may have worked against his American reputation—if, in practicing his art for so long and across the successive loose movements of late realism, modernism, and postmodernism, he produced a collective body of books not readily adaptable to any one specific period or aesthetic category.

Born in France to American parents, Green seemed to have lived out of space as well, a man of conflicted identity: *in* France, but never fully *of* it. He spent his childhood and early teen years in Paris before serving in World War I in the American Field Service and American Red Cross, his first interactions with Americans. After the war Green enrolled at the University of Virginia, in 1919. His parents (his father's people hailed from Prince William County) had left the United States in 1893, and it was the Virginia of that era which, somewhat naively, Green expected to encounter there. He was disappointed when he discovered that particular place no longer existed and he retreated into isolation, his alienation compounded by his French Catholicism, insistent carnal frustrations, and natural reticence. He was a troubled young man in Charlottesville: bothered, in a formal sense, by Professor Thomas Fitzhugh's Latin lectures on the Virgilian appreciation for the beauty of young boys; informally, he was uncomfortable with the frequent sexual trysts of the students he lived with at a Fourteenth Street boardinghouse. Like his artistic avatar Poe, Green left the university without having graduated, departing in May 1922. He had longed for France while in Virginia, yet when he arrived in Paris he was homesick for the Old Dominion. He returned to the United States twice in the 1930s and, again, as an exile during World War II but never visited thereafter, though he clung stubbornly to his American citizenship. He saw himself as the tragic denizen of a vague, beautiful, departed place, which served to intensify his detachment everywhere he went. Although his work would increasingly attract awards and adoration in France, he all but shunned literary politics. He was an outsider-artist if ever there was one. Like most of his characters, Green was a man of constant change and excruciating conflict, which often proved problematic for his personal life but favorable for his muse. He even changed his name from Julian to Julien.

* * *

The particulars of Green's early biography, especially his solitary formative years at the University of Virginia, are significant to us in that they provide an avenue by which to approach and appreciate his work in a decidedly American context—and, most specifically, the United States of late-nineteenth- and early-twentieth-century Virginia. Green's very first novel, *Avarice House* (1926), published in France as *Mont-Cinère*, is set in the Old Dominion, unfolding on an estate, Mont-Cinèreous ("heap of ashes," or Ashley House, as it is called in the novel's English edition), in 1890s Fauquier County. The book relates the psychological alienation and hostility between a miserly aunt, Kate Fletcher, and her sickly fifteen-year-old daughter, Emily. Frail, humpbacked, sick, cold, and (as if all this were not bad enough) mentally and emotionally unstable as a result of her wealthy mother's unwillingness to buy sufficient food or wood to keep the home comfortable, Emily is obsessed both with the warmth of fire and with inheriting Ashley House: an unfortunate combination. She is a figure carefully crafted in the tradition of the grotesque: "the thin lips seemed glued to the teeth and dark shadows marked the line of the cheeks, accentuating the heavy and wilful jaw" (1). Resembling the characters in Sherwood Anderson's *Winesburg, Ohio*, published but a few years earlier, Emily, like her mother, is dehumanized and undone by a single debilitating quality: greed. In an effort to torment and dethrone her dysfunctional parent, she marries the widower Frank Stevens, who succeeds in procuring food for the table and wood for the fireplaces and ultimately in banishing Kate Fletcher, though in many ways he merely replaces her in his own abusively controlling manner. In a mad fit of wrath Emily chokes Stevens's young daughter to death, shortly after which she sets fire to Mont-Cinèreous and joins the coveted estate in its heavily foreshadowed transformation to ash.

The novel, which attracted praise from Rilke, among others, contains in Kate Fletcher a ghostly negative incarnation of Green's own puritanical *mère*, who doted upon the boy (her youngest of eight and only son). Green's childhood, though, was a lonely one. He was an outcast at the French lycées he attended and was dominated at home by the concerns of his numerous sisters and autocratic mother. It was from his mother, whose family hailed from Savannah, that Green inherited a large and sometimes passionately idealized knowledge of the antebellum South (he was not told, for instance, the Confederacy actually had *lost* the Civil War until the age of thirteen). Given his mother's persistent childhood tales, his lonely boyhood, and his formative experiences as a young man at the University of Virginia, there is little surprise in the fact that Green's first novel was a southern one containing both a strong maternal figure—possessed of "a kind of guile which took the place of intellect"—and a lonely maladjusted child, as well as an unrelenting sequence of familial strife almost exclusively involving women (25).

Compounding the hatred between mother and daughter in the novel is the arrival of Kate's mother, Mrs. Elliot, who, "heavy and gross," immediately forms an entente with Emily in regard to all of Ashley House's ugly domestic intrigues (32). The conflict also reveals the monster in Kate, who combats the powerful impulse "to strike her [mother] across the face" even after the elderly woman has suffered a stroke and permanently takes to her bed as a sad, pathetic invalid (50). Mont-Cinèreous, or Ashley House, is based upon Kinloch, a Virginia estate owned by Green's uncle, Loughborough Turner, whom he visited on a number of occasions while enrolled at the university. As in many gothic romances, the house itself constitutes a kind of oppressive character, "dismal and without a single room that was well lighted or inviting" (17). Small-windowed and sparsely furnished, its appearance mirrors the blunted perspectives and spiritual bankruptcy of its inhabitants. The novel is gothic, too, in its indirect reference to a debilitating and crippling past, in this case, the Civil War. Though never fully articulated, the conflict serves as the book's dominant ghostly force, its terrible deprivations constituting the formative root of Kate's compulsive economizing. Green introduces this fact in a subtly symbolic sense when he has the character purchase a used coat at what she believes to be a great value, unaware that it is not only a man's garment but part of an old Confederate uniform. Blind to the war's legacy in a conscious or literal sense, she nonetheless continually wraps it about her.

The women of *Avarice House* are piteous, displaced beings, both realistically and symbolically: Emily from any kind of normal childhood or society, Kate from any degree of humanistic empathy, and Mrs. Elliot from any hope of future health or happiness. They are sad, embittered souls who view the world through selfish darkened glasses, coveting with greed the respective nightmarish visions that constitute, ironically, the very germs of their destruction. We watch in morbid fascination and with more than a little loathing for each of these characters as the conflict between the three women—a multiyear domestic Civil War of sorts—wears on, every new development topping the last in myopic savagery and naked hate. Long before the house succumbs to flames, the distasteful flavor of ash comes to inhabit the reader's mouth. When the Methodist minister of Glencoe incredulously exclaims to Kate, "You cannot betray humanity!" her firm, hopeless reply speaks for most all the characters in the book: "Sir, I am sorry" (183).

Avarice House is a strange novel—a peculiar, ugly book that is nonetheless worth reading. Often first novels tend to be overly crafted and/or too careful in their execution of theme. However, *Avarice House* wastes no time in casting us into a northern Virginia dungeon of odious human suffering and—damn the consequences, structural or otherwise—keeping us there. When the imaginative walls around us thankfully succumb to the purifying flames along with Ashley House and Emily Fletcher, the typical response must be, "Good riddance!" Yet the book's charred conclusion leaves with us something darkly residual, a ghostly token of the relentless human suffering to which we have been subjected for several hundred pages. It remains a novel possessed of an unnatural macabre power that marks the reader and, in doing so, reveals Green's formidable gifts.

In a novella written around the same time, *The Pilgrim on the Earth* (*Le voyageur sur la terre,* 1926), Green—his apprenticeship under Poe still very much in evidence—experimented with shuffling his themes, erasing the occluding mother figure altogether while unfolding the mystery of a young man's suicide at the University of Virginia in 1895. The orphaned son of insane parents, Daniel O'Donovan apparently casts himself into a chasm from a precipice overlooking the Rivanna River shortly after occupying his college quarters. What follows is a slow unraveling of the backlog of evidence (Daniel's diary, letters from acquaintances, etc.), which reveals a past of alienation and terror, including a creepy great uncle who speaks with a voice horrifically damaged during the Civil War. Given these variables, it is not surprising to learn that Daniel is in fact the cousin of *Avarice House*'s Emily Fletcher. Like Emily and some of Poe's more tortured protagonists, Daniel is both repelled and attracted by the grotesque manifestations that surround him, which conspire, slowly and surely, to transform him into a confused and perverse victim. A "severe and willful" young man whom Daniel believes to be guilty of stealing his money and burning his copies of Hawthorne, *Frankenstein*, and *The Vampyre* turns out to be a schizophrenic hallucination (168). Things get worse: a letter from Daniel's uncle reveals that his parents were crazy, his mother having cracked up after his melancholic forty-year-old father perished from a drug overdose. As in *Avarice House*, the narrative wastes no time in plunging itself (and the reader) into a dark abyss—and, as the pages turn, the chasm is made to feel bottomless, for the descent continues.

The novella, composed originally as nothing more than an experimental character sketch, proceeds to drift in a fantastic mode between explanations of madness and outright demonic possession. The last lines of Daniel's journal state, "There will come soon one strong who will take you under his protection and will guide you, if you do not resist him, along life's paths" (190). Yet we are never entirely certain whether this passage has in mind an angel, demon, or some psychological projection. It is clear enough, however, that the narrative's aesthetic guide is Poe (most notably the Poe of "William Wilson")—ever-present yet innocuous enough so as not to take things over or blot out Green's distinctiveness entirely. Hawthorne's residual proximity is felt as well in the story's psychotheological elements. In fact, Green had encountered many of the New Englander's stories for the first time at the University of Virginia during the lonely winter of 1919, an influential immersion that would have lasting consequences, including the publication of a succinct, theologically centered biography of Hawthorne in 1928 (*Un puritain homme de lettres: Nathaniel Hawthorne*). Green likened one story in particular, "The Minister's Black Veil," to

> a frightening subterranean explosion in an indescribable silence . . . it revealed to me the existence of the world of consciousness/conscience. At each moment, I laid the book down and fell as it were into an abyss, because these pages revealed to me the unknowable being that I was and that we all are. . . . As a direct result of that deeply significant reading experience, the path was opened to me into the world of literary creation. (*L'arc-en-ciel* 136)

A novice artist, the young Green was as possessed by the powerful legacies of Hawthorne and Poe as his early protagonist Daniel O'Donovan is possessed by unseen supernatural forces reminiscent of those writers' creations. And author and character succumb in a similar manner, each giving himself over a little reluctantly to a route obscure and lonely, each believing it to be, not without reservation or justification, a path of great risk and promise.

Although it is a dark narrative, *The Pilgrim on the Earth* lacks the gaunt despair—the steadily accumulating bill of suffering—of *Avarice House*. It is a hypnotic, fantastic tale, rife with shadows and secrecy, the main setting of 1895 Charlottesville more suggestive of H. P. Lovecraft's Innsmouth than a bucolic Piedmont Virginia town: "It is a grave and silent place. . . . The people do not rest in the heat of the afternoon, fanning themselves upon their porches, and it seems as if they never go out, for the streets are always deserted" (166). The novella's particular venues and habitations are possessed of a concomitant degree of eeriness. Like Emily Fletcher, Daniel is raised in a cold, uncomfortable room, and the Presbyterian church beyond his window offers "a sinister appearance" rather than any measure of comfort or hope (143). Moreover, the door to the room itself is adorned with a haunting passage set in gothic lettering: "Remember that there is someone in this room ever watching you and silently listening to you" (143). It is both a nod to the reader and a catalyst for Daniel's developing paranoia. We are the watchers and listeners, and the drama unfolding before us is madness.

One might assume Daniel's guardians would remove such disturbing gothic phrases from a child's room; instead they turn out to be a significant part of the problem. Establishing a powerful sense of foreshadowing, Daniel's superstitious aunt recounts to him many times the grim, haunting story of a young boy "driven to death by something irresistible" (149). Ever pursuing a black rabbit into the hills around Charlottesville after nightfall, the child dies mysteriously on each occasion, his body always discovered "lying on the ground in the mountains in the center of a circle he had traced with his stick" (150). Complementing his aunt's weird stories, Daniel reads incessantly from a darkly mysterious collection of books, his aunt never bothering to ask what he is perusing and his uncle continually commenting, "All books are good" (153). Echoing these sinister imaginative variables and the raw motivating hate of *Avarice House* on a visceral level, Daniel's aunt professes an overpowering "desire to strike" his uncle whenever he enters her presence (152). As a result of all this, whatever psychological problems Daniel may have inherited from his mad parents either are indulged or permitted to go unchecked in this unwholesome childhood environment.

The novella concludes with a number of conflicting perspectives on Daniel's life and character, perhaps the most literal and objective coming from a Dr. Thornton, who believes Daniel to possess "the crafty and evasive manner of a person who is going to commit an evil deed" (205). When Daniel departs the boardinghouse for the last time, a quiet and mysterious young woman affords us the tale's supernatural interpretation, remarking that "he has fallen into hands more powerful than ours" (205). However, whether that sublime, ethereal force is a psychological one, the unremitting grip of demonic damnation, or a curious, uplifting salvation remains a mystery that the reader must, regrettably, ruminate over, decide upon, and bear with her. It is a conclusion typical of the best and most tantalizing supernatural fiction, the surety of science reduced to black amid the traceless malignant vagaries of the troubled heart and spirit.

* * *

Although his friend André Malraux would accuse him of having systematically established a pattern for his fiction, Green, from the beginning, was not an elaborate planner, usually confronting the blank page armed only with dream and inclination. He believed his books were his dreams and often described his writing process as a kind of hypnotic, unconscious process resembling slumber. In his early nineties he explained, "It probably makes me sound like a lunatic, but my ideal is to begin with a sort of hallucination. In Europe it's called 'automatic writing.' It's like someone dictating something, and I have to be very careful to write down exactly what I hear" (Riding 106). The beleaguered protagonist Daniel O'Donovan writes using precisely the same technique in *The Pilgrim on the Earth*.

While his method of composition may have been peculiar, Green ultimately conceived of himself as a literary realist rather than a modern practitioner of the novel of ideas. He was but three years Faulkner's junior and admired the Mississippian's work (translated into French by his friend Maurice Coindreau), yet he never believed enough in the tenets of modernism to translate them fully into his own fiction. Even a work like *The Pilgrim on the Earth*, which strays into the fantastic, functions predominantly in the realist mode.

Astute early commentators on Green's work appear to have been more interested in its philosophical concerns than in its formal qualities. Writing in the *Sewanee Review* in 1932, Dayton Kohler said of Green's first few novels, "Terror and despair brood over the pages of Julian Green like shadows of approaching doom. Life holds no escape for his characters, and the sharp shock of tragedy, when it falls, is never blunted by irony or pity" (139). Two years earlier Walter Benjamin had concluded that the hope-crushingly perverse and grotesque elements of Green's fiction were reducible largely to a preoccupation with the philosophical dynamics of Christian suffering.

Torment, both theological and otherwise, would continue to inform Green's work. When he orchestrated a return visit to the University of Virginia in December 1933 he made a point of taking in the campus and calling upon his former professors, including the Poe scholars James Southall Wilson and William Mentzel Forrest. The next year he began a novel set in Virginia and Georgia—revised sections of which would appear more than half a century later in *The Distant Lands* (*Les pays lointains,* 1987)—but abandoned it in the wake of *Gone with the Wind* (1935), which he felt covered excessively much of the thematic ground for which he was aiming. He would not return to Virginia at any imaginative length until the novel *Moira* (1950), considered by some scholars to be his finest fictional achievement. *Moira* explores the agonizing displacement experienced by Joseph Day, an attractive, emotionally disturbed religious zealot from the West Virginia hills, who arrives as a freshman at the University of Virginia only to struggle with the effete culture and incessant debauchery that quickly besiege him there. Overwhelmed by his conflicting carnality and hopelessly impractical religious code, he kills the bewitching stepdaughter of his landlady, Moira Dare, whose name alternately translates as *fate* in Greek and Mary in the Celtic tongue.

Here it is well worth verifying that although his work hardly ever is theologically doctrinal, dogmatic, or inspirational, Green most certainly is a Christian writer whose tendencies bind him to the tradition of Dante, with the biblical references in his novels usually unfolding amid a nightmare struggle of faith. (Green forsook the Episcopal Church at sixteen and embarked upon a rocky and periodically agonizing relationship with Catholicism.) As we have seen, Poe and Hawthorne were his thematic American masters for much of his career, especially early on; Henry James was an exemplar of style until the very end. Green's stylistic experiments, however, remained few, the great bulk of his output adhering religiously to that late-nineteenth-century realist mode, albeit flavored frequently with some of the more grounded work of the symbolists. The structure of his fiction generally lacks variation as well, usually honing in on a single, usually morose, young character and proceeding to single out and investigate the psychological flaw that so often results in his or her undoing. We follow more often out of perverse expectancy than sympathy, eager to learn the black nature of the character's fate—his or her *moira*—before we take up again, as Green sometimes reminds us, "the dark journey" (the English title of his third novel) toward our own.

Although endowed with a similar perversity and violence in its execution of story and theme, *Moira* is a more nuanced work than the early Virginia narratives *The Pilgrim on the Earth* and *Avarice House*. In addition to the simple fact that he had become a more experienced novelist (with a growing knowledge of his weaknesses and a formidable command of his strengths) by this point, Green had begun to range widely and purposefully in search of exemplars for the themes he wished to evoke and capture. After long years of avoiding Dostoevsky for fear of excessive influence, he finally plunged into *Crime and Punishment*. Meaningful readings of Melville's *Billy Budd* and Rilke's *Notebooks of Malte Laurids Brigge* also delivered significant inspiration during this period, as did new theological forays into the works of Jacques-Bénigne Bossuet, Léon Bloy, John Calvin, and the somewhat controversial Abbé of Saint-Cyran.

In *Moira* Green memorably paints Joseph Day's austere theological and psychological struggles upon a canvas of visual calm: the dry, though still lush, neoclassical campus of Virginia in early autumn, late, out-of-season honeysuckle and lavender wisteria blooms perfuming the crisp air even as the earliest leaves turn and fall. Amid this pastoral milieu, Joseph's agonies quickly accumulate: fighting a young man who mocks his red hair, vomiting out of anxiety in the wake of his first class, and refusing the sexual advances of an annoying art student who later commits suicide. Though he negotiates these challenges with mixed results, Joseph clearly is possessed of a heart whose woes are legion, and he is wholly unequipped to resist the manipulations and machinations of Moira Dare, herself a student who has returned home to Charlottesville upon having been expelled scandalously and mysteriously from a nameless woman's institution. Like Rebecca in the Daphne du Maurier novel of that name, Moira dominates the narrative while actually appearing in it very little, the traces of her being always lingering somewhere uncomfortably nearby—her cigarette case, for instance, or her bed (in which Joseph is forced to sleep while she is out of town). Interested in Joseph and bored with life back home, Moira accepts a bet from two students to seduce her mother's humorless boarder. Locking herself in Joseph's room and hiding the key in her bodice, she alternately flirts and reasons with him until he himself is driven past all reason, presumably raping her (the scene cuts away and the text is not entirely clear) before smothering her the next morning.

Although he is faultless in his outward actions for much of the book's duration and serious in his religious dedication, Joseph, from the very beginning, possesses a vaguely felt evil quality that arouses loathing and fear in several of the people he encounters. For instance, on the novel's first page Mrs. Dare notes his "air of defiance" and must "control herself so that he should not notice that he filled her with a sort of repulsion" (1). Later, after his peculiar fight with the student Bruce Praileau, Joseph is told, "there is a murderer in you" (29). In this manner, Green casually plants the promising seeds of unpredictability and violence in his otherwise naïve and rigidly puritanical protagonist.

Green, however, is not entirely humorless in the presentation of his glum, maladjusted antihero, a marked change from his grim treatments of the primary characters in *Avarice House* and *The Pilgrim on the Earth*. He delights in having Joseph blush and avert his gaze frequently, especially when encountering the nude Greek statues on campus, and records with apparent delight his critical reaction to *Romeo and Juliet*:

> What did he care about this quarrel between two Italian families? And this passion of a man for a woman, or rather, for a girl of fourteen? His interest lay in the salvation of souls and where were these people's souls, if they had ever existed? Assuredly they were burning. While he was reading their story in the silent library the two lovers were howling like beasts in the endless pangs of the retributive fire for having thought only of satisfying their desires. (71)

Later Joseph elaborates his belief that "in the hands of poets love became a piece of solemn nonsense; no responsible person could really believe in it" (71). This kind of perspective is indicative of his fundamental problem: an inability to reconcile a literal, evangelical reading of the scriptures with the unknowable complexity of the human heart and all of its conquering irrational desires.

It may be that Joseph Day is Green's most fully realized fictional character; however it should be pointed out that Green is equally skillful in capturing the distinctive feel of a 1920s-era town and campus: the faint echo of a piano playing the last chords of "Swanee" or "Rose of Washington Square," and the disjointed clamor of a group of students setting off downtown to watch Valentino in *The Sheik*. Green strays a bit far, however, in imbuing the rooms on the Ranges and elsewhere with a sustained and occasionally sadomasochistic homoerotic naughtiness that eventually taxes our ability to suspend disbelief. When, for instance, Joseph whips a debauched fellow boarder with his belt while righteously addressing him as the "son of Belial," the reader, depending on her mood and sense of humor, may find herself alternately troubled or attempting unsuccessfully to stifle a chuckle (193).

Readers may be challenged, too, by the possible misogyny of the book, *possible* in the sense that it remains unclear whether the fact that all of the novel's female characters are negative is a nefarious unconscious blunder or part of a purposeful strategy to bring about carefully an intended effect. In his other books Green almost always is sympathetic, convincing, and impressive in his interior monologues involving women. However, *Moira*, perhaps for the purpose of fueling Joseph's overpowering sexual mania, would seem to have us believe that all women are demented whores. The sleazy teaching assistant Killigrew remarks, for instance, that Moira would "give herself to a gorilla if a gorilla made love to her" (163). Later, Moira foreshadows her own demise when she masochistically declares, "nothing is nearer caresses than blows" (202). She also claims to decry love and mutual respect, saying of Joseph, "if ever he fell in love with a woman he would be very boring. He would respect her, which would be worse than anything" (203). Moira is a character both troubled and troubling, though it may be that Green required just this sort of messianic enigma to convincingly bring about his protagonist's destruction.

Symbolic eddies flow beneath these literal dilemmas. As in *Avarice House*, albeit to a lesser extent, the Civil War haunts the pages, Mrs. Dare believing the desultory nature of Moira's generation to be "the fault of the war" (34). History has pushed the occupants of the novel's present era into an immoral age, which makes Joseph's uncompromising religious dogma appear all the more anachronistic. He founders amid the space and time of 1920 Charlottesville, a displaced variable for which assimilation becomes impossible. The outcome is madness and violence; the Psalm passage he contemplates ("Wherewithal shall a young man cleanse his way?") is the same verse that serves as the epitaph for poor Daniel O'Donovan's tomb in *The Pilgrim on the Earth*. They are joined then, these mad protagonists, across a quarter of a century, through the themes of violence and death, through spiritual ambiguity, and through an ultimate question to which they fail to discern an answer that can save them.

It should be noted briefly that beyond its self-contained achievements, *Moira* is significant in the context of Green's entire output for its memorable investigation of the conflict between the purity of the spirit and the baseness of carnal desire in veiled homosexual terms. And not long after its publication, Green would address this theme less indirectly in his composition of the play *South* (*Sud*, 1953), the epigraph for which, drawn from Aristotle's definition of tragedy, speaks to *Moira*'s concerns: "The purification of a dangerous passion by a violent liberation" (23). The play takes place just before the first shots are fired at Fort Sumter in April 1861 and involves the discovery by a Polish-American Northern lieutenant of his desire for a young Confederate planter while visiting southern friends. The lieutenant's confusion amid the faithfully presented tenor of the times forbids any communication of his affection, and, seeking death, he challenges the man to a duel instead; the shot that kills him is followed by the war's opening cannon fire as the curtain closes. Ponderous in the workings of its homosexual subject matter, meandering in its dialogue, and peculiar in its overly long presentation, the play generally confuses audiences. However, despite its somewhat enigmatic formal dramatic properties, *Sud* has received steady critical attention for its cultural importance as one of the first plays in France or the United States to explore homosexuality openly (mostly through nuanced insinuations in the play's *didascalie*). Indeed, beyond Green's artistic achievement, the general conflicting nature of his homosexuality—a topic he often addressed with and in comparison to his strangely appareled friend André Gide—continues to attract as many readers and scholars as his literary work.

Following the mid-century publication of *Moira*, Green would not revisit his imagined Virginia climes until 1987 in *The Distant Lands* (*Les pays lointains*), the first book of a historical trilogy set in the American South during the decades of the 1850s and early 1860s. *The Distant Lands* takes place between 1850 and 1853 and follows a naïve sixteen-year-old female protagonist, Elizabeth Escridge—a comely lass from Devonshire with prosperous relations in Virginia and Georgia—as a means of having the reader encounter and interpret the early 1850s South through the eyes of an alienated, albeit sympathetic, European outsider.

Although she is fascinated by the South, Elizabeth does not fully grasp the whimsical ways of high-class society and plantation life in Georgia; burdened as well by her youthful angst and beauty, she quickly becomes embroiled in love and intrigue. A little more than halfway through the book she is sent to Great Meadow, a Virginia estate, in order to rest and collect herself. As Miss Llewelyn, the self-proclaimed mistress of Dimwood plantation, says of life in the Old Dominion, "the air isn't so stifling, and . . . there is more to talk about than duels and future wars" (504). Later, Elizabeth's host on her sojourn to Virginia, Charles Jones, refers to the Commonwealth as "the most sensible state in the South" (560). Concerned for her well-being, Elizabeth's elder relations feel this is just the sort of environment she requires. Yet Virginia is much more than a quiet retreat. Speaking through Charles Jones, Green relates the changes in the state from Jon Smith's time up through the mid-nineteenth century. Jones, for instance, says of Norfolk, "Rows of fine houses have disappeared in the name of progress, the oysters that are served in restaurants no longer have pearls in them, the witches on broomsticks have become fortune tellers, but the surrounding countryside still dreams of its former paradise" (567). Commenting on Virginia in the early 1850s, Jones delves into and is nostalgic for the Old Dominion of a century or two previous, a range and displacement of historical time that proves slightly mindboggling to the reader.

Of course, it is Green, more than his fictional Virginia characters, who takes obvious pleasure in recounting Virginia's countryside and history, languishing in that lost land and era he had failed to discover in 1919 Charlottesville and had dwelt upon and sought in the realms of his imagination ever after. And it had been a long time coming, for he had begun and then abandoned *The Distant Lands* in 1934. It is a book, then, that contains shrouded forms of the past, for it was, despite its late-1980s publication date, already very old. Among the traces of the past appear time-worn aesthetic inspirations and familiar characters. For example, Green takes obvious joy in having Charles Jones mention Poe's recent death, utilizing it for the purposes of historical irony: "People talk about the story of a walk [Poe] took in the Blue Ridge Mountains with his classmates in 1827 or '28. He predicted a terrible war between North and South, but the boy had a wild imagination, macabre at times" (660). Later, a haughty young man from the University of Virginia, Christopher "Kit" Hughes, is described as having exactly the same red hair and dark eyes of Joseph Day in *Moira*. Moreover, Green's Virginia remains for him a transformative place, just as it had been for Emily Fletcher, Daniel O'Donovan, and Joseph Day—as well as for young Green during his years at the university. And it is the same for the protagonist of *The Distant Lands*: "Amid the more meditative landscape of Virginia," Elizabeth's "riding habit made her a slightly different person" (360).

The Distant Lands and the two books that follow it constituted a large and ambitious challenge for Green the veteran novelist. Attempting his first definitively historical novel in his mid-eighties, he occasionally overpowers the reader with period minutiae and politics, though he is better at establishing the more ineffable and important qualities, especially in his hauntingly resonant portrayal of that culture's slow (slow, at any rate, by the standards of early-twenty-first-century time) way of life. He also is just as exhaustive and nuanced as Henry James or Edith Wharton in capturing the social complexities and manners of the space and time of an occasion. When he delivers the meticulously planned Compromise of

1850 celebration at Dimwood plantation, one feels Green truly is in his element, mixing and matching his large cast of characters with frolicsome intrigue, the subtle flirtations and vague insinuations delivered with great energy and vividness:

> The music was now *accelerando*, announcing a frenzied gallop, enough to take the breath away, then gliding suddenly into a slower, caressing passage. That was the moment for sentimental daring and heavy heartbeats. The fathers and mothers of large families were, needless to say, counting on these traps, so innocent in appearance. (368)

Though its detail at times is exhaustive to the point of inhibiting the narrative's progression, the book's feel—its valiant attempt to capture the esprit of its bygone era—seduces the reader's imagination with skillful and insistent verisimilitude.

Although the trilogy idealizes the South more than it should, its balls and duels should not lead one to conclude that Green was laboring in the much decried tradition of the plantation romance. Indeed, his moonlight and magnolias are of a decidedly variant hue and odor. Once, while wandering the enchanting nocturnal streets of Savannah, Green became powerfully convinced that the devil had taken the form of moonlight and was attempting to seduce him with the pale beauty that lay upon the city. The trilogy's characters, too, often find themselves surrounded by intoxicating splendor, but, true to Green's earlier work, the violent temptation, the misplaced passion, and the grinning skull are nearly always lurking in the shadows, somewhere close by.

Green was less successful, in the end, in making it all click, an inevitability perhaps since he seems to have been going for something on the order of Tolstoy's best historically based work. *The Distant Lands*' nearly nine hundred pages are uneven, the narrative lazing about in a number of parlors and gardens for thousands of lines before rising abruptly and unsteadily to hasten toward its violent conclusion. Unfortunately, the next two installments of the trilogy are of a similar cast, though more meandering and lacking in the delightful range of psychological depth witnessed in Elizabeth's character in *The Distant Lands* as she develops into a woman while becoming acquainted with the ways of the antebellum South. The second book, *The Stars of the South* (*Les étoiles du Sud,* 1989)—its title a reference to the Confederate battle flag (the only sovereign banner Green's mother ever acknowledged)—takes place, with the exception of a brief foray into Virginia at its very conclusion, almost entirely in Georgia and South Carolina, and follows the same cast of characters up through the Confederate victory at Bull Run in 1861, during which Elizabeth loses her second husband. In *Dixie* (1995), the trilogy's final book, Elizabeth, having become widowed a second time, retreats, like so many of Green's protagonists before her, into a world of waking dream, longing, and emptiness.

Odd, if not more than a bit impish, Green's mid-nineteenth-century southern trilogy comes to an end in 1863 with the Confederacy still very much holding its own, which lends a peculiar quality to the sequence as historical fiction. (Imagine a large contemporary German novel that tentatively begins around 1927 and happily concludes in June 1940 with the German military driving three hundred thousand British and French troops into the English Channel.) Beyond its literary achievement Green hoped the trilogy would help to establish him in the United States—at long, long last—as a southern writer with Virginia roots. And despite the fact that it constitutes an uneven sequence and realization, containing as many passages that are middling or troubling as dazzling, Green's late trilogy of southern novels nonetheless forms a large and appropriate bookend to his protracted career and life. By any literary standard, it was an audaciously courageous undertaking: a novelist whose career already spanned nearly seven decades embarking upon a three-volume, two-thousand-page attempt to articulate the dim and timeless land he had failed to discover upon his arrival in Virginia in 1919 and which had eluded him thence.

In finally claiming his land imaginatively, Green had at last discovered and created it after a fashion, and he died not long after the completion of the trilogy's final book. When Elizabeth's fatally wounded husband speaks to her of a possible future life in Europe, he might be the voice of fate as well, addressing Green: "You'll suffer over there because you belong to us. Our South will be the dream that will stay with you until you die, the dream of distant lands where you experienced love" (896). In searching for his dim, remote homeland—a Virginia clime that, in the end, may never have existed—Green gave us a number of extraordinary novels. In exploring and appreciating them, we too may seek and imagine that evasive space and time: the haunted and haunting dreamland of a most unlikely Virginian.

7

Hanging On to Place

The Self-Reflexive Depths of Kelly Cherry's Fiction

Nobody fools
a woman who's plumbed
her own depths. (And hell's.)

Kelly Cherry, "Nobody's Fool," *Hazard and Prospect*

The scholar Matthew Bruccoli once wrote, "It has been justly held that a writer deserves to be judged by his work. Nonetheless, a writer's best work must be assessed in terms of his total work" (xx). This, of course, is a sound and grounded program for literary appraisal, yet one that quickly encounters difficulty when confronting the output of highly prolific writers, especially those who regularly labor in multiple genres. The diverse work of the talented and admired man or woman of letters often becomes for the hapless scholar struck with examining it a dreaded hydra, each head stemming from a common body yet all bobbing and weaving simultaneously in countless different directions, unruly and resistant to easy categorization.

Such a scenario easily may be established for the wonderfully varied work of Kelly Cherry, whose thirty books include poetry, fiction, nonfiction, criticism, several chapbooks in the aforementioned genres, a translation of *Octavia*, a teacher's guide, and a collection of Aggadic children's stories. The reader who journeys (eventually) through all of these books comes away instructed and rewarded on such a dizzying array of levels that it is both very difficult and probably disingenuous to attempt to critically reconcile the books beneath a single moniker across their various genres and decades.

Partly because a penetrating assessment of Cherry's poetry has appeared in the last few years—Fred Chappell's "Kelly Cherry in Her Poetry:

The Subject as Object" (2004)—and partly because I believe Cherry's fiction approaches the merit of her poetry, this essay focuses predominantly on her novels and short stories. However, even with the problem of multigenre totality pared down, there still remains the issue of how best to approach and consider the collective identity of even one of Cherry's genres. Fortunately, Chappell's aforementioned essay provides a clue as to how the rest of her work, or various subdivided aspects of it, might be approached:

> Has the poet achieved her best ambition, the creation of a poetic art analogous to a rigorous philosophical method? We can answer in the affirmative only by accepting the poet's own terms, by granting equal validity to both connotation and denotation, to emotional as well as to logical terms. This is possible when the facts of the poet's life, her basic materials, have been objectified, transformed into terms amenable to treatment by art. We can recognize that accomplishment when we know enough of the life and the art to make a judgment, and that has become possible only after the poet has lived and written a sufficient amount. (Chappell, "Kelly Cherry" 32)

Chappell is theorizing about poetry in particular there, but the general method of inquiry he suggests seems a useful one regardless of genre since it revolves around the ability of the reader to discern the self-reflexive elements of the writer's output across time. Moreover, it is a type of speculation especially well-suited to writers who have produced a number of very different books over a span of decades. Behind the artistic creations, and sometimes informing their most powerful moments and passages, lies the writer's life: her joys, concerns, and traumas. Viewed in this manner, portions of the writer's work become running commentary on the writer's existence, at least to the extent that it is known and/or portrayed. It is perhaps something more than coincidence that in a recent essay on the work of George Garrett, Cherry arrives at a similar approach in conceptualizing that writer's enormous output over a long career:

> What may be *only now* [Cherry's italics] becoming clear is that George Garrett's life's work has been to create a body of literature that comments upon itself, recapitulates patterns, draws connections among parts, and, in effect, mirrors its own grand design, doubling its breadth and depth. That is to say, there is the work, and

> there is the shadow-work, an implied reflection. ("Achievement of George Garrett")

Just as Cherry relates a meta-artistic understanding of Garrett's work that has only become evident after decades of development, Chappell accurately has recognized that the shadow work or implied reflection in Cherry's work most often is herself or the circumstances of her life abstracted for the purposes of art and the narrative at hand. In this way, the person who is the writer places herself, or aspects of herself, in the work in such a manner as to confuse the lines between author, authorial persona, and creative art, yet doing so to the collective benefit of that art, which, at least for writers like Cherry, remains the chief pursuit and endgame of all meaningful writing.

* * *

Cherry's fiction often is informed by the present tense absence of those things which have shaped her and her characters in the past. For instance, the American South backgrounds that lie behind the protagonists of her fist two novels—*Sick and Full of Burning* (1975), whose character Mary "Tennessee" Settleworth is from East Tennessee, and *Augusta Played* (1979), whose Gus hails from North Carolina—function not unlike muted versions of Shakespeare's America in *The Tempest*. They are exotic realms, summoned rarely in the present worlds of the narratives, yet instrumental in having formed the identities of the protagonists who command those narratives.

This harkening back to a vanished formative place, which usually in Cherry's work takes the form of a southern upbringing, continues across her subsequent fiction. That which is often overlooked or pushed to the side with regard to the work of other writers remains a lingering, albeit shadowy powerful force, for Cherry. Yet, her work is far from alone in its references to the formative power of place. As Elizabeth Bowen noted, "Nothing can happen nowhere. The locale of the happening always colours the happening, and often, to a degree, shapes it" (34). In other words, the legacy of the lived in region dictates far flung events beyond the limitations of its temporal and geographical bounds.

Beyond literature, the idea of place has always been of interest, though, admittedly, often of passing interest, to philosophers. Kant considered it as a prehension—a kind of unity of sensation—of the body rather than one of the mind, and thus began a dialogue taken up later by a number of the phenomenologists, Husserl most notably. Place is afforded a powerful physical aspect since it is made up in part by live bodies, which are in turn placially shaped. Our bodies establish space and place by virtue of being in and sensing them. We move about and occupy, yet remain finite in terms of our movements, mass, and perceptions. Space may be infinite but our apprehension of it is not. The boundary inside of which lies our awareness of space is a place. Beyond it are the places and spaces we do not know. Place, then, can move; it can be active.

Place, presence, and feeling function simultaneously in Cherry's art, affording life and immediacy to the philosophical and historical ideas that often provide intellectual form to her work. Her writing speaks to various postmodern debates regarding history and perception, but does not become overly abstract or so enamored of its intellectual agendas as to risk crippling itself by means of its own ideas. Her characters move away from various physical places but imaginatively carry those places with them so that they inform and sometimes determine future actions, and, indeed, this tension between travel and place underlies many of the central dilemmas and epiphanies that appear across Cherry's fiction. As Laurence Buell has observed, "Every modern place is also shaped by the multiple places that inhabitants of a particular place bring with them from a migratory or diasporic past" (18). For the reader, imaginary literary space and place—what Maurice Blanchot called *l'espace littéraire*—can only be realized by immersing oneself in it. And once sensed and recognized it constitutes a powerful avenue by which the reader may understand and embrace the imaginative world in which she finds herself. In *Poetics of Relation* Édouard Glissant asserts that our imagined places are "worth defending against every form of alienation" (153–54). That is because they are essential sites of connection and meaning for writer and reader alike. To give them up, to attempt to estrange experience from our places, is to abdicate a fundamental aspect of our human existence. We lose ourselves.

* * *

So Cherry's characters, beyond her aforementioned first two novels, continue to lurch toward meaning in the present while looking back upon or inadvertently summoning the southern places that have formed them. In the novel *My Life and Dr. Joyce Brothers,* Nina, a highly autobiographical character who resurfaces from time to time in Cherry's fiction, describes a dinner table encounter with her alcoholic brother as the "recent scene of a marathon exercise in Southern nostalgia" (73). The siblings revert to the cultural conventions of their youths as they quarrel in the present. Much later in the novel Nina refers to a specific formative place, recounting her time with her brother "at a Baptist institution in Virginia from which each of us was in turn expelled, one for cutting classes, one for taking more credits than was considered healthful for a clean-minded young woman" (141). Here and elsewhere, Nina's (and Cherry's) southern background is portrayed as a stubborn and debilitating hurdle to overcome. And just when it seems successfully negotiated, there usually occurs some new adversity which triggers a reaction based on that formative time.

Such a recurring convention might come across as overly grim if not for Cherry's rich and generous sense of humor, which has the ability to afford unique comic qualities to even the worst of circumstances. Often the reader giggles even as she shakes her head, such as the occasion when Babette, Nina's delinquent thirteen-year-old pregnant niece, earnestly explains, "If only I hadn't been balancing the beer can on my forehead, I wouldn't have gotten pregnant" (147), a philosophy of getting laid in which truth cannot lie, yet a very humorous one, nonetheless. Later in the novel, Nina's alcoholic brother kisses Nina ardently on the mouth in a bar, gives the *V* for victory sign to their on-looking group of companions, and rhetorically inquires of them, "So who needs Faulkner?" (204). The mingling of intertextuality, incest, and comedy in this scene, grotesque though it may seem, functions appropriately, delivering a complex statement on the haunting southern backgrounds of Nina and her brother that establishes the strangeness of their region while ultimately (and appropriately) raising more questions than answers. "Our ways are not your ways," said Count Dracula, speaking as a southerner might, "and there shall be to you many strange things" (Stoker 20). What appears to the other characters as strangeness constitutes the uneasy foundational aspects of home—the life's blood, if you will—for Nina and her brother. It is part of what it means to be southern.

* * *

Cherry has said of being identified as a southern writer, "I don't like any label when it is applied reductively," and this concern stems at least partially from the depth and volume of her varied artistic achievement (*Writing* 87). It is a fear, not without cause, of being pigeonholed into a single set of assumptions and frameworks that may threaten to limit both readership and appreciation. In her 1995 collection of essays, *Writing the World*, Cherry identifies the "two or three phenomena that inform our understanding of the word *Southern*. Sociologists point to the tradition of Southern storytelling. Then there is the intimacy with defeat which Southerners share. Then there is the Bible Belt" (72). Although it occasionally interacts with and comments upon them, Cherry's work is less overtly concerned with these themes than it is indirectly interested in waving or nodding at them briefly, as they were afterthoughts, while en route to destinations of greater promise. Indeed, her biographical encounters with the South and southern writers seem to have had a stronger influence on her work and evolution as a writer than the region's abstract qualities, traditions, and variable constructs. In *Writing the World*, for instance, she maintains, that "encountering Allen Tate" as a graduate student at the University of North Carolina–Greensboro was "one of the truly lucky events" of her "literary life" (66); later in the book she fondly recounts passing Faulkner on a Charlottesville, Virginia, street only to look back and discover his eyes suddenly fixed upon hers. Indeed, the lives of the writers themselves, how they conducted them—in the classroom, in residence, on street corners—appear to have remained very significant and meaningful gauges for her own career and the relationship between herself and her work.

Like the physicality of these southern writers, southern places frequent Cherry's work in an indirect, referential manner, almost as haunting presences. For example, in her novel *The Lost Traveler's Dream* the southern city of Richmond, Virginia, is described as being slow enough so that "the pace of the place is right" (215); the municipality is associated principally with the measured rate at which time is perceived to pass there. On other occasions, Cherry's perceptions are complicated and lent depth by a qualifying reference to the childhood places in which they were formed. Thus the Moscow cold in *The Exiled Heart* is described as "incredible, at least to somebody from Virginia," the frigidness made more severe by the balmy clime to which it is compared (6). And there are also the people of those places, their lives formed by determinants not unlike those experienced and sensed in the region from which the author hails. In *My Life with Dr. Joyce Brothers*, for instance, Nina believes she relates to the condition of Latvian citizens in part because of "a southerner's identification, with the underdog," a dynamic that invokes the portion of Cherry's definition of southern identity that articulates "the intimacy with defeat" (121).

* * *

In a 2008 issue of the *Oxford American*, Michael Donohue writes:

> On my last night in Yantai, Markis and I went out to eat. The restaurant was Brazilian, the staff dressed like American cowboys, and everything in the all-you-can-eat buffet was Chinese. Markis and I loaded our plates and sat down. On the wall behind Markis there hung a wooden plaque with an old-fashioned door knocker glued to it—the kind of strangely downhome decoration you sometimes see in Chinese places that want to look American. At the bottom someone had painted in bright letters, in English, A SENSE OF PLACE, A SENSE OF PEACE. (130)

Far from home, the familiar echoes of place and culture can have the ability to form the impression of a surrounding safe enclosure for the traveler. We take our home places with us as we wander, and when we return we bear certain essences of the places traversed as invisible souvenirs. Readers partake of the journey when the impressions of the trip are set down in type and published. And then there are the reviewers and scholars who respond to the portrayed places by offering their own versions and critiques of them for their own readerships. So Cherry the writer and traveler finds her work traveled itself by a critical endeavor.

* * *

Cherry's destinations and responses to places, her own and others,' are unique, yet some of her impressions are representative insofar as they are processed by a southern woman of a certain time and place. "Women's lives were so proscribed then," she says of the years of her youth, "especially in the South" (*My Life* 23). Yet, it was in part that very degree of cultural oppression which helped forge her resolve to write. After all, "even Southern girls," Cherry maintains in *Writing the World*, "could be deeply serious about their artistic ambitions" (8). And from that seriousness, cultivated and deepened in an environment that, oftener than not, would rather not have it, comes the tension that fuels the artistic impulse—reactionary at the thought of censure and revelatory at the prospect of expression. Correspondingly, Nina explains the writer's objective in *Dr. Joyce Brothers* as follows: "with a scene here, a simile there, to rewrite the world" (*My Life* 228). And we may easily take this to be Cherry's objective as well since she has described the character Nina as "who I would be if I were living her life. And what a glorious thing it is, a sort of freedom, not women's liberation exactly but a writerly liberation, to be able to step onto the page and say to the reader, 'Here I am. This is my life, which I hope you will want to be part of. It is a woman's life'" (*Writing* 38). This passage not only speaks to the relationship between Cherry and her autobiographical character, but also emphasizes the fact that the formative elements of her autobiographical character and herself—southern background, gender issues, etc.—remain but minor foundational aspects of the fully realized woman: the totality of the existence and the life at hand.

In her essay "Contemporary Virginia Literature's Classical Composer: The Musicality of Kelly Cherry in *The Society of Friends*," Mary Bailey arrives at a similar reading of Cherry's grand design, albeit through different means: "Though perhaps best known as a southern writer, Cherry's writings transcend regionalism through the qualities in her work concerned with general humanistic forces" (Bailey). For Bailey, Cherry's warm humanism arrives to readers of *The Society of Friends* by way of the book's musicality of structure and theme, which helps to deepen the narrative's connection to the places and spaces of its imagined pasts. Beyond Bailey's general argument, it is perhaps worthwhile to note here that "sound space" is a recognized spatial type which has been investigated and studied principally by music theorists. Stuart Jones, for instance, has noted how "the plasticity of sound space, and the very direct way we read it . . . means[s] that sound has a particularly powerful ability to influence the perceptual and thence psychological reading of [an] overall space" (22). Since much of Cherry's fiction and poetry is built upon various musical structures, an arresting book or dissertation angle certainly lies in wait for a reader interested in tracing those fascinating musical underpinnings throughout Cherry's substantial output.

Even without its musical dimension, however, there remains in Cherry's fiction a topical and philosophical dynamic of humanism that pushes the work beyond the sum of its temporal and placially shaped parts. This quality is perhaps most evident in her later fiction, especially the story collection *The Society of Friends* (which serves as a kind of sequel to *My*

Life and Dr. Joyce Brothers) and the novel *We Can Still Be Friends*. Perusing these narratives, even without observing any comparative reference to or having knowledge of Cherry's other books, one is reminded of Matthew Bruccoli's capsulation of F. Scott Fitzgerald's short stories: "They are frankly sensual, though chaste—warm and promising" (xiv). And at their best these narratives sing beautifully and humanely the sad old universal melody of human existence; one can almost hear in the work Gatsby's tuning fork struck upon a star.

"We must begin to prepare ourselves," a character from *We Can Still Be Friends* laments, "for many, many losses now. For you see, we are going to lose so much, and not only friends. We are going to begin to lose ourselves, now. All this time, we have remained more or less who we were, but in the next ten or fifteen years we will become unrecognizable, even to each other, even to ourselves" (204). This, of course, is a very tragic song for a writer to sing, but it also constitutes a key and unavoidable element of existence, and the writer who predicates her art upon her life has no choice but to render the composition as best she can. True, it painfully constitutes a terrible and terrifying challenge, but it is also potentially the trial that promises the most. One is reminded here of the never-ending assignment James Dickey announced to his students during his final class, days before his death: "I want you to fight this thing through. Fight the thing through that we start with your own unconscious and your own dreams and see where it comes out. That's the excitement and the fun of it. Deep discovery, deep adventure. It's the most dangerous game and the best" (Bruccoli and Baughman xxii).

Places evolve and perish; they are born, live, and die—like people. Nihilism and hopelessness are the bedfellows of this reality, and Cherry's fiction, given its themes, would be remiss if it did not give voice to them. Thus there is occasionally that defeated and defeatist character who cannot hear the music of life for focusing on its end result. "*In the long run*," thinks Larry, at length, in *The Society of Friends*:

> *You'll be dead*. In the long run everything just falls apart the house the lawn work love marriage whole impossible cities, even empires. Empires launch wars that are death rattles in their own throats. They think they are making history but history is just something they become. Life's such a swindle. You keep hoping if you play the

> angles right you can come out ahead but all the time you're losing more ground than you're gaining. There's this torrent of events that makes you feel like you're being swept along somewhere a tremendous force carrying you in its current like it matters but then it's all over and where you are is exactly nowhere, nowhere, time goes by and leaves you high and dry. (137)

This is the *SOS* of a man in the process of being crushed by the finality of his mortality. Larry believes the current of life pushes one toward a bottomless waterfall beyond which existence ends, and he is so absorbed by the nature of the endgame that he cannot appreciate life's meaningful moments and pleasures, the gentle shallow eddies and deep pools one moves through along the way.

A testament to Cherry's strength as a fiction writer is that she can give us an eloquent, intelligent, and convincing nihilistic character like Larry in one chapter and then move beyond his worldview in a succeeding one to show the reader precisely what it is his philosophies of life and mortality lack. Thus, near the end of the book, when Nina confronts the death of her best friend, her little dog Tavy, we are afforded a poignant, moving, and beautiful scene which also offers an indirect reply to Larry's hopeless emptiness:

> They put him on the table for the injection. Then she picks him up, holds him, cradles him, and nobody stops her. He gazes up at her with longing, a kind of desire, as if he wants only one thing now—her to stay with him. She holds him next to her heart, which is where he belongs, in this kennel that has always been his. His breathing slows. He seems to become heavier. His eyes are closed, as if he really is simply sleeping. (189)

In this passage death remains the endgame, but its function and the knowledge of it both become secondary to the place where the experiences and love of these two creatures will live on: the kennel of Nina's heart. The lived events of life, as recorded in stark and unavoidable detail by a camera, give way to the sensibility's fanciful rendering of them and the imperfect recollections of those with whom they have been shared. And there they will remain, housed inside us, in a place not set down on any map. "True places," wrote Melville in *Moby Dick*, "never are" (54).

* * *

Cherry's current artistic relationship to place is perhaps best seen in some of her recent poems, which consider and recount her current site of residence and concern in southern Virginia. These pieces—most notably "A Farm in Virginia near the North Carolina Boundary" and the wonderful long poem "Virginia Reel"—differ from much of her other verse in that they are pastoral in nature and landscape-based, leaving the reader with the impression that Cherry may well be discovering new ways of seeing even as she skillfully evokes and comments upon the complexities of her current place.

Of special note among these poems is "Byrd's Survey of the Boundary: An Abridgement," a historical reimagining of passages from William Byrd II's *Histories of the Dividing Line betwixt Virginia and North Carolina*. Byrd, a unique and immensely talented eighteenth-century Virginia planter, is best known today for his frequently anthologized account of surveying the Virginia–North Carolina border as well as for his vividly eventful and highly entertaining personal diaries which he coded in secret shorthand. For the purposes of her poem, Cherry appears interested in Byrd predominantly for his relation of the dynamics of the region which is also her home. Significantly, six of the poem's sections alternate between the headings hazards and prospect, words which also come together to constitute the title of Cherry's 2007 landmark collection of new and selected poems, *Hazard and Prospect*. In 2008 she remarked to me of the title, "The two words seemed to suggest the structure of the whole book: hazards, followed by a new prospect. They also seem to me to suggest my life to this point. And maybe they also suggest that you don't get one without the other." Implicit in the design of "Byrd's Survey of the Boundary" is a matching of observations on—prospects of—a single place separated by nearly three centuries. Residing not far from one of the areas through which Byrd's party passed in the process of surveying the line between the states, Cherry compares notes on geography while deftly offering cultural commentary which speaks to the nature of knowledge and interpretation across the ages. Processing these ideas, the composition of the piece constitutes the true vocational hazard under which the poet labors to assimilate various phenomena into a successful poem. Place and the practice of art come together, the latter offering to the reader a vision of, a journey to, the former.

* * *

Years ago a group of reckless, half-serious undergraduates foolishly struck out southward from Williamsburg late one spring for a weekend of boating and good sport along the Corapeake Ditch, a channel of the Great Dismal Swamp National Wildlife Refuge which runs parallel to and almost exactly a quarter of a mile to the south of the line Byrd surveyed. It was an ill-conceived recreation that quickly exacted from the participants a significant respect for the place at hand as they did their best to fish, hike, and generally enact the roles of young ne'er-do-wells. The air hung heavy and motionless while mosquitoes of prodigious size hovered incessantly, and every time I scratched the pervasive itches about my shins and calves the inner tips of my fingernails came away lined with seed ticks.

For diversion and perspective I had toted along a copy of Byrd's *Histories of the Dividing Line betwixt Virginia and North Carolina*. The volume was destined to become soaked over the course of the excursion and, later, to serve as an accommodating domicile for black mold, but I remain pleased even now to have brought it along, for I distinctly recall sitting around a fire late into the night reading aloud passages while the insects buzzed and bit, and my companions swore at both their physical discomfort and their pronounced distaste for the evening's literary fare.

One aspect of Byrd's account that has always interested me is his dubious theory of the manner in which the Dismal Swamp physically and psychologically alters its human occupants. For instance, in describing an area of the Dismal not far from where our own doubtful expedition unfolded, he reports that the people are "devoured by musketas all the Summer, and have Agues every Spring and Fall, which Corrupt all the Juices of their Bodies, and give them a cadaverous expression, and besides a lazy, creeping Habit, which they never get rid of" (74). What may come across as fanciful perceptions and interpretations to many contemporary readers seemed accurate enough to me the following morning when the young Swamp campers emerged from their tents slowly and stiffly, faces pale in the wake of meager sleep and excessive social recreation, mottled and swollen with mosquito and tick wounds of various shapes and sizes. Try as I might, neither hazard nor prospect could compel them to tarry in the Dismal another night.

* * *

The time and place of that distant sojourn to the Dismal Swamp and Cherry's more recent rendering of Byrd's account of the line coalesced in my thoughts in June 2008 when, to employ some words from Cherry's poem, "a perverse fog / arose" in the Dismal in the form of a massive forest fire which eventually would grow to cover nearly five thousand acres by the middle of July. It was a catastrophe one could not only monitor via the media, but also directly sense a couple hundred miles away from it, though such physical awareness of the fire remained predicated upon the prevailing winds. Thus, a day or two after the fire had reached an alarming size, I walked out of my house in Appomattox County, Virginia, to discover a gray pall of mist had covered the fields overnight so that the sun burned faint and reddish orange behind it. The air remained heavy with smoke for nearly half a week before the wind shifted and began carrying the Dismal's airborne debris into the Tidewater region of Virginia. Two weeks later a visiting family member from Virginia Beach was accused of having camped out the night before, the odor of smoke on his clothes strong enough to fill a room.

Most creatures flee before the flames of such fires, while others linger in wet areas or burrow into damp ground. A few neither depart nor hide and instead take advantage of the natural force's consuming and cleansing power in order to hunt and forage, especially if the wind is low and the flames are of the slow, creeping variety. Grazing mammals scour the burned over areas in search of nuts, roots, and other organic matter, while predators take advantage of the lack of foliage to locate prey. Indeed, some predators have been known to scout along the advancing line of flame for the snakes and other small animals fleeing before it. Ultimately, the soil and fauna benefit in the wake of the destruction as the burned ground stimulates new plant growth, strengthening the overall health of the ecosystem.

Yet it remains that the nature of the place, familiar to so many for so long, is lost. Likely as not, one will find oneself unable to revisit a favorite campsite or stretch of marsh. If I were to revisit the route of my own excursion made years ago, I doubtless would discover the canal but would otherwise find myself greeted predominantly by acres of black ash. However, portions of the nature of that place before the fire live on in the memories of the people who have spent portions of their lives, however small, in it. It might constitute a foolish endeavor indeed to collect reminiscences of the Corapeake Ditch before the great fire of Summer 2008, but bearing recollections of the place and summoning them periodically is not. We can still learn from our places, our imperfect images of them, even when they are forever lost to us. And so once more for me the fire is lit, casting shadows on the surrounding trees and the faces of the eternally young campers, cursing and dancing an uncomfortable jig as the insects plague them and the words of William Byrd drift on the damp night air, informing them it has all happened before, a long time ago. I can see them clear as day when I close my eyes.

Why recount such a place, filling space here? Why do writers bother? Why do they write? Cherry's protagonist and alter ego Nina offers us a compelling answer:

> Because they love life and the world, and it is all vanishing, vanishing more quickly than anyone can say. The people, the trees, the favorite objects, the created art, the puppies, we ourselves are all slipping away; we are falling out of our lives. No clothespin on earth will hold any of us in place, and yet a writer will do anything she can think of to hang on. (*Society* 161)

The finite nature of the world and ourselves, experienced intimately in the places we inhabit, makes us desperate to sustain them—to summon and share them, at all costs.

As if by fate, I recently popped off the cap of a Magic Hat beer bottle and found these words printed on its underside: "It ain't where you're from, it's where you're at!" Traveling through space across multiple landscapes, cultures, and times, Cherry's work possesses the powerful capacity to afford the reader an appreciation of her own. I can think of few bodies of work that articulate the journey from a point of origin to various inhabited places with more perceptiveness, feeling, and artistry. It remains, of course, partly the story of a woman writer's singular development and concerns, but it also constitutes a portion of that grand, endless narrative which recounts the artist's perpetual attempt to shrug off the limitations of self in pursuit of giving utterance to the universal. The reader who endeavors to take up the trip eventually will find herself someplace else, a place all her own, and, having come there, will regret neither the journey nor the nature of its terminus. She will have arrived.

8

Here, There, Where

David Huddle's Appalachian Virginia

> After all, the great majority of people are destined to be, in some sense, provincials—and so why not make them good provincials, not provincials by prejudice, but knowing something about their own province for good or for bad, and, therefore, better able to function also as citizens of the world?
>
> George Stewart, "The Regional Approach to Literature"

Much as that mountain culture along the New River near a village called Ivanhoe in southwest Virginia has and does trouble(d) him, David Huddle can't seem to help but return to it again and again in his work, repeatedly conjuring up that small portion of hilly rural Virginia in print using a number of fictionalized names, including, most recently, Glory River, the title of a 2008 volume of poems which very well may prove his best collection of verse—perhaps his best book altogether—through the first decade of the twenty-first century.

"Professor Nelson can't get free of Stevens Creek, Virginia," (*La* 1) declares the narrator in the first line of Huddle's second novel, *La Tour Dreams of the Wolf Girl*. This utterance ascribes yet another fictional name to the same region of Virginia explored in Huddle's other works, while the phrase "can't get free" suggests the protagonist's binding fate—-a debilitating psychological prison sentence, at its worst, a muse's blessing, at best—is true enough for Professor Nelson's creator as well. And is this not as it should be, especially for writers? Much as we yearn to escape our formative places, occasionally fooling ourselves into believing we have succeeded, they surface from time to time, or, to regionalize a cliché, come back to *haint* us in ways so subtle we frequently fail to understand or even discern them. Fortunately, however, the relationships between formative places and artists remain a little easier to ponder and trace because of those created bodies of work that possess the capacity to serve as conduits or translators between the two. Paradoxically, then, many of the qualities David Huddle and writers of similar upbringings (self included) tend to shut out, lament with embarrassment, and/or outright despise about their parochial points of origin—qualities such as meanness, savagery, patriarchy, violence, countless manifestations of numbing small-mindedness, a smothering overriding xenophobia—often function as or among the most powerful catalytic variables in the workings of a writer's craft. After all, our bodies have digested and continue to carry the trace elements of the soil, flora, air, animals—as well as the often-unconscious psychological impacts of sound, weather, topography, and human interaction—long after we have departed. A connection remains, some of the dimensions of which tend to make our places almost indistinguishable from ourselves, to the extent that we might even be known to others and ourselves by the same names as the land. It is no fiction at all, for instance, that about five miles northwest of Ivanhoe—in the shadow of Raven Cliff, just off State Route 619, along Cripple Creek—there is a place on the map consisting of little more than a scattering of homes called "Huddle."

There exists a fundamental tension, then, a mixing or confusion of formative being, location, and identity, which has the potential to prove most favorable for the concerns of artists but also destructive to human beings, including artists, in the contexts of their everyday lives. "I don't!" *Absalom, Absalom!*'s Quentin Compson famously repeats in ascending manic manner as he attempts to ward off his friend's question, "Do you hate the South?" Of course, it is himself as much as the South of his mind that Compson both loves and unconsciously hates. The two have become unceremoniously and awkwardly welded within him, and since, unlike his authorial creator, he is possessed of no satisfactory medium to reconcile or even investigate the crippling identity he has come to embody, it annihilates him—metaphorically and, later, literally. It might be remembered here, too, that despite possessing an artistic outlet—despite having written those astonishing books—Faulkner was himself a tortured, even agonized, unhappy drunk of a man much of the time.

In 2007, while participating on a panel of writers entitled "The Perils of Regionalism: Labels and Their Limitations," Huddle explicitly addressed how his ongoing uneasy relationship with his home region continues to benefit his art: "There's a whole lot about southwestern Virginia that I don't get along with, at all, and I think that's a good thing for my writing.

I think I need that friction, that being at odds with Appalachian culture in the way that I am" (Norman 25). Huddle's choice of the word *need* in this context seems especially meaningful. His perpetual artistic tug of war with Glory River/Stevens Creek/Rosemary/Ivanhoe, that imaginary landscape of his formative past, whatever he or we might call it, is not simply nice or good or troubling or burdensome for his art; it may embody some or all of those things, but it most definitely is "needed." In other words, it is necessary.

Below the idea of artistic necessity lies an additional, deeper layer—sometimes troubling and painful, though also often very productive—which informs the relationship between writer and place, and which we might best approach by way of a comment Huddle makes near the end of his introduction to a collection of much of his best work up through 1994 entitled *A David Huddle Reader*. Comparing the process of writing to participating in a sport, Huddle emphasizes, "what matters is that I'm *there* [his italics]—as completely as I possibly can be" ("Introduction: Confessions" 4). Functioning in his composition process is an implied duality of being, of action, in which Huddle is both there as the man sitting before a computer and as an artistic entity seeking to give itself over to the work it is imagining into existence to the greatest degree that it can. In an essay called "What You Get for Good Writing," from his collection *The Writing Habit*, Huddle switches from *there* to *here* while retaining much of the insinuated connotation from his earlier description: "It may not be much, but at least I'm here by the page and a half that I wrote this morning. . . . I set down a word and then another beside it. I am here" (*Writing* 209). Again, Huddle is present in two respects: as a proximate man who has concluded his writing day and is perhaps finishing the last of his coffee, and as that artistic entity who stands by with the work it has just created. Yet *here* also is wedded to an intimate idea of real and imagined place in a way that *there* is not. Having scribbled from time to time on my own notion of the former, the conceptualization of it that satisfies me most, the one that seems closest to right (some passages from a book called *The Warrior's Path),* is, sadly, also the most abstract:

> "Here" is usually something we take for granted but its simplicity of connotation ever blurs in our minds its inherent insinuations of both position and time. The traveler asks himself, "How do I get there from here?" or, measuring the position of the sun against his

> fatigue, suggests to his companions, "Let us stop here for the night and resume our journey at dawn." It may also refer to a minute topic or specific subject, as in "Here, I must disagree with you"; yet, more dynamically, it may too demand action: "Come here!" Beyond, in all these things, the word embodies an affirmation of life, of being, now. To the one who, uncertain of our presence, calls our name, we reply, "Here."
>
> "Here" is the bashful and more shadowy companion of "place." As with here, the idea of place, any place, remains one of our most basic yet slippery of concepts: it is a space with boundaries but its limits may be definite or indefinite; it might be construed as an abstract mental or spiritual location, "There is a place for you in my heart," or a literal blank domain, "This is the place where you write your name"; it may also refer to a small particular occupied spot, your finger touches the place where your head hurts, or a point someone has achieved or come to only to then lose it, as in this book: "I've lost my place." Place is irrevocably wedded to context, for the space your body occupies is a place, but so is the earth and what scientists call the solar system. And, at once more abstract and more central, it is also a proximity of yearning, of desire. . . . (1)

As ultimately unanswerable as the shifting and overlapping relationships between the natures of *here*, *there*, and *where* often may prove (and they nearly always prove different for each of us), they constitute among the most fundamental recurring variables that any serious writer—any passionate liver of life—might deign to dwell upon, much less take as a primary subject and attempt to explore and evoke through craft.

There exists also the tantalizing prospect that an artist might come to occupy neither *here* nor *there* at all, but rather somehow disappear into, become the work itself. This is a noble and romantic idea shared by a number of writers across time, and perhaps the best anecdotal manifestation of it—the story that stays with me has been recounted to me on more than one occasion by more than one person—involves a visit that the novelist and historian Shelby Foote once made to the University of Virginia, during which he was asked by a student, "What was William Faulkner really like?" Foote, who had endured a kind of irregular literary apprenticeship under that fellow Mississippi scribbler, is purported to have countered with a question of his own: "Have you read his books, young man?" "Yes, sir," replied the student. "Well," Foote concluded, "that is all there is." A younger literary contemporary of Foote's, George Garrett, later would evoke a similar notion in reference to his own work by describing his ambitious attempt to write books "into which 'the real me' (whatever that might be) could vanish forever, wholly transformed, leaving only ghost and flesh, finally mere shadows behind" (Garrett, "Garrett, George Palmer" 104). Readers familiar with Garrett's last published writings, particularly his final novel, *Double Vision,* might acknowledge that he came as close as any writer to doing so.

During a memorable moment, perhaps *the* memorable moment, in Huddle's 1993 fiction collection *Intimates*, the protagonist of the short story "Mister Mister" describes a powerful instance in which he watches his pet rabbit, Dr. Bones, at the very instant the animal crosses over from drowsy consciousness into slumber: "There was a fraction of a moment there, with Dr. Bones's minute eyelids drooping and my finger brushing along the frontal bridge of his skull, when the lower threshold of my identity just dropped out of me and I became something only one or two evolutionary stages up from protoplasm" (132). What is occurring here, whether ultimately explainable or not, what is intimated, is a kind of primitive existential transmission involving these two mammals that also comments indirectly on the shared relationship between an artist and his or her art. What would it be like if, for a split second—the span of a hard-hitting albeit abbreviated epiphany or eureka—the writer were to lose all self and become his or her work? True, the experience might prove akin to any number of things for different writers, but I can assure you that more than one of the possibilities would constitute something close to what Huddle's character experiences while running his finger along the skull of that rabbit.

In order to flesh this concept out a little more successfully, we might consider briefly another fictional rabbit, a feral one, from another, longer book of fiction published the same year as Huddle's *Intimates*: James Dickey's novel *To the White Sea*. The protagonist of that book, Muldrow, whose father left Virginia for unclear reasons, has endured a childhood of almost total isolation from other humans while living in the Brooks Range of northern Alaska. As a result, from a very early age Muldrow studies, kills, and comes to identify very closely with the animals of that formative place, among them the arctic hare. This is a creature whose fur changes with the seasons and who comes to match the snow of a white landscape so precisely that a human traversing a snowfield might nearly step upon the animal and yet never glimpse it so long as it keeps its eyes, the dark color of which otherwise would prove a dead giveaway, fully closed. In the novel Muldrow ponders at length the metaphorical significance of this natural ability, concluding:

> From watching the animals and birds up on the muskeg, on the tundra, and on the Brooks, I've always believed that if camouflage is good enough, if it is right *exactly*, the bird or the animal will not just be invisible, it won't be there. . . . Like that or just about, it was almost somewhere else, or just not. (112)

Later, in an interview, Dickey would elaborate on the significance this natural phenomenon holds for his largely "ahuman" protagonist:

> Muldrow wants to achieve the perfect camouflage. He believes that the perfect camouflage will enable him to cease to exist and merge with the landscape. The only thing that will give him away is his eyes. When he closes them, he thinks he can become the place. (Suarez 130)

A romantic, perhaps even a mad, conceit? Possibly, but the concept remains a most alluring one, nonetheless, and I cannot think of a creative writer who would consciously choose to pass up an opportunity to be that vanishing bunny—to close one's eyes and become, in all its feeling and scope, if only for a moment, the thing one has written.

So it happens that the *here, there, where* of a work of art may sometimes function less as a formal variable for the sake of the composition at hand and more as a necessary, though often unconscious, catalyst in the artist's compulsion to understand himself and his art. Moreover, the witnesses to the art, the readers, stand to benefit as well when place is created not as backdrop but as the invited artistic experience of something through the medium of a painting, or a poem, or, as in Huddle's novella *Tenorman*, a song which asks the listener to enter into it and exist with the performer: "to *stay* [Huddle's italics] there with him in the song" (*Tenorman* 119).

Sadly, such an approach is not the most lucrative one for an artist to adopt, and it tends to make one's audience rather selective—as discerning and eclectic, perhaps, as the artist—but this is a decision, consciously or unconsciously, every artist eventually must make. As Huddle says of the writer's existence in this seemingly shrinking literary world of ours, "Since literary justice and excellence have very little to do with money and fame, I know that I might as well write what I want and let it all get sorted out by the big crazy machine. The great mistake—whether because of success or of failure—is to try to write for the machine" (Wickett). There is Huddle's decision, explicitly enough, and a fortunate one it is for his readers. Young writers struggle to understand or appreciate the value of such a resolution, and the unfortunate truth is that most never do. It is not an easy thing to accept, after all, that the reward for good writing—or, in any event, the best writing you can muster—may prove little more than the printed thing you hold in your hand, but such an acceptance, I would argue, is one of the things necessary in making it good or, failing that, making it at least true.

* * *

Although often concerning itself with the power and nuance of place, Huddle's earliest collected fiction focuses on regions other than his formative one. It is as though the young Huddle was possessed of the conviction that consciously rejecting or ignoring those phenomena he knew best was a necessary exercise in improving and distinguishing himself as a writer. Partially for this reason, however, the stories in the 1975 collection *A Dream with No Stump Roots in It* do not rank among Huddle's finest, though they do constitute sound fiction in their own regard and come to gain significant and unique luster for readers who make the worthwhile investment of time to familiarize themselves with the rest of Huddle's output.

The opening story "Luther," for example, may possess arguably the best, or at least the most outrageous, first line of any of Huddle's stories. "They sent me to Africa," proclaims the narrator, "to teach the word of God the Almighty to the Black People" (*Dream* 1). As in well-known colonial Africa narratives such as Conrad's *Heart of Darkness*, however, the protagonist's focus on the words and concepts he has been charged with importing to the continent quickly give way to the powerful nature of it. "The sun shines better in Africa than it does in other parts of the world, I think," observes the narrator, a comment which suggests that the place enables him to see and sense more (9). And what he does perceive, most of it described in strongly natural terms, is anything but settling. During a storm, for instance, the protagonist remarks how the "great huge trees that stood outside the village were being stirred and swirled and twisted and whipped up like all nature had gone berserk" (12). Of course, it is merely a nocturnal African storm that is transpiring, but the experience of it is so different from the storms of the places with which the speaker is most familiar that it manifests itself in his particular mind as ungovernable and frightening. Indeed, in the wake of a nearby thunderclap, the protagonist notes that it seemed as though "a bolt of lightning was hunting for my body and had just found it, lacking a foot or two" (11). Truly this visitor to Africa is one for whom the word *alien* is not misapplied, and indeed much of the story's power stems from his displacement and paranoid discomfort, particularly as they relate to his natural surroundings.

A similar sense of alienation spills over into some of this inaugural collection's other narratives as well. In "The Interrogation of the Prisoner Bung by Mister Hawkins and Sergeant Tree," for example, the flatness of Vietnam is evoked in terms that contrast it mightily with the wooded hills of Huddle's Appalachian youth. "The land," observes the narrator, "in these provinces to the south of the capital city is so flat that it would be possible to ride a bicycle from one of this district to the other and pedal only occasionally" (*Dream* 17). This is an open, naked country, possessed of a certain sameness of terrain, in which there are few places to hide, and, correspondingly, character and intention in the story eventually are laid bare as well. "He is alone," reads the description of Sergeant Tree near the conclusion of the tale, "the highway behind him and in front of him as far as he can see and nothing else around him but rain and the fields of wet, green rice" (25). This character and his concerns come to dominate the setting because . . . well, because they have to: there isn't anything else there that can. Indeed, were the sun to break out on poor Sergeant Tree he might cast the longest shadow of anything around him for miles, and if he were to wave his arms in the air, the shadows they cast would sway on the ground like branches. A shallow, unremarkable man, he towers out of the text like his namesake on account of his surroundings. He is the featured sentinel of that place, because he has to be.

Huddle's early stories seem to project a certain amount of pleasure stemming from the ways in which they use their settings in relation to vastly diverse characters. In another Vietnam tale, "Rose Baby," the narrator describes, with a certain measured disgust, an American military garbage dump he finds himself stationed near: "one square mile of mud and stagnant water and rotten piles of U.S. Army trash" (35). Yet, for the Vietnamese people living in the area who are brave enough to infiltrate the dump and rummage through its detritus, the garbage constitutes a wonderful opportunity for acquiring food and supplies to which they otherwise would not have access. What constitutes trash to the destructive Americans has come to function as an important resource to the area's South Vietnamese residents, another irony in a war that had more ironies than most.

Huddle continues to evoke how different people respond to strongly felt surroundings in a couple of stories that take place in New York City, "Waiting for Carl" and "The Proofreader." The former opens by calling attention to the protagonist's dislike for the city's frigid northern winters in light of his southern background: "The insane winters in New York, particularly the days when the wind on Seventh Avenue became very nearly unbearable, brought Partridge his best business" (27). In describing the winters as "insane," the narrator accentuates the degree to which they lie beyond the protagonist's ability to process and articulate in light of his more balmy point of origin. Although the story is also concerned with urban manifestations of nature, particularly as they apply to humans, deeper questions are at stake in "The Proofreader," in which the stale, voyeuristic approach with which the male protagonist experiences New York City is contrasted with young Leslie's likening of love to "the way your hair and your fingernails and your toenails grow, which are things you can't do anything about" (75). Even in this tale's cityscape of trashed playgrounds and cramped apartments, it is the connection of the people to each other by virtue of their experience (or lack thereof) of the natural which enables them, or at least the ones like Leslie, to meaningfully lead their lives even as they are aware there is very little will or purpose or meaning to guide them.

The consummation of Huddle's use of place and people in the context of the natural world in his first fiction collection arrives at last in its final story, which he initially composed as a poem but appears here as an impressionistic single-paragraph vignette of just over two pages. Despite its brevity, the piece is the collection's most important, if for no other reason than it draws the others together. Out of this narrative's destructive opening—"I took a long-handled ax and made myself a stump out of an oak tree" (107)—there eventually arrives the narrator's "most beautiful vision," which constitutes also the vignette's and the collection's final lines: "In animal skins I am walking with my wife and child over a plain of freshly mown grass. . . . A gentle, pale blue wind is at our backs, and there is sunlight all around us. Our feet pass without sound over an earth that is smooth and endless" (109). This is an image of primitive, natural human togetherness the possible over-idealization of which is justified, or so I would argue, by the manner in which it draws together many of the book's themes in a setting that is, well, placeless. Only in and through this nowhere land of dream may a connective principle be arrived at for the collection's sibling narratives. It is less a narrative or structural cop-out—as dream sequences often are in writing—and more an ambitious grasping for meaning by way of those timeless, placeless domains we stray across in our slumber.

Reluctant to embrace his home place in earnest, Huddle did not begin publishing extended material focused on his region of origin until the 1980s, perhaps in part since he finally had been away from it long enough in terms of his own life and perhaps because he sensed and felt artistically drawn to the depth of setting, character, and overall feeling he could generate by affording it prolonged literary consideration. The results of this shift, as book reviewers and the books themselves across the last three decades demonstrate, have been very favorable. Whatever the reason(s), writing about rural Virginia seems to have been the right decision to make.

Some of Huddle's best evocations of southwest Virginia are in the form of poetic snapshots. Lines from the last poem in the collection *Stopping by Home*, "Things I Know, Things I Don't," (later anthologized in Summer Lake), offer one such example:

> Virginia in early October
> is a soft countryside, color not yet
> in the trees but the leaves' green going pale,
> the sunlight's angle sharp, the birds about
> to move. (*Summer Lake* 56)

This is a pastoral image of expectancy, its mild languor carrying the hints of the slow death of foliage to come and the migratory departure of some of the area's inhabitants. However, because Huddle rarely provides much sustained detail on place for place's sake—rightly, I would argue, since he spares readers the potential problem of having setting get in the way of character, story, and theme—we are left, even in the wake of having perused all his books, with only an indirect idea of it, as rendered by a handful of characters by way of their experiences or as captured through the abstract medium of poetry.

Although Huddle makes the sound authorial decision not to journey too far back into the history of the place he is portraying, we might, before proceeding further and in the interests of appreciating the region's relevance in history and the depth it lends to Huddle's overall work, note a few things about it here. One would have approached the Ivanhoe area in colonial times either by following the New River upstream and southward or, more likely, by way of the valley to the north which Route 11 and Interstate 81, built atop much older traces, follow. Travelers bound for Ivanhoe or thereabouts using the valley would have turned south at a place called Fort Chiswell, the proximity of an outpost built under the direction of William Byrd III in 1759, largely on account of its position in a natural pass between Lick Mountain and Ramsay Mountain, the northwest tip of which pushes up against the village of Max Meadows, notable as the location of one of the earliest North American frontier academies, founded in 1792. The fort was named for Byrd's friend John Chiswell, who in the 1760s would discover lead mines several miles to the south along the New River—just north of Ivanhoe, near present-day Austinville, which would later supply colonial forces during the American Revolution. Ivanhoe too would eventually benefit, at least economically, from the growth of a small regional mining industry, but in the eighteenth century the area constituted little more than just another wild place along the New. Belying the region's political significance as an outpost, on January 30, 1775, the "Freeholders of Fincastle County" met at Fort Chiswell to establish a number of local resolutions in concert with the wishes of the First Continental Congress and to celebrate their joyful relief at the Indians in the area having been "now happily terminated" (Clabough, *Warrior's* 114)

It is the local descendants of such people—independent, stubborn, not averse to violence—who make up many of the characters in Huddle's writing. His second short-story collection, *Only the Little Bone*, constitutes perhaps the most in-depth study of them, as a result of the book's linked evocation (in the tradition of Sherwood Anderson's *Winesburg, Ohio* and Fred Chappell's *I Am One of You, Forever)* of a small place and its singular, yet often archetypal, ways. As Virginia Moore notes in her book *Virginia Is a State of Mind*, "In Virginia towns are not encouraged. They are put up with" (57). But that attitude is precisely what makes rural Virginians worthy of note and investigation. Among other things, the diverse characters of a place serve to remind us that, quite apart from its weather, topography, and other factors, a place is never really static or fixed. As Enrico Baraldi notes in *Taking Place: The Spatial Contexts of Science, Technology, and Business*, "The boundaries of a place are not . . . definite or unproblematic. Rather, they are permeable and constantly negotiated, disputed and maintained by the interests and actions of people. Places relate to the surrounding world and are perceived differently by different people" (Baraldi, Fors, and Houltz xiii). Places, then, are given character by the people who inhabit them just as much as they influence the development of character, and Virginia, as a state, is perhaps one of the best North American exemplars of this concept. This interdependency has deepened the tragedy of the state's history but also benefited its literature. Virginia's topography—from the low-lying coastal areas to the red-clay Piedmont to the mountain and valley region—lent it to diverse cultures and patterns of settlement that often came into conflict. Of special note, in his lively book *The Virginia Tradition*, Marshall Fishwick articulates the Old Dominion's Tidewater-Appalachian dichotomy as follows:

> Here are the much-advertised manor houses, surrounded by unpainted shacks and sub-marginal farmers; pink-coated sportsmen, concerned with their well-bred horses, and half-clothed hill people, concerned with their poorly-bred children. In a few hours one can drive not only from region, but from century, to another. (iii)

Of course, this is hyperbole meant to shock, titillate, and possibly enrage readers, yet it inhabits a district not overly remote from truth.

Huddle's region falls on the half-clothed, poorly bred side of Professor Fishwick's outrageous binarism, but it cannot be lumped in so easily with the rest of southwest Virginia or Appalachia. One distinguishing feature that serves as a central literal and metaphorical force throughout Huddle's work is the New River: from the descriptions of the local drunks lounging on its banks and the children who tragically drown in its waters to its more symbolic and abstract insinuations of discovery, rebirth, and navigation elsewhere. It is true that such uses and themes might be applied to any stream or brook (and have been by numerous writers across time), yet the New is no ordinary river. One of the most venerable bodies of water on the planet, it is over 250 million years old—more ancient, in fact, than the Atlantic Ocean, which did not exist prior to 180 million years ago. On account of its having been shaped in another epoch, the New River runs in an odd direction, west and north, from the Blue Ridge Mountains in North Carolina to the Mississippi. It even predates Appalachia, its waters already flowing when the continent of Africa collided with that of North America, resulting in the great, rippling, continental cataclysm that birthed our eastern mountains. While glaciers spread and receded around the New over the course of several centuries, animals congregated on its banks, safe from the freezing wastelands and privy to abundant plant and animal life. Because of this insulated quality, immensely old species live along the New River even now, attracting scientists and enthusiasts, such as the harried researcher in Huddle's poem "Screech Owl," from around the world.

The land around the New shares some of the distinctiveness of its river. In another story from *Only the Little Bone*, "The Undesirable," the narrator affords an elevated view of the fictional small town based on Ivanhoe:

> It looked like pictures I'd seen of villages where they made wine in Europe, except their hillsides were lined with vineyards and ours were mostly fields of broomsage and scrub cedars, cow pastures, corn fields, trash piles, gatherings of junked cars, and back behind us the smoke of the carbide plant rising up from the two tall stacks. (*Only* 48)

Establishing European wine country—or at least postcard depictions of it—as an ideal for human participation in such landscape, the description then captures the ragged pastoralism indicative of overly aggressive but now largely defunct agricultural practices and the waste products of industry that might apply to countless places in Appalachia. Yet, once again, although similar to these places in a cursory, surface sort of manner, the Ivanhoe area is somewhat different in substance. For one thing, its industry, its form of mining, is not the gas or coal variety responsible for the endless miles of horrific moonscape destruction in the mountains further west. It is, instead, a true mineral-based type of excavation that nonetheless affects the area's people in a similar, if more benign, manner. As Huddle writes in his wonderfully titled poem "Holes Commence Falling":

> The lead & zinc company
> Owned the mineral rights
> to the whole town anyway. (*Summer Lake* 4)

And as in West Virginia, Kentucky, East Tennessee, and elsewhere, the foreign ownership and ensuing exploitation unfortunately becomes a kind of cultural emblem of local self-importance and esteem:

> We were proud
> Of all that digging,
> Even though nobody from
> Town got hired. (*Summer Lake* 4)

Yet, as in most mining communities everywhere, the complex interrelationship between natural resources and developmental industrial planning in the area never comes to embody its greed-inspired potential. As a result, the protagonist of *Only the Little Bone* relates his ghostly experience of wandering through forested roads and developments in the area that had never been occupied or, in some cases, completed: "Many of those roads had turned back to dirt roads and then turned further back to grass paths that were used only occasionally by people walking" (59). Failing to realize their projected human functions, these phenomena and the minds that designed them lie fallow in long defeat by the place they would change—an inspirational scenario now, perhaps, for citizens in Evington, Virginia, concerned about the new quarry or those in Pittsylvania County uncomfortable about their proximity to a uranium mine.

If anything, such haunting and occasionally menacing industrial elements only serve to enrich the natural descriptions that inform Huddle's work. In fact, he seems to enjoy playing along the edges where civilization and nature blend. In the title story from *Only the Little Bone*, for example, the yard of the protagonist's childhood home is described in the following terms: "an acre of mowed grass, an old tennis court gone to honeysuckle, and a bushy patch of woods far below the house that we call the jungle" (201). Characteristics of both a wild and a suburban youth are at work here, the mowed lawn and tennis court indicative of any American family that might inhabit a bracket of the upper-middle class or above. But, then, consider these things alongside the animals of Huddle's youth as listed in his poem "A History of the Pets":

> Small possums loose in the house. Short-Circuit,
> Affectionate cat that walked crooked, that'd been
> BB-shot in the head. Goat. Skunk. Some snakes. (*Summer Lake* 46)

These are the creatures of a country boy's childhood, maimed and casually abused by the standards of animal treatment we employ today, but nonetheless cared for and loved by their keepers after a fashion. Many contemporary readers will be troubled by this scenario, but that is to the purpose: it lends power to the poem.

Rich descriptions of the natural world continue to appear in Huddle's third collection of short fiction, *The High Spirits*, the title story of which vividly captures the feel of a Virginia May: "the air smelled like freshly-plowed fields with intermittent gusts of lilac and wisteria" (130). However, at least one reviewer of the book, Dennis Jovenetti, writing in a 1991 number of the *Hollins Critic*, asserted that the collection's close attention to dynamics other than human interaction come at the expense of its overall achievement: "While these are stories of men and women, the reader is ultimately removed from these men and women" (14). Whatever the degree of accuracy in such an interpretation, Huddle, whether as a result of conscious or unconscious factors, soon would vanquish such objections to his fiction by enlarging his cast of characters and deepening readerly knowledge of their inner lives by way of a first novel that would turn out to be his most commercially successful book to date: *The Story of a Million Years*. A novel that, according to reviewer John Kennedy, "peels away the dying skin of suburban, middle-class life, revealing the quiet loneliness that stalks so many" (245). *The Story of a Million Years* breaks away from the natural world and Huddle's place of origin in order to investigate the quandary of late-twentieth-century American life. Although the manner in which the novel is written sacrifices some of the good things readers had come to expect from Huddle's work up to that point, it gains much in other areas and is indicative of a mid-career author healthily and successfully experimenting with new forms and ways of thinking about prose and character psychology. As one anonymous reviewer concluded in *Publishers Weekly*, "the setting is really incidental; the real action takes place internally. It is this inner terrain to which Huddle is most sensitive: the ways we reconcile or fail to reconcile ourselves to our moral lapses" ("Review of *The Story of a Million Years*" 71). Outer terrain, then, abandons center stage to inner terrain in *The Story of a Million Years*, and the immediacy of place becomes secondary, all with new and favorable results.

While Huddle abandoned some of his earlier signature techniques for the good of the story at stake in his first novel, he did not give them up altogether, and, in fact, a remarkable blending of his new interest in the trials of suburban adults and his traditional natural concerns takes place in the title narrative of a three-piece collection published a year after his debut novel, entitled *Not: A Trio*. At least to my mind, *Not* is unlike anything Huddle has written before or since and easily stands as the darkest and most ominous of his prose works. It does not prove an easy book for many readers to love, but I have grown very fond of it.

Toward the end of *Not* the beleaguered narrator, a Vermont psychologist beset by unsatisfying relationships and a general lack of purpose, journeys to an old overgrown farm she has inherited in order to reflect on her life and, one initially supposes, establish a new direction for it. What ensues are some of Huddle's most stunning prose meditations on nature and time, often triggered by vivid sensory-based moments that seem to stand still on the page. When, for example, the narrator experiences a powerful urge to take the morning off from work, it is the smell of the surrounding landscape, as well as its memory-stirring appearance, that compels her: "A sky that reminds me of mornings in my childhood, green valley land and mountains, cows and the smell of the Vermont springtime—which is to say the smell of cow manure" (58). Moreover, her impressions of the natural world are deepened by the repercussions of contemporary industrial civilization and the inner forlornness that accompanies it, all of which have become mixed up and confused inside her. At one point, for instance, when she senses a "slight current of air," she likens it to a "motor running quietly in the distance" (79). The protagonist's ambition for correcting such unnatural associations and her overall situation is to give herself over to nature—metaphorically, we think, at first. She would like to become, for example, what she believes a mountain constitutes to the road that ascends it: "The mountain barely tolerates the road. It makes the road squirm. If it wished, the mountain could heave this asphalt scab off its skin. If people wanted to drive cars up its side, they would have to start over again, they would have to build another road" (64). Of course, this is an impossible thing to want, but that does not restrain her from desiring it, a sign perhaps that she has broken loose a little from those strands that hold us to our existences.

Given its themes and ambitions, *Not* is not a very accessible book, particularly for readers unfamiliar with the concerns and overall trajectory of Huddle's writings. Another anonymous reviewer for *Publishers Weekly* concluded, "Huddle's formal choices here obscure the shape of his plot"

(Review of *Not: A Trio* 84). However, I could not disagree more with this phantom appraiser and, indeed, would argue the opposite: that it is the protagonist's impressions of the natural world, delivered through her truncated journal entries, which make it possible for the reader to sense her deepening depression and growing resolve to take her own life. When, for instance, she recalls the time during her girlhood when she entered the dairy (the farm's subterranean storage chamber) with her father, she compares the room's odor to that of "a plowed field on a rainy night. I am remembering it because we seemed to have penetrated into its essence. It is to that fragrance I mean to return to" (56). What this protagonist wants is to *be* an odor, a place: "to be still on a sunny day. To spend hours watching the wind stir the leaves on the trees" (67). What she desires is a consciousness of belonging paradoxically predicated upon timelessness and an absence of self. "Less than a hundred years ago," she says of her remote inherited homestead, "this mountainside was a working farm. Thousands of years ago, after the glaciers melted away, there were no trees here at all. The landscape looked like the arctic tundra" (76). In other words, it was a place of vast frigid nothingness; it was, in essence, *not*.

Remember the arctic bunny? This woman wants to close her eyes.

* * *

> Fairies there, thought I, once more; the queen of fairies at her fairy-window; at any rate, some glad mountain-girl; it will do me good, it will cure this weariness, to look on her.
>
> Herman Melville, "The Piazza"

Why not add an additional layer to the deepening and perhaps ultimately inarticulable concoction of lived-in, remembered, and evoked place that is perhaps the most Prometheanly ambitious of aims in this essay? Why not recount our own journeys into those particular southwestern mountains, my own having occurred just a little over a decade and half ago? Why not let our own lids droop a little?

Actually they were squinting since I was driving westward into the sun, having departing the central part of the state, roads curving evermore, terrain drawing itself up with the passing of miles, constricting into hills and vales—in league with them—as the sun kept up its swinging round from the south, sliding slowly, angling imperceptibly, down toward the horizon.

Mountains rising all about me on the other side of the New as I drew nearer the home of the girl who, unlikely circumstances behind and in front of us, had seen fit to have me escort her to her school's senior prom. Road leading up to her mountainside home a tangle of bends, passing in and out of great acres-long swaths of rock-cast shadow. And then my own whimsy, ever at war with the rest of me, especially in those years, infecting me with the notion of driving round the backside of the mountain—to drive up it and then descend upon this girl's home from above rather than approach it by way of the shorter and more direct route from below. I already knew how the twisting fence-lined driveway of gravel led up to where the long one-story house sat upon a knoll; set almost into the slope, barn off to the side—hillside pasture rising in back so as to loom outward overtop the house as though it might bite down and devour it.

Perhaps because I already knew what it was like to arrive at that place, I resolved to go about it a little differently, selecting a route lonely and obscure: less direct, wayward—narrow road coiling itself about the base of the mountain, passing far below the place where sat that house on its knob, looking out eastward.

Around then and in back of. Ascending not at all until I gained the base of the sun-facing western slope. Scaling then, driving up and gearing down, engine at a low rumble, winding my way ever higher, crumbled fragments of rock crunching beneath the tires as my ears popped.

At the crest of the peak I pulled off the road, perpendicular to it, onto a bare gravel spot, so that I might have a beer or two and look back westward over the wind-dwarfed trees at the last of the sun. Hills, green with leaves of spring, shone against the afternoon sky, dotting the horizon, spanning off toward West Virginia. Little wooly clouds drifted not far above them; thin air around me sweet, cool, and damp with the odor of the springs trickling forth from the black roadside mountain rock.

Crushing of cans, glancing back at the ebbing light a final time, rolling the windows down all the way, before tuning the stereo to "Love's Theme" by Barry White and turning the volume all the way up. When the second chord progression began, I accompanied it with my favorite lines from *Thus Spoke Zarathustra*, read for the first time over my own mostly ill-spent senior-year spring vacation.

"*Du grosses Gestirn*!" I sang heartily in my bad German to the tune's bubbling wah-wah peddle, "*Was wäre dein Glück, wenn du nicht Die hättest, welchen du leuchtest*!"

Then stabbing the accelerator, outward fountain of fragmented rock and dirt signaling the engine's protest as I jerked back out onto the road and started down the dark side of the mountain.

"*So segne mich denn*," I yelled, pounding my forehead with my fist, before leaning into a switchback curve, "*du ruhiges Auge, das ohne Neid auch ein allzugrosses Glück sehen kann*!"

"*Siehe*!" I shouted toward the canopy passing then at eye-level. "*Dieser Becher will wieder leer werden, und Zarathustra will wieder Mensch werden*!"[1]

And the evening side of the mountain still and silent, not another traveler in sight: mute and unpeopled save for the music, my words, and the irregular tradeoff of engine and brake—echoing off the rocky roadside walls and along all the hemlock-lined gorges like the mating call of some odd species of animal that perhaps would remain always a little out of the time and place at hand, regardless of where it roamed.

* * *

> Never having vanished into Space (or Time) altogether, place is abounding: this is so even when it is called by various names, and itself names different events and experiences.
>
> Edward Casey, *Getting Back into Place*

While his fiction, including his most recent stories published in literary magazines, increasingly has focused on the rich inner landscapes of characters rather than their visceral surroundings, Huddle's poetry has continued to balance the two concerns. One anonymous reviewer of Huddle's volume of selected and new poems, *Summer Lake*, articulated this balance admirably, noting how the volume's "formally unremarkable free verse and deliberately muted vocabulary seek the clearest possible understandings of his feelings and motives, and of [Huddle's] eccentric, pathetic or brave regional characters" (Review of *Summer Lake* 100). As though commenting upon such a reading (not without a certain measure of irony), one of the poems from *Glory River*, "The Mayor of Glory River," adopts the voice of an academic in describing the Ivanhoe-area people as:

---

1 Sung passages translate as follows:

You great star, what would your happiness be had you not those for whom you shine?
Bless me then, you quiet eye that can look upon all-too-great happiness without envy!
Behold! This cup wants to become empty again, and Zarathustra wants to become man again!

> embodying a contemptuous attitude
> toward authority tacitly
> shared by residents of Glory River,
> a convergence of Appalachian humor,
> dialect, and the shared values peculiar
> to their microregion. (*Glory* 30)

At work here and, indeed, at work across several of the poems in *Glory River*, is an implicit or explicit tension between the portrayed doings of the people in this southwest Virginia "microregion" and the various interpretations they are subjected to by each other, outsider figures, and different narrators. Moreover, it is a tension often sought after and explored, consciously or unconsciously, by southern and Appalachian writers—and minority writers everywhere—seeking to portray the value of their places and/or cultures in the face of national and/or global ignorance and hostility without coming across as sentimental, nostalgic, or polemical. This can be a difficult and perhaps implicitly self-defeating task for a writer to take up. For example, one need look no further than manifestations of everyday contemporary American media to discern that characters either explicitly from the southeastern United States or possessed of overblown accents meant to identify them as such almost always function negatively in the narrative at hand, as a result of their ascribed ignorance, laziness, bigotry, or any number of other debilitating stereotypes. All this persists in the face of evidence that the American South as a region, including the southern mountains, disputed as its boundaries may be, has produced art of a high order, particularly in the areas of music and literature, in equal or greater proportion to some of the planet's continents in their entirety, and certainly up to the standard of the other regions of the nation with which it long has endured an uneasy relationship.

It is safe to say that the writers who portray their places are the ones who largely ignore the loudest and most prevalent cultural appraisals made of them, and instead draw on their own knowledge and resources to evoke these places, albeit sometimes indirectly, as best they can. In a review of *Glory River* in the *Southern Review*, Philip Deaver noted that Huddle "tells stories about this place from the point of view of its people, writing in long riffs of the mountain country vernacular that we know, from reading this, is deep-rooted in him" ("Writing to the Center" 785). This mountain country is deep rooted though not always explicitly evident in terms of its function. Huddle's novel *La Tour Dreams of the Wolf Girl*, for example, takes place mostly in France and the northeastern United States, and proceeds in its feel and focus on character from the precedent established by *The Story of a Million Years*; yet, as reviewer Paul Evans remarked of the book's female academic protagonist, "She's a misfit intellectual from backwoods Virginia who experiences an epiphany in her youth" (Evans 75). Switch the gender here, and this protagonist sounds a lot like David Huddle.

There remains, then—whether he likes it or not, and/or is always aware of it or not—a persistent place-signature across most all Huddle's work that powerfully benefits the work and, I believe, benefits his formative place as well. Perhaps it is something more than coincidence that Huddle acknowledges this association most explicitly in "Water," the poem that concludes his most recent book:

> Valley farmland
> beside a mountain:
>
> A spring up there sent down
> the coldest, sweetest water—
>
> fifty years since my last sip,
> my tongue still remembers
>
> that black-dirt-dogwood
> taste of the Blue Ridge. (*Glory* 65)

To round out this chapter, we'll afford a few more words to Huddle that come from a book of his that never mentions southwest Virginia but at times reads like his own love letter to it. "*Here we are,*" a recorded voice utters near the end of the novella *Tenorman*. "*Here we are, indeed. With what we have brought with us*" (90).

Epilogue

Writing for a Place

A Writer's Workshop for McDowell County, West Virginia

There were two of us, charged, as part of a National Endowment for the Humanities initiative, with devising a writing workshop manual to be housed at the Caretta Community Center, in McDowell County, West Virginia. Ours was one of many service projects aimed at applying the latest studies in regionalism, globalization, and public policy to the community needs of McDowell County, considered at the time the poorest and most illiterate district in West Virginia, and the sixth poorest county in the United States. Having spent three weeks in the Virginia Blue Ridge Mountains on the campus of Ferrum College absorbing theoretical and artistic notions of southern Appalachia, in general, and coal country, in particular, we had traveled west, faced with the challenge of attempting to translate our intellectual themes and techniques into some variety of community benefit. We had studied the history, culture, and economics of the region very closely. We arrived with a sound grasp of globalization theory and a new understanding of public policy. We hoped we could employ these abstractions as means of doing some good for the people of McDowell County. We were two very ignorant and naïve young scholars.

LET'S WRITE!

A community-based writing workshop is a good way to encourage local folks to create and tell stories, and to receive helpful advice from writers and friends. The writer's workshop should be a safe place where people can communicate without fear of harsh criticism. It is important to remember that the purpose of such a community activity is to be supportive of writers, both artistically and emotionally. Everyone's writing improves when you help each other.

Community workshops may be run in a number of ways. For instance, community members may feel a need to offer a "Women's Writing Workshop," a "Men's Writing Workshop," or even a "Children's Writing Workshop." Ideally, the group interested in promoting and maintaining these kinds of support groups should weigh the wants and feelings of the community members. This may be done by advertising the possibility of a writer's workshop to the community. Flyers may be posted at highly public places, such as the local restaurants, grocery stores, and libraries. It is also good to spread the word at churches, schools, video stores, and community social groups (such as sewing circles and hunt clubs). Share the idea and see what folks say.

After advertising to the community and getting a group together, the creative work begins. Here are some ways to start workshops; they have worked well in other places.

WORKSHOP MEMBERS

A Moderator or Group Leader: the group leader is in charge of introducing the writer and his or her work, giving out copies of the writer's stories to readers/respondents, and shepherding the group discussion.

A Writer/Author: the writer provides copies of his or her short fiction, poetry, or nonfiction for the group. Copies are handed out one week before the piece of writing is talked about; this gives each member time to read and think about the writing. If the writing group can't or doesn't want to make copies, it may simply have writers read their work aloud at the meeting.

A Group of Readers/Respondents: the reader's job is to give the writer opinions or ideas he or she can use. The reader should begin by explaining to the writer what "works" or what is "praiseworthy." Feedback is helpful, but be sure to give ways to make the piece better and avoid attacking the author's work or person. Be a friend to your fellow writer. We are all in it together.

We were in it alright, for sure—well over our heads, for southern Appalachia is a different kind of South, and coal country is a different kind of southern Appalachia. My colleague and I each possessed centuries-old ancestral ties to the Smoky Mountains of Sevier County, Tennessee—the cartoon hillbilly capital of southern Appalachia: Dollywood, Gatlinburg, and a menagerie of mountain stereotypes hemmed in by the stunning beauty of misty peaks. Yet our rural and commercial experiences in the Smokies left us wholly unprepared for West Virginia coal country: those crumbling landscapes with mountains toppling evermore, from which the centuries will burn rich loads under which the people of those places have groaned. These are remote wastelands of the industrial era, twisted nightmarish episodes of rural Appalachia briefly turned modern and then abandoned: small dilapidated company houses pressed against rusty railroads, centered by a slightly less-decomposed company store; all—the homes, the railroad, the store, even the roads that lead to them—now partially sunken in and defunct, the rare figure or vehicle that moves among them suggestive of an unlikely survivor from some apocalypse.

For the land that is mined, there is no recompense, advantage, or silver lining: it is irrevocably maimed and torn, though the wounds may be so deep as to appear all but invisible, save for the brackish, acidic groundwater and befouled wells, the inexplicable sinkholes in the terrain, the uprooted trees, the suddenly eroded slopes, the deadly floods. It is a place fraught with many trials and dangers, yet it was our visceral ignorance of it that placed both us and our project in the greatest peril.

ONE WAY TO HOLD A WRITING WORKSHOP

Create a Safe Place

The first and most important task is to create a sanctuary where group members feel comfortable enough to share their writing with others. Here are some things to do: 1) sit in a circle to help create a sense of fellowship among members; 2) allow the members to talk and decide on rules for the meeting, like making time limits for author's readings and audience comments; 3) let the members figure out the way to run the workshops; 4) allow members to speak about trust and support in the group; honesty and fellowship are important parts of any writers group. Respect the other writers and you will earn their respect.

Leading the Workshop: The Moderator

Next, workshop members elect a leader, also called a moderator, to help shepherd the group during the meeting. The moderator's job is to: 1) introduce the writer and his or her work; 2) hand out copies of the story/poem (if there are any—remember, the writer may just wish to read aloud); 3) make sure the reader and the people who give feedback stay within time limits; 4) take notes for the author on what members liked or disliked about the author's work.

Reading before Reviewing

At the end of each group meeting, the moderator can hand out a new piece of writing by a new author. Group members should

1) take these pages back home and read them carefully; 2) make notes about the story or poem that will help the writer understand where his or her work "entertains" or "confuses" the reader. If there are no copies to be had, it is always good to check out a novel or book of poems from the library in War (the name of a nearby slightly larger coal village). Good writers are good readers; books will give you ideas about how to sow your own writing.

Make Comments about the Work, not the Author

Members of the writing group must keep in mind that writing is often times very personal. A bad comment by a group member can easily be taken as an attack on the author. Each member should take extra care always to refer to the story or the poem, not the author, when making comments. Remember that the person you are judging will be judging your work at some point. It is helpful to use the following words when describing the author's work: *clear/unclear*; *accurate/inaccurate*; *organized/unorganized*. Also, phrases such as these work well: "this verse touches my soul" or "this verse leaves me cold"; "this passage works for me" or "this passage doesn't work for me." It is always good to be detailed about why a verse or sentence does or doesn't "work." Quoting a passage may help to explain what you mean. It is best to avoid words that attack such as *wrong, stupid, ignorant*. These words bring doubt and strife to the writers.

We were nervous about encouraging too much conflict, even though a writing workshop would seem, at least on the surface, a harmless, abstract activity. The region was home both to a romanticized tradition of feuding and a very real legacy of domestic violence fueled mostly by pervasive poverty, lack of education, and drugs (crystal meth, in particular). Home to broken promises and crippling frustrations, the West Virginia coal region is where pain and rage often simmer just below the point of boiling.

Once flourishing towns, home to every modern convenience, many of the local coal villages such as Caretta are now ghostly places, hollows where steel cankers and vines wrap about the broken sidewalks and abandoned railroad tracks. Trees have grown up through roofless houses and schools, among the best that could be built when their foundations were laid in the 1920s and 1930s. The population is largely aged, the youth having fled in search of work, a different kind of life, propelled by an indefinite need to escape. Many of those who remain are indigent and unemployed, drugged out and uneducated; they have been subjected to conditions worse than those in many Third World countries, while living in a county just three hundred miles from the capital of the United States.

The people who settled McDowell County in the early nineteenth century were similar to my own Germanic frontier ancestors: independent, stoic, poor folk arrived to a place where they could finally afford land and carve a living, however humble, out of the close-pressed ridges and hollows of the southern Appalachian Mountains. And so they got by, enduring rather than prospering, but doing so on their own terms, decade after decade. The arrival of modern coal operations dramatically altered the traditional local economy from one of hardscrabble agricultural subsistence to an even more tenuous, crude and industrial one. The land and/or what lay beneath it was steadily acquired—coercively as well as forcibly—by absentee coal barons, while the local people were herded into coal camps, and they or their children were eventually compelled to mine, the terraced hillside rows abandoned for dark subterranean passages, cribbed with lumber, water dripping amid the creaking of timbers: the clink of pick or shovel as a crew shuffles past, hunched and silent in the pale glow of headlamps.

The Author Reads the Work

When the group gets together, the moderator reminds the group of the rules so that everyone can work together. The moderator then asks the author to read his or her work aloud to the group. The author should always respect the time limits set by the group. Here are some things the author might think about before reading the work: 1) if the story or poem is long, the writer should select two or three sections of the work to read aloud; 2) the writer should select passages that the author wants feedback on. Always show polite attention while the writer reads.

The Author Hears the People

After the author reads his or her work, the author needs to stay silent and listen carefully to comments made by members. This is very important. It keeps the session from getting bogged down in discussions or arguments. As the author listens, he or she should: 1) write down the comments; 2) avoid strong emotional reactions to the comments; 3) consider carefully what each member says and try to understand; 4) write down questions for members who make comments that are unclear.

Give Positive Feedback First

When members talk about the author's work, members should first make good comments about the writing. Members should focus on what the author should not change. It is also helpful to be as clear as possible about what is "good" about the writing. Commentators should 1) point to words, sentences or paragraphs that are pleasing to read; 2) point to passages that explain tough feelings and emotions; 3) point to sections in the writing that help create strong feelings in the reader. Such comments help the author know what is good about their work.

Offer Ways to Improve

The purpose of a writing workshop is to make a piece of writing better. But members need to be gentle with their advice because authors sometimes become angry when their work is attacked. Remember: the writing workshop is a sanctuary of safety, and you have entered into a covenant of respect with your fellow writers. Here are some ways to make comments about improvements without hurting the author's feelings: 1) tell the group and author one problem with the story or poem that you had as a reader; 2) next, suggest how a writer might try to solve the problem; 3) remind the author that the suggestions are "just suggestions" and are not "commandments" for making the story or poem better. Remember that the author is the only one who can change his or her writing. Never holler out comments without thinking.

Here are some things group members might look for when reading the work and making comments to improve it: 1) when reading, watch how the story or poem moves from one happening to another. Then ask whether it is believable or not; 2) watch what might be missing from the story or poem. Maybe the author's work could get better by adding more information to make certain parts clearer; 3) at other times, a story or poem can be improved by taking things out. Things that do not help the story or poem move forward can sometimes be cut, making the writing better.

The best thing to remember about giving advice is that no one but the author can change or write the story or poem. The writer will meet their fate on their own terms. It is not our place to judge or interfere. The group should not try to rewrite the work for the author. Group members are there only to help the writer see the story or poem from other people's points of view.

The last thing we wanted to do was make the workshop manual overly obtuse or heavy handed, yet that is precisely what we unknowingly had been doing. The kind woman who read over a draft at the Caretta Community Center stunned us with the comment, "Y'all realize the person who will be running this thing might only have an eighth-grade education." There was much our academic training had caused us to take for granted and a lot we still didn't understand.

During McDowell County's company era, people often were paid for their underground labor in script, which allowed them to buy goods only from the company store. The company provided everything, ensuring that all or most of the real money it paid and spent upon miners and their families eventually made its way back into the coffers of the company, one way or another: if not the company store, then the company doctor, the company church, etc. The psychological impact of living in such a society was much worse than the nefarious exploitation it practiced on its victims, for over time the coal-mining system encouraged and produced an unhealthy culture of paternalism in which miners expected the company to provide everything, a dynamic that stripped them of the formidable initiative and independence of their forefathers. When industry failed and the companies pulled out of the region, few locals even knew where to begin—the lucky ones moving away, those who remained struggling with poverty and unemployment, their communities slowly disintegrating. Many people yearned in despair for the return of the very system that had exploited them.

Today, in McDowell County—three hundred miles from Washington, D.C., yet rated one of the top ten poorest counties in the United States, eight-tenths of its land owned by people who don't live there, home to staggering rates of illness and illiteracy—there exists, to some degree, a troubling marketing of victimization, an advertised human deprivation that openly attracts and recruits philanthropic groups and tolerates their various ideologies for the purpose of attaining whatever material benefits may be involved. Sometimes, a measure of genuine good is accomplished. Overall, though, one can't help but feel troubled that those who arrive with aid are, in some sense, not all that different in their paternalistic material capacities from the coal companies of old: a new benevolent crutch to replace the old malignant one, though a crutch remains a crutch, as the saying goes.

My fellow manual-writer and I worried about slipping into this trap and agonized over the best ways to apply our knowledge in a manner that would be helpful without appearing unduly prescriptive or outright incomprehensible. The previous summer we both had attended a month-long seminar on the globalization of culture at Research Triangle's National Humanities Center. One of the recurring questions that kept coming up in our discussions involved how exactly to apply the theoretical salves and prescriptions of globalization theory through the visceral arm of public policy. One of our visiting lecturers, Rey Chow, had confessed that this was something that troubled and haunted her with regard to her own work, especially her writings on China. Another visiting scholar, Tim Brennan, had appeared less concerned, offering that theorists should probably just do their jobs and let policymakers do theirs.

Back in West Virginia, in our particular case, we had received sound, informed feedback on our endeavor; now it was up to us to transform our document—readable to our eyes but obtuse to those that mattered—into something that might actually be useful. We wracked our skulls a good while before coming to the somewhat unlikely realization that the Bible held the answer. Not a particular passage, mind you, or divine illumination of insight, but rather the book's general vocabulary and the way it was written. Literacy may have been tenuous in McDowell County but religion was not, and the language of King James, the foundation of western literature, is a rich, descriptive utterance. As you perhaps already have surmised in perusing parts of the manual, biblical rhetoric became our unlikely compositional model. And behold! All who read our newly altered passages were able to discern their meanings. . . .

Making Things Clear: The Author Asks for Clarification

As group members comment on the writer's work, it is good for the author to keep note of comments that are not clear. Sometimes it is hard to behold where someone else is coming from. If some members are not very clear with their comments, the author should ask the group member to explain again her comment of praise or improvement. The understanding of words is the beginning of meaning.

Review Changes

During the time when members are commenting on the author's work, the moderator should be remembering or keeping brief notes of good comments and suggestions for improvement. These notes do not need to be detailed, but they should help the author remember some of the comments after the meeting is over.

The Readers Thank the Author and the Author Thanks the Readers

At the end of the session, it is nice for the author to thank the other group members for their interest and goodwill. Also, members should thank the author for presenting the story or poem at the workshop.

Hand Out Copies of Next Author's Work

Next, the moderator should ask the author who is going to read during the next meeting to hand out his or her writing, or simply to be ready to read next time. The moderator also reminds the group to read the work and make comments, or check out a library book in War. It'll be time soon for everyone to read and write again!

Clear the Air

Because writing workshops can cause emotions to run high, it is good to end the meeting on a light note. It is good for the moderator or author to redirect the conversation by telling a joke or making announcements of other cultural activities in the community.

NOW LET'S ALL GO WRITE!

Mining operations persist in many regions of Appalachia today, the black specter of coal omnipresent though often shy, the smaller, modern operations tucked back among the hills, grinding and clanking, loaded down Mack trucks hustling along, brakes burning—the odor of roasting rubber and hydraulics—as the heavy vehicles rumble down the mountain, going in slow, bursting out of, switchback curves. Schopenhauer said, "The world is my idea—this is a truth for every man, since the world as it is depends for its character and existence upon the mind that knows it." Our notions of the coalfields remain ill-defined, incomplete, for it is an Appalachia we still struggle to know and to which we remain foreigners, despite our own Appalachian heritage. We are strangers with other pasts, for whom the people of these areas are, by turns, familiar and alien. Appalachian coal country is a different kind of southern Appalachia, from what people eat and think about, all the way down to the traditional means of heating one's house, the smell of coal smoke on the evening autumn air having long ago replaced the sharp sweet odor of kindling aflame or the slow, smoky simmering of wet wood, set for the night at the back of the woodstove. In southernmost West Virginia, at day's end, the waning sun sinks behind hollowed mounds—tragic, riddled peaks, the wounded heights West Virginia writer William Hoffman once called "the dark mountains."

Yet there are people who know this land and remain willing to share. Among them: the Muncy sisters, leaders in their local church and dedicated ATV enthusiasts, who have constructed a family compound in the hills above War and spent an entire afternoon helping us forget our project. They rode us around the summits and gas fields of all the local ridges, telling us about the people who once had lived there, showing us the rusty ruins of an old still. "Virginia is way over there on the other side of them hills," one of the sisters told me, pointing into the evening sun from the mountaintop where we stood. "We can take four-wheeler trails anywhere you want to go. Point and we'll go there. . . . I could ride you all the way to Grundy." There are still such people in McDowell County, those who gaze beyond their poignant history and suffering, even in the wake of its telling: oracles scanning the horizon, for whom there are still possibilities.

Strange and wonderful stories hover and drift amid West Virginia's southern hills and hollows, and the people there have been sharing them with each other for generations. The stewardship of local tales rests in strong, capable hands. Surely one of the most humbling and fundamental lessons we learned is that no one needed us to help tell them.

Recommended Web Links

http://www.wvexp.com/index.php/McDowell_County
General Information on McDowell County
http://www.geocities.com/mcdowellcounty/photoindex.html
McDowell County Photo Album
http://www.appalachianwomen.org
Appalachian Women Writers Group
http://www.hillside.net/patterns/

Much of the compositional theory in this document is drawn from pattern-based applications of architectural concepts as formulated by computer programmers. They argue that all spaces are inundated with interrelated patterns that repeat, which is useful in creating computer programs and robotics. Such patterns generate solutions to problems indirectly, a necessary approach for the most difficult problems of design. They describe largely irresolvable relationships involving deeper system structures and mechanisms. Since all software/theory serves human comfort or quality of life, the best patterns explicitly appeal to aesthetics and utility.

Works Cited

Abram, David. *The Spell of the Sensuous: Perception and Language in a More-Than-Human World.* New York: Pantheon, 1996.

Adams, Sheila Kay. *My Old True Love.* Chapel Hill: Algonquin, 2004.

Alhazred, Abdul. *The Necronomicon (Al Azif).* No publication information available for this private edition (originally published in Damascus, c. 730 A.D.).

Amis, Kingsley. *Lucky Jim.* New York: Penguin, 1954.

———. *Memoirs.* New York: Summit, 1991.

Anderson, Sherwood. *Winesburg, Ohio: A Group of Tales of Ohio Small-Town Life.* New York: B. W. Huebsch, 1919.

Aristotle. *Physics.* Qtd. in Helen S. Lang, *The Order of Nature in Aristotle's Physics: Place and the Elements.* Cambridge: Cambridge UP, 1998.

Ayers, Edward. "The Inevitable Future of the South." *South to the Future: An American Region in the Twenty-first Century.* Ed. Fred Hobson. Athens: U of Georgia P, 2002. 87–106.

Bailey, Mary. "Contemporary Virginia Literature's Classical Composer: The Musicality of Kelly Cherry in *The Society of Friends.*" *Nantahala Review* 3.2 (Fall/Summer 2007) 9 Sept. 2008 <http://nantahalareview.org/issue2-3/view/marybailey.htm>.

Baraldi, Enrico, Hjalmar Fors, and Anders Houltz, eds. *Taking Place: The Spatial Contexts of Science, Technology, and Business.* Sagamore Beach, Mass.: Science History Publications, 2006.

Baughman, Ronald C. "James Dickey at Drury College." *James Dickey Newsletter* 5.1 (Fall 1988): 16–25.

Bell, Madison Smartt. Novel Panel. Southern Literature Festival, A Celebration of the Life and Work of George Garrett. U of Tennessee, Knoxville. 2–4 Oct. 2003.

Bell, Robert. "'True Comic Edge' in *Lucky Jim.*" *American Humor: An Interdisciplinary Newsletter* 8.2 (1981): 1–7.

Benjamin, Walter. "Julien Green." *Neue Schweiser Rundschau/Nouvelle Revue Suisse* 23 (1930): 259–64.

Berry, Wendell. "The Poetry of William Carlos Williams of Rutherford." *Sewanee Review* 119.1 (Winter 2011): 30–42.

Blackbourn, David, and James Retallack. *Localism, Landscape, and the Ambiguities of Place.* Toronto: U of Toronto P, 2007.

Bowen, Elizabeth. *Pictures and Conversations.* New York: Knopf, 1975.

Brinkmeyer, Robert H. Jr. *Remapping Southern Literature: Contemporary Southern Writers and the West.* Athens: U of Georgia P, 2000.

Brown, Peter. Introduction. *Literature and Place, 1800–2000.* Eds. Peter Brown and Michael Irwin. New York: Peter Lang, 2006. 13–23.

Bruccoli, Matthew. "$106,585." Introduction. *The Price Was High: Fifty Uncollected Short Stories by F. Scott Fitzgerald.* Ed. Matthew Bruccoli. New York: MJF Books, 1979. xi–xv.

Bruccoli, Matthew, and Judith Baughman. *Crux: The Letters of James Dickey.* New York: Knopf, 1999.

Buell, Lawrence. "The Timeliness of Place: Response to the Presidential Address." *American Quarterly* 58.1 (Mar. 2006): 17–22, 265.

Buffington, Robert. "Tolerating the Short Story." *Sewanee Review* 102.4 (Oct.–Dec. 1994): 682–88.

Burchfield, R. W. *A Supplement to the Oxford English Dictionary.* Vol. 1 (A-G). Oxford: Clarendon, 1972. 3 vols.

Byrd, William II. *William Byrd's Histories of the Dividing Line betwixt Virginia and North Carolina.* New York: Dover, 1967.

Casey, Edward S. *The Fate of Place: A Philosophical History.* Berkeley: U California P, 1997.

———. *Getting Back into Place: Toward a Renewed Understanding of the Place-World.* Bloomington: Indiana UP, 2009.

Chambers, Ross. *Room for Maneuver: Reading the Oppositional in Narrative.* Chicago: U of Chicago P, 1991.

Chappell, Fred. *Castle Tzingal.* Baton Rouge: LSU P, 1984.

———. *Earthsleep.* Baton Rouge: LSU P, 1980.

———. "Fictional Characterization as Infinite Regressive Series: George Garrett's Strangers in the Mirror." *Southern Literature and Literary Theory.* Ed. Jefferson Humphries. Athens: U of Georgia P, 1990. 66–74.

———. *The Gaudy Place.* New York: Harcourt Brace Jovanovich, 1973.

———. "Kelly Cherry in Her Poetry: The Subject as Object." *Mississippi Quarterly* 58.1–2 (Winter 2004): 255–77.

———. Interview with the author. 6 Aug. 2001. Greensboro, North Carolina.

———. "Taking Measure: Violent Intruders in William Hoffman's Short Fiction." Frank 9–23.

Cherry, Kelly. "The Achievement of George Garrett." *Blackbird* 7.1 (Spring 2008) <http://www.blackbird.vcu.edu/v7n1/nonfiction/cherry_k/garrett.htm>. 6 June 2008.

———. *The Exiled Heart.* Baton Rouge: LSU P, 1991.

———. *Hazard and Prospect.* Baton Rouge: LSU P, 2007.

———. *The Lost Traveler's Dream.* New York: Harcourt Brace Jovanovich, 1984.

———. *My Life and Dr. Joyce Brothers.* Chapel Hill: Algonquin, 1990.

———. *The Society of Friends.* Columbia: U of Missouri P, 1999.

———. *We Can Still Be Friends.* New York: Soho, 2003.

———. *Writing the World.* Columbia: U of Missouri P, 1995.

Clabough, Casey. *Elements: The Novels of James Dickey.* Macon: Mercer UP, 2002.

———. *The Warrior's Path: Reflections along an Ancient Route.* Knoxville: U of Tennessee P, 2007.

———. Core, George. Introduction. Frank 1–8.

Cresswell, Tim. *Place: A Short Introduction.* Oxford: Blackwell, 2004

Daiches, David, and John Flower. *Literary Landscapes of the British Isles: A Narrative Atlas*. New York: Paddington, 1979.
Deaver. Philip F. "Writing to the Center: *Glory River* and Other Works by David Huddle." *Southern Review* 44.4 (Autumn 2008): 785.
de Certeau, Michel. *The Practice of Everyday Life*. Trans. Steven Rendall. Berkeley: U of California P, 1988.
Depta, Victor. *A West Virginia Trilogy*. Ashland, Ky.: Blair Mountain, 2004.
Dickey, James. *Alnilam*. New York: Doubleday, 1987.
———. *Deliverance*. Boston: Houghton Mifflin, 1970.
———. Foreword. *Living in the Resurrection*. By T. Crunk. New Haven: Yale UP, 1995. ix–xi.
———. *Self-Interviews*. Ed. Barbara and James Reiss. New York: Doubleday, 1970.
———. *To the White Sea*. Boston: Houghton Mifflin, 1993.
———. *The Whole Motion: Collected Poems, 1945–1992*. Hanover: Wesleyan UP, 1992.
———. Unpublished notes for *To the White Sea*. James Dickey Papers. Series 2.3, box 91k. Special Collections. Woodruff Library, Emory U, Atlanta.
Dillard, R.H.W. "Letters from a Distant Lover: The Novels of Fred Chappell." *Hollins Critic* 10.2 (Apr. 1973): 1–15.
———. *Understanding George Garrett*. Columbia: U of South Carolina P, 1988.
Dixon, Terrell F. "Chance and Closure in *Lucky Jim*." *Ball State University Forum* 17.4 (1976): 75–80.
Donohue, Michael. "Exile in Yantai." *Oxford American* 60 (Spring 2008): 126–31.
Edmundson, Mark. *Why Read?* New York: Bloomsbury, 2004.
Einstein, Albert. Preface. *Concepts of Space: The History of Theories of Space in Physics*. By Max Jammer. 3rd ed. Cambridge, Mass.: Harvard UP, 1970. xiii–xvii.
Eliot, T. S. "Gerontion." "*The Wasteland" and Other Poems*. New York: Harcourt Brace, 1934. 17–22.
Escobar, Arturo. *Territories of Difference: Place, Movements, Life, Redes*. Durham: Duke UP, 2008.
Evans, Paul. Review of *La Tour Dreams of the Wolf Girl*, by David Huddle. *Book* (Mar.–Apr. 2002): 75.
Fallis, Richard. "*Lucky Jim* and Academic Wishful Thinking." *Studies in the Novel* 9 (1977): 65–72.
Feld, Steven, and Keith H. Basso, eds. *Senses of Place*. Santa Fe: School of American Research P, 1996.
Findlay, J. N. *The Philosophy of Hegel*. New York: Collier, 1958.
Fisher, Vardis. *Dark Bidwell*. Boston: Houghton Mifflin, 1931.
———. *Mountain Man*. New York: Morrow, 1965.
Fishwick, Marshall. *The Virginia Tradition*. Washington, D.C.: Public Affairs P, 1956.
Fletcher, Marvin. Review of *Goodbye, Darkness: A Memoir of the Pacific War*, by William Manchester. *Ohio History* (Jan.–Dec. 1982): 95–96.
Frank, William, ed. *The Fictional World of William Hoffman*. Columbia: U of Missouri P, 2000.

Freud, Sigmund. "The Aetiology of Hysteria." 1896. Trans. James Strachey. Freud, *Freud Reader.* 96–111.

———. "Anxiety and Instinctual Life." 1932. Trans. James Strachey. Freud, *Freud Reader.* 773–83.

———. "Beyond the Pleasure Principle." 1920. Trans. James Strachey. Freud, *Freud Reader.* 594–626.

———. "Draft K." 1896. Trans. James Strachey. Freud, *Freud Reader.* 89–96.

———. "Fragment of an Analysis of a Case of Hysteria ('Dora')." 1905. Trans. James Strachey. Freud, *Freud Reader.* 172–239.

———. *The Freud Reader.* Ed. Peter Gay. New York: Norton, 1989.

Fussell, Paul. *The Anti-Egotist: Kingsley Amis, Man of Letters.* Oxford: Oxford UP, 1994.

Gadamer, Hans-Georg. *Truth and Method.* Trans. W. Glen-Doepel. New York: Continuum, 1975.

Gardner, Phillip. *Kingsley Amis.* Boston: Twayne, 1981.

Garrett, George. "A Life without End: Two Novels about World War II by William Hoffman." Frank 88–97.

———. *Cold Ground Was My Bed Last Night.* Columbia: U of Missouri P, 1964.

———. "Don't Try and Sell Me No Pink Flamingos: An Introduction." *White Trash: An Anthology of Contemporary Southern Poets.* Ed. Nancy Stone and Robert Waters Grey. Charlotte: New South, 1976. xi–xii.

———. *Double Vision.* Tuscaloosa: U of Alabama P, 2004.

———. *The Finished Man.* New York: Scribner's, 1959.

———. "Foote's *The Civil War*: The Version for Posterity?" *Mississippi Quarterly* 28 (Winter 1974–75): 83–92.

———. "Garrett, George Palmer." *Contemporary Authors.* Vol. 202. Detroit: Thomson-Gale, 2002. 97–132.

———. "George Garrett." *The Fugitives, the Agrarians and Other Twentieth-century Southern Writers.* Charlottesville: Alderman Library (U of Virginia), 1985. 21–25.

———. George Garrett Papers. David M. Rubenstein Rare Book and Manuscript Library. Duke U.

———. Interview with the author. 9 July 2003. Charlottesville, Virginia.

———. *King of the Mountain.* New York: Scribner's, 1957.

———. "Literary Ladies of Dixie." *Virginia Quarterly Review* 79.1 (Winter 2003): 161–66.

———. Review of *Promises: Poems 1954–1956*, by Robert Penn Warren. *Georgia Review* 12.2 (Spring 1958): 106–108.

———. *The Sorrows of Fat City.* Columbia: U of South Carolina P, 1992.

———. "The South." *American Libraries* 3.1 (Jan. 1972): 24–39.

———. *Southern Excursions: Views on Southern Letters in My Time.* Baton Rouge: LSU P, 2003.

———. *Whistling in the Dark: True Stories and Other Fables.* San Diego: Harcourt, Brace, Jovanovich, 1992.

Gelfant, Blanche Housman. *The American City Novel.* Norman: U of Oklahoma P, 1954.

Gioia, Dana. *Can Poetry Matter?* Saint Paul, Minn.: Graywolf, 1992.

Glissant, Édouard. *Poetics of Relation*. Trans. Betsy Wing. Ann Arbor: U of Michigan P, 1997.
Gohn, Jack Benoit. "The Novels of Kingsley Amis: A Reading." Diss. Johns Hopkins, 1975.
Goldsmith, N. Kent. Review of *Goodbye, Darkness: A Memoir of the Pacific War*, by William Manchester. *United States Naval Institute Proceedings* 107 (Apr. 1981): 91.
Graham, John. "Fred Chappell." *The Writer's Voice: Conversations with Contemporary Writers*. Ed. John Graham and George Garrett. New York: Morrow, 1973. 37–50.
Gray, Richard. "Foreword: Inventing Communities, Imagining Places: Some Thoughts on Southern Self-fashioning." Suzanne W. Jones and Sharon Monteith xiii–xxiii.
———. *Southern Aberrations: Writers of the American South and the Problems of Regionalism*. Baton Rouge: LSU P, 2000.
Green, Julien. *Avarice House*. Trans. Marshall A. Best. New York: Harper, 1926.
———. *The Distant Lands*. Trans. Barbara Beaumont. New York: Marion Boyars, 1991.
———. *L'arc-en-ciel: 1981–1984*. Paris: Seuil, 1988.
———. *Moira*. Trans. Denise Folliot. London: Quartet, 1950.
———. *The Pilgrim on the Earth* in *Christine and Other Stories*. Trans. Courtney Bruerton. New York: Harper, 1930.
———. *South: A Play*. Trans. Robin Buss. New York: Marion Boyars, 1991.
———. *The Stars of the South*. Trans. Robin Buss. New York: Marion Boyars, 1996.
Hanly, Charles. *The Problem of Truth in Applied Psychoanalysis*. New York: Guilford, 1992.
Heidegger, Martin. "Art and Space." Trans. Charles H. Seibert. *Man-and-World* 6 (1973): 3–8.
Heise, Ursula. *Sense of Place and Sense of Planet*. New York: Oxford UP, 2008.
Hoffman, William. Interview with author. Charlotte Court House, Virginia. 3 Aug. 2001.
———. *Lies*. Montgomery, Ala.: River City, 2005.
Hubbell, Jay B. "The Decay of the Provinces: A Study of Nationalism and Sectionalism." *Sewanee Review* 35 (1927): 473–87.
Huddle, David. *A Dream with No Stump Roots in It*. Columbia: U of Missouri P, 1975.
———. *Glory River*. Baton Rouge: LSU P, 2008.
———. *The High Spirits*. Boston: Godine, 1989.
———. *Intimates*. Boston: Godine, 1993.
———. "Introduction: Confessions of a Multi-Genre Writer." *A David Huddle Reader*. Hanover: UP of New England, 1994.
———. *La Tour Dreams of the Wolf Girl*. Boston: Houghton Mifflin, 2002.
———. *Not a Trio*. Notre Dame: U of Notre Dame P, 2000.
———. *Only the Little Bone*. Boston: Godine, 1986.
———. *The Story of a Million Years*. Boston: Houghton Mifflin, 1999.
———. *Summer Lake: New and Selected Poems*. Baton Rouge: LSU P, 1999
———. *Tenorman*. San Francisco: Chronicle Books, 1995.
———. *The Writing Habit*. Salt Lake City: Peregrine Smith, 1991.
Humphrey, William. *The Spawning Run*. New York: Knopf, 1970.

Hurm, Gerd. *Fragmented Urban Images: The American City in Modern Fiction from Stephen Crane to Thomas Pynchon*. New York: Peter Lang, 1991.

Israel, Charles. "Interview: George Garrett." *South Carolina Review* 6.1 (Nov. 1973): 43–48.

Jacobson, David. *Place and Belonging in America*. Baltimore: Johns Hopkins UP, 2002.

Jammer, Max. *Concepts of Space: The History of Theories of Space in Physics*. Cambridge, Mass.: Harvard UP, 1970.

Jefferies, Richard. *The Story of My Heart*. Portland, Maine: Mosher, 1900.

Jeffers, Robinson. *The Selected Poetry of Robinson Jeffers*. New York: Random House, 1937.

Jones, Stuart. "Space-dis-place: How Sound and Interactivity Can Reconfigure Our Apprehension of Space." *Leonardo Music Journal* 16 (2006): 20–27.

Jones, Suzanne W., and Sharon Monteith, eds. *South to a New Place: Region, Literature, Culture*. Baton Rouge: LSU P, 2002.

Jovenetti, Dennis T. Review of *The High Spirits*, by David Huddle. *Hollins Critic* 28.1 (Feb. 1991): 14.

Kaplan, Eugene H. "Adolescents, Age Fifteen to Eighteen: A Psychoanalytic Developmental View." *The Course of Life*. Vol. 4, *Adolescence*. Ed. Stanley I. Greenspan and George H. Pollock. Madison: International UP, 1991. 201–33.

———. "Development of the Sense of Separateness and Autonomy during Middle Childhood Adolescence." *The Psychology of Separation and Loss*. Ed. Jonathan Bloom-Feshbach and Sally Bloom-Feshbach. London: Jossey-Bass, 1987. 136–64.

Kemmis, Daniel. Foreword. *Bioregionalism*. Ed. Michael Vincent McGinnis. New York: Routledge, 1999. xii–xvii.

Kennedy, John. Review of *The Story of a Million Years*, by David Huddle. *Antioch Review* 58.2 (Spring 2000): 245.

Kirschten, Robert. "Interview with James Dickey." *"Struggling for Wings": The Art of James Dickey*. Ed. Robert Kirschten. Columbia: U of South Carolina P, 1997. 65–77.

Kohler, Dayton. "Julian Green: Modern Gothic." *Sewanee Review* 40 (1932): 139–48.

Kooser, Ted. *The Official Website of Poet Ted Kooser*. Web. 6 June 2006. < http://www.tedkooser.net/>.

Kort, Wesley A. *Place and Space in Modern Fiction*. Gainesville: UP of Florida, 2004.

Krisham, R. S. "Closure in Kingsley Amis's *Lucky Jim*." *Studies in Contemporary Satire* 18 (1991–92): 18–25.

L'Amour, Louis. *Last of the Breed*. New York: Bantam, 1986.

Lee, Ernest. *Discovering Place: Readings from Appalachian Writers*. New York: McGraw-Hill, 1997.

Lieberman, Laurence. "James Dickey: The Deepening of Being." Introduction. *The Achievement of James Dickey*. Ed. Laurence Lieberman. Glenview: Scott, Foresman, 1968. 1–21.

Lodge, David. Introduction. *Lucky Jim*. By Kingsley Amis. New York: Penguin, 1992. v–xvii.

Lopez, Barry. *Arctic Dreams: Imagination and Desire in a Northern Landscape*. New York: Charles Scribner's Sons, 1986.

Lucretius. *On the Nature of the Universe*. Trans. E. Latham. Harmondsworth: Penguin, 1951.

Lutwack, Leonard. *The Role of Place in Literature*. Syracuse: Syracuse UP, 1984.

Machor, James. *Pastoral Cities: Urban Ideals and the Symbolic Landscape of America*. Madison: U of Wisconsin P, 1987.

Malpas, J. E. *Place and Experience: A Philosophical Topography*. Cambridge: Cambridge UP, 1999.

Manchester, William. *American Caesar: Douglas MacArthur, 1880–1964*. Boston: Little, Brown, 1978.

———. *Controversy: And Other Essays in Journalism*. Boston: Little, Brown, 1976.

———. Foreword. *Chronicle of 20th Century Conflict*. By Neil Grant. New York: Smithmark, 1993. 9.

———. *The Glory and the Dream: A Narrative History of America, 1932–1972*. Boston: Little, Brown, 1973.

———. *Goodbye, Darkness: A Memoir of the Pacific War*. New York: Dell-Laurel, 1987.

Matthiessen, Peter. *Nine-Headed Dragon River: Zen Journals 1969–1982*. Boston: Shambhala, 1986.

Mazmanian, Adam. Review of *The King of Babylon Shall Not Come Against You*, by George Garrett. *Library Journal* 121.3 (15 Feb. 1996): 176.

McDermott, John. *Kingsley Amis: An English Moralist*. New York: St. Martin's, 1989.

Melville, Herman. *Moby Dick*. New York: Harper, 1851.

———. *The Piazza Tales*. New York: Modern Library, 1996.

Mendelsohn, Jane. "Paints with Wolves: A Novel Involves the 17th-century Artist Georges de La Tour and an Art Historian Studying Him." *New York Times Book Review* 17 Feb. 2002: 7.

Meriwether, James B. "George Palmer Garrett, Jr." *Seven Princeton Poets*. Ed. Sherman Hawkins. Princeton: Princeton U Library, 1963. 26–39.

Miller, Danny L., Sharon Hatfield, and Gurney Norman, eds. *An American Vein: Critical Readings in Appalachian Literature*. Athens: Ohio UP, 2005.

Moore, Virginia. *Virginia Is a State of Mind*. New York: E. P. Dutton, 1943.

Nietzsche, Friedrich. "On Truth and Falsity in an Extra-Moral Sense." *Early Greek Philosophy and Other Essays*. Trans. M. A. Mügge. Ed. Oscar Levy. *The Complete Works of Friedrich Nietzsche*. Vol. 2. New York: Russell and Russell, 1964. 171–92.

———. *Werke: Kritische Gesamtausgabe*. Berlin: de Gruyter, 1967.

Nin, Anaïs. *The Novel of the Future*. New York: Macmillan, 1968.

Norman, Gurney (moderator), with Denise Giardina, David Huddle, Sharyn McCrumb, and Lee Smith. "The Perils of Regionalism: Labels and Their Limitations" [panel discussion, Appalachian Literary Festival, 21–23 Sept. 2006].

O'Brien, John. *At Home in the Heart of Appalachia*. New York, Knopf, 2001.

Owen, Guy. *Journey for Joedel*. Winston-Salem: Press 53, 2010.

Palmer, Tersh. "Fred Chappell." *Appalachian Journal* 19.4 (Summer 1992): 402–11.

Palumbo, Carmine. "Folklore and Literature: The Poetry and Fiction of Fred Chappell." Diss. U of Southwestern Louisiana, 1997.

Poe, Edgar A. "Dreamland." *The Works of Edgar Allan Poe*. Vol. 1. Ed. Edwin Markham. New York: Funk and Wagnalls, 1904. 128.

Powell, Mark. *Blood Kin*. Knoxville: U of Tennessee P, 2006.

"The Perils of Regionalism: Labels and Their Limitations." *Iron Mountain Review* 23 (Spring 2007): 25–31.

Review of *The Gaudy Place*, by Fred Chappell. *Kirkus Reviews* 41.1 (1 Jan. 1973): 17.

Review of *The Gaudy Place*, by Fred Chappell. *New Republic* 168.22 (2 June 1973): 30.

Review of *Not: A Trio*, by David Huddle. *Publishers Weekly* 247.36 (4 Sept. 2000): 84.

Review of *Summer Lake: New and Selected Poems*, by David Huddle. *Publishers Weekly* 246.39 (27 Sept. 1999): 100.

Review of *The Story of a Million Years*, by David Huddle. *Publishers Weekly* 246.31 (2 Aug. 1999): 71.

Rivers, W.H.A. "The Repression of War Experience." *The Lancet* 2 (Feb. 1918): 173–77.

Roberts, Diane. "Afterword: The South of the Mind." Suzanne W. Jones and Sharon Monteith 363–74.

Robinson, William R. "George Garrett Discusses Writing and His Work." *Mill Mountain Review* 1.3 (Spring 1971): 79–102.

———. "Imagining the Individual: George Garrett's *Death of the Fox*." *George Garrett: The Elizabethan Trilogy*. Ed. Brooke Horvath and Irving Malin. Huntsville, Tex.: Texas Review P, 1998. 34–44.

Rose, Marilyn Gaddis. *Julian Green: Gallic-American Novelist*. Frankfurt: Herbert Lang, 1971.

Russell, Bertrand. *A Critical Exposition of the Philosophy of Leibniz*. London: George Allen and Unwin, 1900.

Salwak, Dale. *Kingsley Amis: Modern Novelist*. Lanham: Barnes and Noble, 1992.

Santayana, George. *Three Philosophical Poets*. Cambridge, Mass.: Harvard UP, 1945.

Sartre, Jean-Paul. *The Philosophy of Jean-Paul Sartre*. Ed. Robert Denoon Cumming. New York: Vintage, 1965.

Schöne, Hermann. *Spatial Orientation: Spatial Control of Behavior in Animals and Man*. Trans. Camilla Strausfeld. Princeton: Princeton UP, 1984.

Snyder, Gary. *Axe Handles*. San Francisco: North Point P, 1981.

Spencer, Benjamin T. "Wherefore This Southern Fiction?" *Sewanee Review* 47 (1939): 500–513.

Staggs, Sammy. Review of *The Gaudy Place*. *Library Journal* 98 (15 Feb. 1973): 563.

Stewart, George R. "The Regional Approach to Literature." *College English* 9 (Oct. 1947–May 1948): 370–75.

Stoker, Bram. *Dracula*. London: Constable, 1897.

Stuart, Dabney. "Mary Poppins's Mouth." Frank 98–120.

Suarez, Ernest. "An Interview with James Dickey: Poet and Novelist." *Texas Review* 17.3–4 (Fall/Winter 1996–1997): 128–43.

———. "'Real God, Roll': Muldrow's Primitive Creed." *James Dickey Newsletter* 10.2 (Spring 1994): 3–14.

Terr, Lenore. *Too Scared to Cry*. New York: Basic Books, 1990.

———. "Who's Afraid of Virginia Woolf? Clues to Early Sexual Abuse in Literature." *Psychoanalytic Study of the Child* 45 (1990): 533–46.

Tuan, Yi-Fu. *Space and Place: The Perspective of Experience.* Minneapolis: U of Minnesota P, 1977.

Turner, Frederick. *Spirit of Place: The Making of an American Literary Landscape.* San Francisco: Sierra Club, 1989.

Valéry, Paul. "Note." *Variety.* Trans. Malcolm Cowley. New York: Harcourt, Brace, 1927. 27–53

Van Noy, Rick. *Surveying the Interior: Literary Cartography and the Sense of Place.* Reno: U Nevada P, 2003.

Warren, Robert Penn. *All the King's Men.* New York: Harcourt, Brace, 1946.

Wickett, Dan. "Interview with David Huddle." *Emerging Writers Forum.* 20 Mar. 2002. Web. 25 Jan. 2010.

Woolf, Virginia. *To the Lighthouse.* New York: Harcourt, Brace, 1927.

"World War II Writers' Symposium at the University of South Carolina, 12–14 April 1995" (participants included James Dickey, William Price Fox, Paul Fussell, Joseph Heller, William Manchester, Mary Lee Settle, Mickey Spillane, William Styron, and Albert Wertheim). *Dictionary of Literary Biography Yearbook: 1995.* Ed. James W. Hipps. Detroit: Gale, 1996. 138–92.

"Writer-in-Residence Garrett Takes Sabbatical for Next Two Semesters." *Cavalier Daily* 12 Jan. 1967: 1.

Yardley, Jonathan. Review of *The Gaudy Place*, by Fred Chappell. *New York Times Book Review* 13 May 1973: 36.

York, Lynn. *The Piano Teacher.* New York: Plume, 2004.

Index

Casey Clabough serves as editor of the literature section of *Encyclopedia Virginia* and as general editor of the *James Dickey Review*. He is the author of the historical novel *Confederado* and the travel memoir *The Warrior's Path: Reflections along an Ancient Route.*

Other books by Casey Clabough:

Elements: The Novels of James Dickey
Experimentation and Versatility: The Early Novels and Short Fiction of Fred Chappell
Gayl Jones: The Language of Voice and Freedom in Her Writings
The Art of the Magic Striptease: The Literary Layers of George Garrett

The University Press of Florida is the scholarly publishing agency for the State University System of Florida, comprising Florida A&M University, Florida Atlantic University, Florida Gulf Coast University, Florida International University, Florida State University, New College of Florida, University of Central Florida, University of Florida, University of North Florida, University of South Florida, and University of West Florida.